THRIVE IN GRIEF

GRACE RICHARDSON

"Copyright © 2024 by Graceful Wellness Co All rights reserved. No part of this publication may be reproduced, distributed or transmitted in any form or by any means, including photocopying, recording, or other electronic or mechanical methods, without the prior written permission of the publisher, except in the case of brief quotations embodied in critical reviews and certain other noncommercial uses permitted by copyright law. Although the author and publisher have made every effort to ensure that the information in this book was correct at press time, the author and publisher do not assume and hereby disclaim any liability to any party for any loss, damage, or disruption caused by errors or omissions, whether such errors or omissions result from negligence, accident, or any other cause. Adherence to all applicable laws and regulations, including international, federal, state, and local governing professional licensing, business practices, advertising, and all other aspects of doing business in the US, Canada, or any other area, is the sole responsibility of the reader and consumer. Neither the author nor the publisher assumes any responsibility or liability whatsoever on behalf of the consumer or reader of this material. Any perceived slight of any individual or organization is purely unintentional. The resources in this book are provided for informational purposes only and should not be used to replace the specialized training and professional judgment of a health care or mental health care professional. Neither the author nor the publisher can be held responsible for the use of the information provided within this book. Please always consult a trained professional before making any decision regarding treatment of yourself or others. All Scripture quotations are taken from You Version Bible, New King James Version (NKJV), English Standard Version (ESV) 2016. Copyright © 2015 by The Lockman Foundation, La Habra, CA 90631. All rights reserved. English Standard Version (ESV). The Holy Bible, English Standard Version. ESV ® Text Edition: 2016. Copyright © 2001 by Crossway Bibles, a publishing ministry of Good News Publishers. THE HOLY BIBLE, NEW INTERNATIONAL VERSION ®, NIV ® Copyright © 1973, 1978, 1984, 2011 by Biblica, Inc. ® Used by permission. All rights reserved worldwide. Scripture taken from the New King James Version ®. Copyright © 1982 by Thomas Nelson. Used by permission. All rights reserved. Scripture quotations marked NLT are taken from the Holy Bible, New Living Translation, copyright © 1996, 2004, 2015 by Tyndale House Foundation. Used by permission of Tyndale House Publishers, Inc., Carol Stream, Illinois 60188. All rights reserved.
— Thrive In Grief
Heal the Ravages of Loss Through 5 Proven Steps

eBook ISBN: 979-8-89694-112-5
Paperback ISBN: 979-8-89694-113-2

CONTENTS

Redeemed xiii

Doxology xiv

Reviews xv

Foreword xxiv

Dedications xxvii

Introduction xxix

Chapter 1 1

Understanding Grief and Its Impact on You 1
   Anatomy of Grief: Acknowledge Your Journey 10
   Let's Take a Personal Reflection 12
   The Days After 16
   Ethan at the Services 17
   The First Weeks 20
   What Kept Me Going 21
   Is It Possible to Normalize the Grief Experience? 23
   Reflection Exercise 24
   Emotional and Physical Symptoms of Grief 25
   Make an Effort to Create a Routine 27
   Grief Can Make You Question Your Faith 28
   Accepting Grief as a Part of Life 30
   Share Your Story of Loss 32

Chapter 2 34

Faith and Healing 34
    Embracing Faith in Times of Loss 34
    The Power of Prayer and Meditation on Scripture 35
    Scripture for Grieving Hearts 40
    Use of Psalms and Scriptural Prayers 41
    Prayer Journals 43
    Create a Time for Daily Devotion 44
    Engaging with Scriptures for Deep Comfort 45
    Finding Comfort in Biblical Promises 45
    Trust in God's Plan 47
    Renewing Faith Through Promises 48
    Faith and Gratitude 48
    Songs and Hymns of Comfort 49
    Faith Reminders 51
    Memorization for Quick Access 51

Chapter 3 53

Faith and Community 53
    The Value of a Supportive Community 53
    The Importance of Community 54
    Treasured Friendships 55
    Grow Your Community by Networking 58
    Finding a Faith Community 65
    Starting From Zero 67
    "The Know Like and Trust" Principle 68
    Building Community Through Know, Like, and Trust 68
    The Blessing of Engaging in Your Church and
    Local Community 70
    A Secular Community:
    An Opportunity to Share Your Faith 71

    Intercessory Prayer 74
    Sharing Scriptures in the Community 81

Chapter 4 83

The Impact of Grief on Health and Beauty 83
    The Devastating Impact of Stress 83
    I Was a Mess. 88

Chapter 5 94

AromaReflex Healing™
Method – Step 1: Essential Mindset™ Cultivating a
Positive Mindset Through Faith. 94
    Faith as a Foundation for Healing the Mindset 95
    Using Faith to Frame the Grief
    Experience and Improve Your Mindset 96
    Biblical Examples of the Power of Mindset to
    Triumph Over Grief 96
    Case Studies 98
    An Essentially Essential Mindset Is Key 99
    Overcoming Common Mental Blockades to
    Healing the Mindset 100
    Identifying Blockades 101
    More Blockages to a Healthy Mindset 102
    Essential Oils for a Healthy Mindset 104
    Strategies for Overcoming Blockades. 106
    What Is Aromatherapy? 107
    What Are Essential Oils? 109
    Two Ways Essential Oils Can Support Emotional Healing 110
    Safety First 112
    Selecting Essential Oils for Emotional Support 112
    Daily Aromatherapy Routines to Ease Grief. 116

Chapter 6 119

AromaReflex Healing™ – Step 2: Essential Beauty™ 119
   Aromatherapy for Physical Healing 119
   Fragrance Is in Everything. 121
   Defy Nature: Build Up Your Collagen, Naturally! 122
   Collagen Decreases After a Certain Age 122
   Rejuvenating Essential Oils for Your Beauty and
   Health Routine 123
   Why Dilute and What Is the Role of Carrier Oils? 126
   Hydrate and Rejuvenate 127
   Look to Your Skin to Tell You What's Going On 127
   Application Techniques for Maximum Benefit. 128
   Emotional and Physical Connection 128
   Routine for Morning and Night 129
   Essential Oils for a Restful Sleep 130
   Beautifying Self-Care Rituals with Oils 132
   Bath and Body Care 132
   Beautifying Facial Care Routines 133
   Face Stimulation Techniques. 133
   These Rituals Have a Power to Ease 134

Chapter 7 136

AromaReflex Healing™ – Step 3: Essential Stimulation™ 136
   Interesting Facts 137
   Some of the Benefits of Face Reflexology 137
   How Face Reflexology Works 139
   Let's Recap with Emphasis on Ease. 142
   Key Reflex Points for Alleviating Grief 142
   Targeted Points for Grief 143
   Frequency and Duration 143
   Combining Breathing Techniques 144

Personal Anecdotes.................................. 144
Integrating Reflexology into Your Daily Routine........ 145
Combining Aromatherapy with Reflexology to
Enhance Healing.................................. 147
Synergistic Effects................................ 148

Chapter 8... 150

AromaReflex Healing™ – Step 4A: Essential Breathing
and Exercise 150
What Is Proper Breathing?........................... 150
Some Dangers to Shallow Breathing 151
How Serious Is Shallow Breathing? 152
Breathing and Chronic Stress? 153
So What Do We Do?............................... 153
My Recommendations to Support Breathing 157
AromaReflex Healing™ – Step 4B: Exercise............. 158

Chapter 9... 161

AromaReflex Healing™ – Step 5 - Essential Nutrition/
Hydration/Supplementation............................. 161
Nutritional Support for Skin and Body 161
Holistic Approach to Nutrition....................... 161
Essential Oils in Cooking............................ 162
Hydration and Essential Oils......................... 163
Supplemental Support 163

Chapter 10.. 165

Embracing Life from a Fresh Perspective................. 165
Healthy Grief...................................... 165
Grieving My Father, Keeping His Legacy Alive 166
Mourning Our Beloved Pet 167

Recognize and Honor Your Loved Ones and Your Grief. . 168
The Importance of Self-Care. 170
Stay Connected in the Community 171
A Note on Self-Compassion 172
Lessons Learned 173
"See the Forest for the Trees". 174
Establishing a Daily Routine for
Continued Spiritual and Physical Wellness:
Continue to Grow and Progress 175
Guided Recipes and Face Reflex Points. 177

Chapter 11. 179

Embracing A New Normal 179
Redefining Identity After Loss: Identity Shifts 179
Step 1: Essential Mindset™. 182
Step 2: Essential Beauty™ 183
Step 3: Essential Stimulation™. 183
Step 4: Mindful Breathing and Exercise. 184
Step 5: Nutrition and Hydration 184
Embracing Change 184
Embracing the Future. 186
Incorporating Healing Practices into Your Goals
for the Future. 186
Creating a Vision for the Future 186
Maintaining Your Healing Practices Long-Term 187
Celebrating Small Victories on the Path to Recovery 188
Recognizing Progress. 188
Lori's Story: A Journal of Healing. 188

Chapter 12. 195

Real Stories, Real Victories 195

Thanking God for the Intercessory Work of Jesus
on our Behalf.................................... 207
Finding New Purpose After Loss 208
There's Victory in Jesus............................ 210
My Final "Restore" 211
God Will Not Allow Those Who Love Him Without Help 211
A Family's Betrayal 211
God Is in the Story!............................... 216
Embracing the Future.............................. 217
Incorporate Healing Practices into Your Goals for
the Future.. 218
Creating a Vision for the Future 218
Maintain Your Healing Practices Long-Term........... 218
Recognize Progress................................ 219
Celebrate Small Victories on the Path to Recovery 220

Chapter 13.. 223

Ethan's Story 223
   Introduction...................................... 223
   Remembering Mom 223
   Letter to Mom 226
   Remembering Papa 227
   Letter to Papa..................................... 229
   Life Now.. 231
   My Talents - What I Love to Create 233
   Drawing with Pencil............................... 233
   My Comic Books................................... 233
   Painting.. 235
   Building with Legos 235
   How Creating Helps Me............................ 236
   My Message to Other Kids.......................... 237
   Talk About Your Feelings........................... 238

    It's Okay to Cry 238
    Remember the Good Times 239
    Do Things That Make You Happy 239
    Believe in Heaven 239
    You're Stronger Than You Think..................... 240
    Hold On to That Promise 241
    Ethan and His Faith Amazes Me!.................... 242

Conclusion 244

Epilogue.. 247

Thriving In Grief 247
    The Blessing in Disguise 248
    Seeing the Fleas in Ethan's Story..................... 249
    Life Today - God's Restoration Continues.............. 250
    Ethan's Creative Healing............................ 251
    The Book's Impact - God's Global Reach............... 251
    My Continued Education - Equipped to Heal 252
    My Mission Today................................. 254
    What Restoration Looks Like 254
    The Journey Continues - Living with Hope 256
    Still in the Battle 256
    The Power of Community in the Long Haul............ 258
    Using Our Pain to Help Others...................... 259
    The Purpose of Ongoing Suffering................... 261
    Thriving While Still Struggling...................... 262
    A Final Word 263
    To You, Dear Reader.............................. 263

Resource Page 265
    Introduction..................................... 265
    Chapter 1 265
    Chapter 2 266

Chapter 3	266
Chapter 4	266
Chapter 5	267
Chapter 6	267
Chapter 7	267
Chapter 9	268
Chapter 10	268
Chapter 11	268
Chapter 12	269

Acknowledgements 270

ABCs of Salvation. 271
   A – ADMIT that you are a Sinner. 271
   B – BELIEVE on the Lord Jesus Christ 272
   C – CONFESS with your mouth. 274
   Now do the Sinner's Prayer:. 275
   D – DEPART from evil. 275

References 279

REDEEMED

O God, Author of Ages,
how many times have humans, such as I,
disobeyed You, denying Your glory?
And still, You harbor the mercy to forgive,
bridling Your wrath until it's due.

I look around at all You have created:
sunlight, blue sky, clouds as a garnish,
plants and tree branches growing upward
as arms reaching out in praise, and yet,
You chose to save someone.
Leaving the ninety-nine
You sent your Son to die
a martyr and ransom for many
to find and save me,
that I who am poor may be heir
to the throne of grace.
— Seth Kronick

Seth Kronick is a poet and journalist from Southern California. He currently studies as an MFA student at CSU, Long Beach. He is also a member of the Haiku Society of America. Seth's poetry has appeared in journals such as Trash Panda, Frogpond, Vessels of Light, IAMB, and the Pomona Valley Review among other publications.

Instagram: @sethkronickpoetry
Website: https://www.sethkronick.com/

GRACE RICHARDSON

DOXOLOGY

Greek word described as a "short hymn of praise to God"
Praise God from Whom all blessings flow
Praise Him all creatures here below
Praise Him above ye heavenly hosts
Praise Father, Son, and Holy Ghost!
Written by Thomas Ken 1674

REVIEWS

I will never forget the message I received late one night in September 2021 from Grace, "I need you." I didn't know Grace all that well, having met her briefly at a networking event or two and exchanged business cards. I called her within moments, and what she told me was shocking and heartbreaking.

Throughout the following months I witnessed her grief, legal battle, and incredible strength as she turned her unimaginable loss into something positive, empowering, and healing. Our relationship morphed from service provider/client to dear friends, like sisters.

In her book, "Thrive In Grief – Heal the Ravages of Loss Through 5 Proven Steps" you'll witness Grace's grit, strength, tenacity, huge giving heart, and genuine belief in the Lord. She shares her deep faith without being preachy and her AromaReflex Healing method without being too salesy.

Grace has poured her heart and soul into this book, as she does in her spiritual and personal lives. She encourages you to embrace your community, be it by attending church, networking, or simply spending time with friends and family. You do not have to go through your grief or healing process alone.

Grace shares her vast knowledge openly and in an encouraging way. As her friend, I know she has followed the steps in this book and continues to do so. These are not just words but rather how she lives her life. On many occasions, she has dropped what she was doing to help a friend or acquaintance with serums and techniques to assist with their ailments, including helping me many times with my cancer and diverticulitis treatment.

Grace, I am so honored to call you my dear friend, who is not ever solely a client. You inspire me daily in so many ways, as I know you inspire many others.

Congratulations on this book which shows you are truly a victor, not just a survivor.

> **Lynda Bergh Herring, Author, Child Advocate, Board Member and Speaker (MillionKids.org), Owner/ Qualified Manager, L.J.B. Investigations**
> **ocladypi@gmail.com**

My friendship with Grace began at a Kay Arthur Precept Conference in 2011. I remember her excitement about the Lord and her eagerness to study God's Word inductively. I invited her to join a Precept study I was teaching, and she and her husband, Doug, began attending the evening classes. Over the years, they became ardent students and wonderful friends, often treating my husband and me to dinner. I cherished seeing Grace's passion for God's Word and the deep love she and Doug shared.

Then came COVID-19 in 2020. Classes stopped, and so did everything else. Grief and sorrow swept through so many lives, robbing us of loved ones and even the comfort of family and friends due to the restrictions. My own husband passed away at the end of 2020—not from COVID-19 but during a time when hospitals were closing their doors to visitors. I had to fight to stay with him, but others were not as fortunate. The pain and loss were overwhelming.

In 2021, during the worst of the pandemic, Grace faced unimaginable loss when Doug and her daughter, Joanne, both passed away within days of each other. We were all in shock. How does one overcome such grief? Where does one find comfort and strength during such immense pain? Is there hope? Is there life after such loss?

Grace has walked this long, hard road and found answers to these questions. Through her journey, she has written about her experiences and the stories of others who have also endured deep loss. She shares how faith and hope can be restored and strengthened even in the face of tragedy.

As both a widow and a funeral director, I am no stranger to grief. I've experienced it firsthand and walked alongside others in their sorrow. Over the years, I've read many books on this subject and shared countless resources with those in pain. What makes Grace's book stand out is the fresh insight she brings to this deeply personal and painful journey. She offers practical tools for those beginning this lonely path and gently guides readers toward healing and a renewed sense of God's love.

I believe this book will not only provide comfort and encouragement but will also become a trusted resource—one to be kept close and revisited often.

Peggy McAulay, Bible Teacher, Funeral Director, Widow
pjmcaulay@newopt.com

When I first met Grace as a greeter at church, I had no idea about the incredibly tragic loss she had faced just a few years prior. She has chosen to surrender her despair to the Lord, who has transformed her ashes into a beautiful story of hope and healing. This narrative serves to bless and encourage those navigating their own painful journeys of grief.

Her book is filled with deep faith and unwavering hope, emphasizing the precious biblical truths of a God who loves us and longs for us to draw close to Him in our heartache. It highlights the blessings and unexpected triumphs that come from making Him our focus and strength.

I found encouragement in my daily spiritual walk through the meaningful scriptures that Grace shares, which reflect the strong faith foundation she has built since childhood. This is an uplifting account of hope and victory in the Lord, paired with practical tools to help women age gracefully amidst the pains of life. Grace's carefully developed AromaReflex Healing method, centered around a holistic approach, offers a clear plan for grief recovery and overall health. Her journey challenges the reader to "let your pain be your purpose", and that's exactly what she has done in her incredible true story.

Julie Boswell, Secondary Teacher:
Excel Academy Charter School

"I highly recommend Grace Richardson's book. If you've experienced grief in any form—no matter how severe or overwhelming the loss—it can often feel insurmountable, affecting every aspect of your personal and professional life. I strongly encourage you to dive into this captivating and inspiring work as a travel companion on your journey through grief.

As a survivor of domestic violence and victim of long-term post-separation violence, I found her personal anecdotes and profound insights deeply touching. This book brought me to tears, and, at the same time, gave me glimmers of hope and joy. Grace's holistic approach to grief strongly resonated with me and her words have been a balm of comfort to my heart and soul."

Charlotte Habegger -VP Heartlink Network Worldwide, Canada, President/Founder Women Expo at Salon Femmes

WOW! Such an incredibly impactful book I am so honored to be a part of. The content is so valuable, I learned a lot and now I can't wait to get my hands on a copy and to share it with others. Your life story is so powerful, it honors Doug so well too. It's hard to believe you went through that. And not hard to believe God carried you through. All the "restores" and the significance of 7 are perfect examples of how Jesus delivers when you're faithful. I love all the scriptures which are perfectly placed to affirm the content from Him. This book is even better than I imagined. Congratulations my friend on the impact you will have on people with all the glory for God. xo

For those who have suffered loss and are seeking healing, "AromaReflex Healing" by Grace Richardson offers a holistic approach to managing grief and finding inner peace. Grace explores the powerful combination of aromatherapy, reflexology, and faith-based practices as tools for emotional and physical well-being. Through personal anecdotes and practical guidance, this book provides a compassionate and empowering roadmap for navigating grief, embracing change, and rediscovering a sense of purpose and joy in life.

Caprice Crebar, CEO, Heartlink Network Worldwide, USA, Certified Nutritional Coach

As I read each chapter of Grace's book, I was drawn in more and more because of her faith in God through such heartbreak and tragedy. Having never lost a loved one in such tragic circumstances or faced the family adversity and persecution Grace endured, I was encouraged by her fortitude to find peace and strength through the truth of God's word. Grace shares the many stages of grieving and how she found healing, spiritually, physically and emotionally. I am grateful for her writings because it gave me a new understanding and compassion for those who have experienced such loss and a resource to share with others.

Sandy Hart

"Thrive In Grief" is a heartfelt and practical guide that draws from Grace's own deep loss, offering a faith-based path to healing. Through her unique AromaReflex Healing™ method—combining aromatherapy, face reflexology, and spiritual practices—Grace addresses both the emotional and physical aspects of grief, showing that true healing involves the whole self.

What stands out is the balance of faith and actionable steps. Scriptures are woven throughout, offering comfort, while tools like journaling, prayer, and daily routines offer a way to actively participate in your healing journey. Grace beautifully reminds us that we don't have to walk this road alone—community and faith are vital to recovery.

Her compassion and strength shine in every chapter, making this book a valuable resource for anyone navigating grief. It's more than just surviving; it's about thriving, with God's promises lighting the way.

Grace, your unwavering faith and holistic approach to healing will change lives. Thank you for offering your heart to help others find peace and strength in the hardest of times.

Mary Barnett, Marketing Advisor, Author, Speaker | Another Brilliant Idea, Inc.
AnotherBrilliantIdea.com

In a world that often moves too fast, where challenges can seem insurmountable and grief can feel like an endless journey, Grace's words come as a much-needed embrace. In this book, she generously shares her wisdom, offering not just tools but a roadmap for healing—one that is rooted in faith, love, and the incredible power of community.

Grace's journey through grief isn't just her own; it's a testament to the strength we all possess when we tap into our deepest resources. She guides us with gentle hands through prayer and scripture, showing us how to lean on our spiritual foundation when the weight of the world feels too heavy. Her stories of community support remind us that we are never truly alone, no matter how isolating our pain might seem. And then there's the soothing balm of essential oils, an ancient remedy brought into the present, offering comfort in its purest form.

As you turn the pages of this book, let Grace's voice be a companion on your path. She speaks with the kind of wisdom that can only come from someone who has walked through the fire and emerged not just whole, but with a heart more open than ever.

-Leisa Reid, Author
Founder of Get Speaking Gigs Now & CEO
of The International Speaker Network
https://GetSpeakingGigsNow.com
https://iSpeakerNetwork.com

From the very first chapter I was captivated by Grace's words. Even though I have not experienced a recent turbulent event, Grace's book was still very relatable to my past experiences and was an invaluable source of tools to help heal from events that I didn't realize were still affecting me so deeply. I highly recommend having *Thrive In Grief* as part of anyone's collection of resources for reasonable and easily implementable steps for healing mentally, physically, emotionally, and spiritually.

Dakota Dixon, DC

RECOGNITION & GRATITUDE

The journey of *Thrive In Grief* has been shaped by lived experience, deep healing work, and the women who have walked alongside this message. I am deeply grateful for the recognition this work has received and for the opportunity to continue supporting others through grief, growth, and restoration.

FOREWORD

"Grief is the price we pay for love; yet when we embrace the power of our faith and community, it is also the path that can lead us back to joy, hope, and purpose." — Diana Sabatino

"Thrive In Grief – Heal the Ravages of Loss Through 5 Proven Steps" is a heartfelt guide that speaks directly to you. Grace, who has faced profound loss, offers a compassionate and practical roadmap to help you through the turbulent waters of grief. Her goal is not just survival, but true healing and empowerment.

In the book, Grace introduces the AromaReflex Healing™ method, a faith-based approach that combines aromatherapy, face reflexology, and spiritual practices. This method addresses both the emotional and physical impacts of grief, providing a comprehensive path to recovery.

As you turn each page, you will find that faith plays a central role in Grace's journey, and she encourages you to draw strength from your own spiritual beliefs. She also emphasizes the importance of community—we don't have to do it alone. Personal connections and faith groups can offer support when you need it most.

Grace doesn't just leave you with theory; throughout the book, she provides practical tools like journaling, prayer, meditation, and self-care to help you actively engage in your healing.

Her message is clear: grief is part of life, but it doesn't have to define yours. With resilience, faith, and holistic practices, you can emerge not just as a survivor, but as a victor.

As the Executive Managing Director of eWomenNetwork, I have witnessed Grace's remarkable strength and generosity as she navigates her new normal. Even while mourning her husband and daughter, she remains dedicated to helping others on their own journeys, offering invaluable tools and resources to guide them from loss to healing and renewal.

Grace, your wisdom, faith, and holistic approach to healing will empower and impact so many lives. Congratulations, my friend!

Diana Sabatino, Executive Managing Director
EWomenNetwork OC dianasabatino@ewomennetwork.com

It is with heart-filled acclaim that I introduce this book by my dear friend, Grace Richardson. Through her beautiful prose, Grace expresses the profound depth of grief that accompanies loss, while also offering rays of hope through simple, consistent, and viscerally impactful actions.

In these pages, you will find that prayer and nourishing self-care are key components of the healing process. Grace eloquently demonstrates how God provides us with both spiritual connection and physical tools to help our bodies navigate the new seasons and layers of life that follow a loss.

Having personally experienced poignant and deep layers of grief over the past few years, my husband and I have relied on many of the practices Grace outlines. Yet, as I read this book, I discovered even more tools that empower me to release the waves of grief when they come, moving forward.

GRACE RICHARDSON

Grace's work is a testament to the strength and resilience that can arise from our darkest moments. Her insights will guide you toward healing and renewal, offering a gentle reminder that while grief is a part of life, so too is the hope that follows.

Dr. Melissa + Evan Esguerra
The Wellness Abode
+1-415-740-7841
|www.thewellnessabode.com
thewellnessabode@gmail.com

DEDICATIONS

To God, my Father, my Provider, my Protector, "Husband to the widow."
To Jesus, my Lord and Savior, Redeemer, and Intercessor.
To the Holy Spirit, my Guide, and my constant Companion.
Thank You for Your abundant grace and mercy and bountiful provisions!

To my beloved grandson Ethan, who is the joy of my life on earth, I love you to the moon and back!

Doug, my dearest husband, my best friend and my spiritual mentor. How grateful and blessed I am you chose me to be your wife. You provided in abundance, I never lacked anything, especially of the overflowing love you joyfully showered me with every day, obeying God's word: *"Husbands, love your wives, just as Christ also loved the church and gave Himself for her," Ephesians 5:25 NKJV*

Joanne, my precious and awesome daughter, a Proverbs 31 woman: *"Strength and honor are her clothing; She shall rejoice in time to come. She opens her mouth with wisdom, and on her tongue is the law of kindness. "Many daughters have done well, but you excel them all." Charm is deceitful and beauty is passing, but a woman who fears the Lord, she shall be praised." Proverbs 31:25-26, 29-30 NKJV*

And my mom, Aila, who set my strong spiritual foundation and has prayed diligently and fiercely for me over the course of my life. It is what brought me back to Jesus after a prodigal life. I am so blessed that you taught me to have integrity, Biblical work ethics, loyalty, generosity, sharing and compassion. You were a Proverbs 31 woman: *"Who can find a virtuous wife? For her worth is far above rubies. The heart of her husband safely trusts her; So, he will have no lack of gain. She seeks wool and flax, and willingly works with her hands. She is like the merchant ships, she brings her food from afar. She girds herself with strength and strengthens her arms. She extends her hand to the poor, yes, she reaches out her hands to the needy. Strength and honor are her clothing; She shall rejoice in time to come."* Proverbs 31:10-11,13-14, 17, 20, 25

"Train up a child in the way he should go, And when he is old he will not depart from it." Proverbs 22:6

Thank You, Lord, for blessing me with such a precious trio as my loving support in life, a godly grandson, my inspiration for this book.

I miss you all and I am looking forward to the day we will be reunited to be together forever!

INTRODUCTION

In a single, heartbreaking week in September 2021, I lost both my precious husband of thirty years and my cherished daughter at only forty-one years of age. These losses did not offer gentle goodbyes, but unwritten chapters of my life abruptly cut off.

In the wake of such unbearable grief, I saw how my life could have spiraled out of control from the extreme sorrow, depression, hopelessness, and pain I was drowning in. Doug and Joanne were two of my life's four most important people. They were my support system. We did everything together.

Doug and Joanne lost their lives under circumstances that left us reeling; in the merciless hands of doctors we should be able to trust! Looking back and recounting the events and the evil that was done to my loved ones was disturbing and horrifying. Their deaths shouldn't have happened.

To make matters worse, I became embroiled in a legal fight for my grandson, Ethan, in the Orange County family court after his father told me I would never see my grandson again. Top that off with the loss of my mom in April 2023 under despicable and unnecessary circumstances.

Searching for comfort, healing, and relief for a broken heart, I turned to the only place I knew could give me true peace, at the foot of the Throne. My confidence that God would hold my hand through this, as He has done many times before, triggered my resilience.

The gift of healing that I gained over the years, along with my strong spiritual foundation, was what I needed to help me through this "wilderness" of loneliness and uncertainty.

I created AromaReflex Healing™, a faith-based method, from a burning desire to rise above intense sadness and hopelessness to an unwavering hope. My focus was and is to restore my physical and emotional health so I can help others traverse their paths through grief.

> "As each one has received a gift, minister it to one another as good stewards of the manifold grace of God." I Peter 4:10 NKJV

AromaReflex Healing™ is not just a technique. It is a testament to the power of integrating natural healing practices with deep and unshakable faith. This book intertwines aromatherapy's powerful soothing and rejuvenating essence, face reflexology's healing and restorative stimulation, and the empowering strength of trusting in the One True God.

> "... casting all your cares upon Him, for He cares for you." 1 Peter 5:7

Each element of the five simple steps of the AromaReflex Healing™ method outlined in this book is integral. They work perfectly in harmony to ease the physical manifestations of grief and address the spiritual and emotional wounds that often go unspoken.

My trek through loss is not just my story—it is a shared story for many of us, particularly women who grapple with similar heartaches, be it the death of a loved one, the end of a marriage, losing a valued relationship, or a terminal diagnosis, like cancer.

> "God is our refuge and strength, always ready to help in times of trouble." **Psalms 46:1 NLT**

I was grateful to God that I had my faith. The solid spiritual foundation laid in my childhood by my mother became my lifeline, guiding me toward therapeutic practices that included faith and reliance upon the Great Physician, His providence and sovereignty; through prayer and scriptural promises that offered me absolute, tangible assurance of restoration.

The song "I Trust In God" written by Elevation music based on Psalm 34:4 written by David, reminds us why we need to thank, praise, and worship God:

> "I sought the Lord, and He heard me, And delivered me from all my fears." **Psalms 34:4 NKJV**

This book promises to be a nurturing guide filled with compassionate insights, success stories, and actionable, effective, and proven advice.

Even if you are not a follower of Jesus Christ, this guide will help you navigate the grieving process through its many inspiring stories of redemption and restoration and practical holistic tools for overcoming grief and rejuvenating emotionally, physically, and spiritually.

It's crafted for you, a woman in the throes of grief who is searching for holistic ways to heal without relying on expensive therapy sessions and prescription medications. It's a guide if you don't know what to do or you have the will but lack resources and support.

If you want to take responsibility for your healing process, this is for you. It includes the restorative power of essential oils, the therapeutic benefits of face reflexology or stimulation, the transformative assurance and peace of God's Word, prayer, and an encouraging, loving, supportive faith and secular community.

This book is both a companion and a beacon of hope. Its goal is to walk you through understanding the multifaceted nature of grief, introducing you to the AromaReflex Healing™ method, and showing you how to incorporate these practices into your daily life toward recovery and a graceful aging journey.

I pray you will allow me to help walk you through your grief and empower you to emerge with a renewed sense of purpose and fullness through faith and the holistic tools that helped me in my recovery.

I invite you to join me on this healing adventure. Open your heart to the possibilities of future renewal and happiness. You are not alone in this. Yes, healing, moving forward with your life, and using your exploits as a testimony to those who are grieving is not just a possibility but within your reach.

Let this book be your first step toward a journey back to wholeness and a life where grief has a place but doesn't dominate. Engage fully, practice diligently, and keep your heart open to the life-changing experience of healing through faith in God, aromatherapy, face reflexology, proper breathing, exercise, and nutrition.

Visit the Resource page

CHAPTER 1

Understanding Grief and Its Impact on You

Have you ever felt like the world should stop spinning for a moment, just long enough for you to catch your breath? Grief is like everything continues around you, yet time seems to freeze.

I remember the song written by Eddy Arnold: "Make the world go away, lift it off of my shoulders." The weight of all the world's miseries piled one on top of the other, crushing me. I wasn't sure I could get up again.

I miss my husband. Doug was a perfect husband, friend, lover, mentor, cheerleader, and support for me. He was a blessing from day one of my meeting him. Everyone who knew Doug has fond memories of him. He was compassionate, with a dry sense of humor. He had joy. Doug teased me often and called me "grumpy." I didn't wake up with joy like he did.

My husband did not have parents who could afford to send him to law school. His mom raised four kids as a single parent. Doug worked as a janitor for World Vision, an international Christian relief organization for impoverished children, to pay for his education. He rode the bus to UCLA in Los Angeles, where he went for his undergraduate, from La Puente, California, where his family lived. Doug then went on to Loyola University to get his law degree.

He was a remarkable man who worked hard to achieve his goal of serving and bettering other people's lives. I admired this trait most about Doug. His humility and compassion for people stem from his deep faith and humble upbringing.

As a real estate and business attorney, Doug was honest. We weren't rich because he was not your typical attorney. Money did not motivate him. He was unique in that he saw every problem as an opportunity to stretch his knowledge and find the most creative and least costly solution for the client.

Therefore, Doug had clients that stuck with him for years, many of them since he started his law practice. They were more than happy to be sources of referrals, so he never lacked business.

Doug was loyal to a fault. He expressed his love through sacrificial giving, which, to me, defines true love. He still got mad and impatient, and we argued—but he was a good, godly man. I knew he loved me; he loved us. He was faithful to his role as a devoted husband, a loving father, an adoring "papa" for Ethan, a friend, and a lawyer to those who relied on his ability for years.

Honestly, I don't know how Doug put up with me. I was not a great homemaker. I didn't like to cook or do housework. This stems from my childhood when I did a lot of housework and even cared for my younger siblings on my own for a couple of years from age thirteen.

Doug did most, if not all, of the cleaning and cooking. I used to tease him and tell him I'm grateful to God for giving me an excellent "wife." He would just laugh. I believe he actually relished it.

Here's an adorable fact about Doug. In all the years we were together, Doug never went to bed without me. No matter how long it took me to get done with the work I was doing, he waited up for me.

Joanne was my only child. For many years, our relationship was strained. My frustration comes from knowing she was smart but not motivated and she didn't apply herself. Her focus was on having fun with her friends, and she lost good jobs because of this.

Although Doug and I supported her financially and helped her find a career, we didn't approve of the choices she made in her life. Her lack of "stick-to-itiveness" required to build a successful future disappointed us. For example, she signed up for a cosmetology course and only lasted six weeks. Her lack of ambition bothered us.

Doug and I later realized that Joanne was a "late bloomer". She changed as she got older, especially when she got pregnant with Ethan. Little did we know she had honed skills we did not realize she had.

Joanne's creativity was stunning, and she had a knack for graphics and technology. She created websites and funnels. She expertly assembled my brand board, colors, and logo, creating a beautiful and highly professional appearance that identified my brand perfectly. Her skills amazed me, and I felt a deep sense of pride!

Joanne became my tech and graphic support. She created design ideas for my website, marketing materials, and technology activities. Doug and I were pleased to see her finally uncover her talents, and her skills impressed us. I leaned on her, so you can imagine the loss, both personally and for the business I was trying to build.

Even though Joanne was not Doug's flesh and blood, he treated her like his own daughter. He never referred to her as his stepdaughter. When she had Ethan, Doug was totally over the moon in love. He was thrilled to be grandpa!

On one of our trips to Vallejo, California, to visit them, I asked Doug if he would be willing to let them move in with us. I was relieved that we both wanted a better place for Ethan to grow up in.

Their house in Vallejo was so small and had no yard area for a little one to run around and play. With Joanne working with me while living with us, she could spend more time with Ethan. And we could help her raise Ethan while Todd went to school.

Joanne, Todd, and Ethan moved in with us in October 2016. Doug was ecstatic. Even though it would be difficult for us financially—expenses would double, and sacrifices would need to be made—Ethan and Joanne were with us, and that was worth whatever hardship we had to endure.

Doug spent all his available time with Ethan every day. He took him outside to the backyard and taught him how to garden. He also showed Ethan what each tool was called and how to use it. Ethan learned a lot from his papa.

We went on our walks every afternoon, with Doug pushing Ethan in his stroller. As Ethan got older, he would ask Doug to stop so he could get out and walk on his own to explore. He picked flowers for me and his mommy and looked for bugs. The five years Doug spent with Ethan were the happiest years of his life, and I'm grateful for that.

Meanwhile, Joanne started going to church. She gave her life to the Lord and encouraged her husband, Todd, to attend church with her and Ethan. Finally, he succumbed to her urging and started going. They were both baptized together. Doug and I were joyful. God finally answered our prayers!

For years, we prayed for Joanne's salvation, Doug even more diligently than me.

"If you abide in Me, and My words abide in you, you will ask what you desire, and it shall be done for you." John 15:7 NKJV.

Joanne was active at their church, serving in ministries, volunteering at worthwhile events, leading Bible studies, and encouraging women with toddlers like her. I loved that she also taught Ethan about having a servant's heart by bringing him along when she volunteered at church events.

She was a great mom. We were all on lockdown in May 2020 during the C19 pandemic, yet Joanne made a memorable celebration for Ethan's fourth birthday. She had friends and their kids drive by, wish Ethan a happy birthday, and drop off birthday gifts. Plus, she had the Anaheim fire truck drive by with the siren blaring!

Many of Joanne's peers from church and in her local women's communities liked her. They saw her as a wonderful mother, a loving human being, and a good friend.

We worked at home, so we were together twenty-four-seven. We did everything together. It was always "Doug and Grace," with Joanne and Ethan in tow—or "Joanne and Grace," with Doug and Ethan following behind. Doug and I didn't take separate vacations or go anywhere without each other.

We were extremely close. Doug went to all kinds of doTERRA and networking events with me and Joanne, always the one tasked to watch Ethan while we talked to people. This was the happiest time of our lives.

Ethan brought us all so much joy. He loved to sing and dance, and I have many videos of him entertaining us. Joanne encouraged his talents.

Ethan was very artistic, and he still is today. I have many pictures that he painted for me. I pray daily for the Lord to soften his father's heart and give me more time with Ethan. I love and enjoy the time we spend together. I read Bible stories to him, teach him to spend time with the Lord, and pray to intercede for others, not just his needs.

I have learned to step out in faith, commit to scheduling time with Ethan, and pray for God to bless it with a miracle.

> **"For with God nothing will be impossible."**
> **Luke 1:37 NKJV**

As if the loss of my loved ones wasn't enough, you will read below how many more challenges I went through. The enemy seemed to win, but none were successful from God's perspective.

> **"'No weapon formed against you shall prosper, And every tongue which rises against you in judgment You shall condemn. This is the heritage of the servants of the Lord, And their righteousness is from Me,' Says the Lord." Isaiah 54:17 NKJV.**

After Joanne went to be with Jesus, Todd got hold of her cell phone and saw negative communication between me and Joanne about

Todd during her hospital stay. He was furious. He started taking Ethan to work with him every day to keep us apart.

I couldn't understand why Todd would rather have his five-year-old son, Ethan, sit in a room at his workplace for hours every day than leave him with me. But I knew it was the beginning of his emotional campaign to separate Ethan from me.

But God. I fought, and God, my Savior, prevailed.

The merciful and loving God who chose me as one of Ethan's stewards would not allow Todd to keep us apart. It was a challenge, but as prayers continued to go up to Heaven from many, miracles poured down on me and Ethan.

Todd turned people at his church, Doug's mom, the judge, Ethan's legal advocate, and the probate investigators against me. His family threatened to reveal my "secrets" to newspapers, as if I mattered to anyone, if I didn't stop the legal pursuit of my rights to see and have time with Ethan. He was able to turn everyone against me. They took his side without hearing mine.

Doug's mom even tried to extort me by threatening that she would go after me for fraudulently opening a PayPal account in her name. I told her, "Go ahead, I have done nothing!" Doug opened the account on her behalf, which was and is being paid for by the corporation.

Please continue reading. Chapter 12 uncovers this so-called "secret" and explains why Todd's family thought I would be so ashamed and afraid for people to know my ugly past, forcing me to withdraw the lawsuit.

Todd's attorney was *ruthless*! I don't know if the legal declaration papers the lawyer conjured up and filed in court were words from

Todd or if he created a narrative from a story Todd told him. Just the same, everything written and submitted to the family court by his lawyer was cruel, untrue, and with no hint of gratitude for everything Doug and I sacrificed for five years. The family court system in California is the worst.

Doug's brother, Dave, also played a role in my persecution. He has always hated me and was eager to get his dirty little fingers in my grandparents' right case. He told Todd about what he considered my "dirty little secret". Dave was not happy with Doug for helping their mom when Dave defrauded his mom and her husband Ron many years ago for over $100,000, so this was his opportunity to exact his revenge.

The moment Dave learned Doug was helping their mother untangle from Dave's fraud and advising their mom how to deal with the million-dollar check Dave wrote from his mom's bank account to the IRS for his debt, he was furious and beside himself. He immediately forbade his ex-wife from letting us see his little girls, who we were close to.

So, Dave was more than happy to feed Todd all the salacious details he believed would hurt my credibility in court. They were successful in poisoning everyone against me. Even though I had many character witnesses who have known me for many years write letters to the court under penalty of perjury supporting me and attesting to everything I submitted based upon what they saw over the years. Our neighbor directly across the street from us, who saw the four of us every day, wrote a letter. She said she always thought Joanne was a single mom because she never saw Todd until after.

I thought church is supposed to help bring families together during difficult situations. Joanne's so-called "good friend," Stephanie, from Eastside Christian Church, immediately took Todd's side and refused to talk to me, if only to find out a way she could help us reconcile our differences. Instead, she fed into Todd's anger and thirst to hurt me. No one from his church came to talk to me about how they could help resolve our issues, especially for Ethan's benefit.

They fell hook, line, and sinker for every lie Todd told them. It's sad that Christians take sides when they're called to promote peace and reconciliation.

"Therefore, as we have opportunity, let us do good to all, especially to those who are of the household of faith." Galatians 6:10 NKJV.

Todd's attorney was rabid and totally without a conscience. Once you read the legal papers in the resource page for Chapter 1, you will understand what I was up against. Had it not been for Jesus holding me together, I'm not sure where I would be today.

One statement in a paper filed by Todd's attorney was, "She wants to kill herself and Ethan so they can go to Heaven and be with Doug and Joanne." We all know that willfully killing someone is murder, a sin in God's eyes, and would keep me out of Heaven.

Another statement said, "She's so crazy, she runs around the house screaming and yelling. She shouldn't even be allowed to drive."

Meanwhile, it was his client who had already been involved in two car accidents within a short period of time. I do appreciate God's sense of humor! The ugly comments about me in the court papers filed by Todd's attorney, which you can find in the resource page, were hideous, cruel, and without merit.

But God. In my obedience, He heard my prayers and supplications, as well as the prayers of others for Ethan and me.

> **"Blessed are all who fear the Lord, who walk in obedience to him." Psalms 128:1 NIV**

I lost in man's court despite having the law on my side. But I won in God's court. He rewarded my obedience and continues to do so.

Experiencing grief in such a violent way should have broken me beyond repair. But as I look around me, so many others are suffering and hurting much more with no one to turn to.

Grief is not a stranger to many of us. It comes in many forms, whether through the loss of a loved one or something you value deeply, the end of a significant relationship, a divorce, a terminal diagnosis like cancer, or a life-changing event that leaves a void.

As someone who has experienced grief, I will gently walk you through the often-misunderstood panorama of grief to help you recognize the unfamiliar terrain and share with you the tools that God gave me to experience my grief with hope and healing.

Anatomy of Grief: Acknowledge Your Journey

Grief is a complex, multifaceted experience that each person encounters uniquely. No book or expert can tell you precisely what your grief feels or should feel like. Only someone who has experienced it can. Even then, how you respond to the manifestations of grief can be vastly different from the next person. Understanding what grief is and how it affects you can provide a comforting framework to help you make sense of your feelings and how they can change daily.

I knew this lonely path would not be easy. Doug was my best friend. We were seldom apart. We went everywhere together. If you saw Doug, I was soon to follow. Our strong bond, cemented by our love for Christ, united us. We knew a huge part of this was because of our nightly practice of reading the Bible and praying together. We worshipped with one heart and included Jesus in everything we did. I miss Doug so much. I continue to do the nightly devotional, even on my own.

Let's Define Grief

Grief is more than just emotional pain following a life-altering event. A deep mental, emotional, and physical response can turn your entire world upside down and disrupt your life and plans for the future. It affects how you feel, think, behave, interact with others, and perceive your life in the future.

The pain of grief might feel crushing and endless. During these moments, you fight against hopelessness and look to victory by toppling "the giant" in front of you.

> **"In the Bible, patience is not a passive acceptance of circumstances. It is courageous perseverance in the face of suffering and difficulty." - Warren Wiersbe.**

Stages of Grief

I read that the journey through grief often follows several stages: denial, anger, bargaining, depression, and acceptance. Elisabeth Kübler-Ross first proposed these stages in her 1969 book *On Death and Dying*. It's crucial to understand that these stages are not straightforward.

You might move back and forth between feelings, experiencing several stages at once or perhaps none at all. It's okay. These stages are based on observations of people encountering grief. Each person's experience with grief is as unique as their fingerprints.

You might feel fine one day, only to slip back into sadness the next. This is normal and part of the grieving process. There is no right or wrong way to experience these stages. They are simply a guide to help you understand and put into context what you might be feeling.

Let's Take a Personal Reflection

As you read this book and ponder the suggestions given here, take a moment to assess where you are in your grief process and how you can incorporate the tools in this book to help you with what you're going through.

Will there be days when denial seems the only way to cope, not wanting to acknowledge the pain of your loss? Or maybe you grapple with memories, pondering the "if only" or "what if" scenarios? These moments bring a deeper self-awareness and understanding of your emotions.

Doug's death at the hands of doctors in the hospital was unbelievable and tragic. He went in healthy, as indicated in the medical records from the hospital. He complained of difficulty breathing after just experiencing COVID, and he thought the hospital could help him. The doctors admitted him and immediately administered Remdesivir, opiates, and medications that made his breathing worse.

Looking at the side effects of the opiates, many of them restrict breathing. They did not adequately feed or hydrate Doug, causing him to lose ten pounds in eleven days. He was bedridden and developed deep venous thrombosis (DVT). When a patient is bedridden, hospitals use a type of leg massager to keep the blood flowing as a prophylactic, but they did none of that for Doug. Instead, they loaded him up full of morphine every day to keep him docile and compliant.

I think about how my daughter Joanne met her ultimate fate in the same hospital that Doug was in. The doctors convinced her to intubate, I'm not sure if they told her and Todd that her chance of surviving intubation is less than 1 percent. The doctors were giving her massive doses of dangerous medicinal "cocktails" to keep her alive or her systems "functioning." Her body couldn't possibly hold up to that and didn't. She ultimately suffered a massive stroke. I will leave the rest to your imagination after reading the article about Greg Eyerly in the Resource page.

I blame myself when I think of what Doug and Joanne went through. The memories haunt me, but I have to resign myself to the fact that there was nothing I could have done.

When Joanne went into the hospital on August 7, 2021, I should have stopped her and talked to her about using the essential oils and other recommended non-toxic solutions. I didn't even interfere with the decision she and Todd made, and I wasn't consulted. Plus, I was also recovering from COVID, and my brain wasn't working as it should. I wasn't myself at all. My first response to addressing medical concerns is always natural, but at that moment, I had to admit I couldn't think clearly.

And then a week later, Doug said he needed to go to the hospital due to breathing difficulty. He grew concerned that he would suffocate. The oxygen tanks that we rented him didn't improve his breathing. So, on August 14, 2021, he called the ambulance, and they took him. I wasn't even worried. I thought he would be home in a few days. That's what the doctors were telling Doug and Joanne every other day while they were plotting their deaths, the "scamdemic." Doctors and hospitals were getting paid big money for every "COVID" death, even when it wasn't COVID.

They wouldn't let me see Doug or Joanne. Our loved ones were held "hostage", and this was going on all over the country. They had the process down pat. Which protocol will hasten the patient's demise? They were able to convince Joanne to accept the ventilator, just as other hospitals did to many of their patients. Doug refused it, so they did him in with opiates, starvation, and dehydration. This is how many victims were treated by the hospitals in other states. The incentives were too good to turn down.

I couldn't be with Doug in the hospital but they allowed us to talk on the phone or FaceTime, but Doug couldn't speak because of the oxygen contraption they had him strapped into, the conversations were never meaningful or fruitful. Doug was frustrated and tired easily from lack of proper hydration and nutrition.

The only time they allowed me to see him was if I agreed to let them shut off his oxygen permanently. What could I do? The doctor kept saying, "He is dying. He won't live more than a couple more days." They let me see him for two hours the day before, and then the next day, I was there to go through the final moments with Doug.

September 5, 2021—the worst day of my life!

"The Lord is close to the brokenhearted and saves those who are crushed in spirit." Psalm 34:18 NIV

At some point, Joanne was on a ventilator. I wasn't allowed to see her, and her husband made no effort because he was so afraid of catching COVID. Even after she had a massive stroke on September 12—four days after Doug went to Heaven—Todd was told he could see her, but he didn't want to. He was too afraid. Ultimately, he was forced to.

September 12, 2021—the second-worst day of my life.

You can't imagine my shock. I was numb. In a matter of four days—just four days—I lost the two of the four most important people in my life.

They're with the Lord, and I am grateful that one day, I will see them again and be with them for eternity. I find comfort knowing that they escaped the evils of this world. As *Isaiah 57*:1 says:

> **"The righteous perishes, and no man takes it to heart; merciful men are taken away, while no one considers that the righteous is taken away from evil."**

Joanne Eyerly lost her husband Greg under the same circumstances as I lost Doug. When I last spoke with Joanne, she said life has been difficult to go through alone. She remains steadfast in her faith but finds the sadness and the pain of loss overwhelming. Joanne is still young; I pray she finds happiness again.

Click the link in the Resource page for Chapter 1 to the article about Greg Eyerly's untimely death from the inhumane hospital protocol.

GRACE RICHARDSON

The Days After

I don't even remember the exact dates of the celebration of life for Doug and Joanne. I was so traumatized, so shaken, that time became meaningless. Days blurred together in a fog of tears and unbearable pain. I invited as many people as I could remember to celebrate Doug's life, but honestly, I could barely think straight.

Warren Wiersbe wrote, "The fact that God permits suffering in our lives doesn't mean He enjoys it or that He is blind to our tears. He sees, He cares, and He comforts." I hung onto those words during those first impossible days.

We held Doug's service at Calvary Chapel Chino Hills, followed by a reception at a restaurant called Papa Chino's up the street. But I didn't plan any of it. I couldn't. I was completely incapable of making decisions or handling even the most insignificant detail.

Cindy Bennett was the one who managed and orchestrated everything. She took me to my church to talk to Gaby, the lady in charge of the celebration of life services. She ordered the photos and had them all printed and framed. She arranged for the restaurant. She and Case paid for everything—the service, the reception, all of it.

I just cried. I was still in shock. I couldn't speak during Doug's service; I would have broken down completely. Even now, years later, it's easier for me to write about him and Joanne in this book than to talk about them out loud. I couldn't do it at the celebration of life. The pain was too raw, too overwhelming.

If you could ever think about a friend who just took your hand and made your unbearable pain a little less unbearable, it was Cindy. I don't know what I would have done without her.

"A friend loves at all times, and a brother is born for a time of adversity." **Proverbs 17:17 NIV**

At Doug's service, we also celebrated Joanne's life. We had photos of her made and brought them to my church. Brad, the elder who conducted Doug's service, also mentioned Joanne, so we were able to honor them both together in a way that felt right. They left this world four days apart, and we celebrated their lives side by side.

Joanne's service was held in October 2021 at Eastside Christian Church, where she and Todd attended. But I was not included in the planning. I wasn't consulted. I wasn't asked for input. He invited me to talk to the lady in charge of events merely for show, but I was never asked for input.

At the service, Todd and his family sat up front, along with Doug's mother and brother. None of them spoke to me. As I recall, this was after I had already filed the custody case for Ethan. I was "persona non grata", my name was mud!

Cindy Bennett took me. She held my hand through that service too. I'm not even sure if there was a reception afterward. I think we left right after the service. I was so grateful for Cindy—she was my anchor through both services, through everything.

I was numb, shocked, angry, confused, and devastated! Unimaginable pain. It's a pain so deep that words can't capture it. Your mind can't process it. Your heart can't hold it.

Ethan at the Services

Ethan was able to attend Doug's service. They were still living with me then, before Todd spirited him away without even a hug or a "goodbye". But by the time Joanne's service came along, the legal battle had already started, and I was the most hated person in the room. Ethan wasn't even allowed to talk to me.

Ethan was the recipient of many unfair, and heartless actions during that time. The cruelty he was put through were meant to separate us, and without concern for his well-being.

Shortly after Ethan got done telling me, "Grandma, I'm glad you didn't go to Heaven," he was yanked away from me so brutally and without regard for his feelings. That was devastating for me and Ethan. And then the brainwashing started—intimidating this little boy into hating his grandma, even forcing him to call me a "liar."

Ethan apologized to me for the negative way he treated me then, I told him it wasn't his fault. He was just a little kid. He was only five years old, still a toddler. I told him I knew he was intimidated and afraid of the physical pain he knew an adult could inflict on him if he didn't obey. I have no reason to believe that Ethan has not been the receiver of this physical and verbal abuse, knowing the character of the person. He definitely has the fear of a child who has already experienced the cruelty first hand.

Even today, Ethan doesn't show me affection or tell me he loves me in front of his father. His father is very jealous of me so he avoids his father's anger by being nonchalant around me. He gets mad at Ethan when Ethan doesn't respond back with "I love you, too." Joanne once told Todd: "Ethan can love more than one person."

Ethan was never prepared for their deaths. He was never given the opportunity to talk to someone impartial to express how the loss affected him. During the legal battle, I begged for Ethan to be allowed to see a therapist. I know the pain, the agony, the questioning, the confusion, I went through, the wondering what I could have done differently. All of those thoughts went through my head constantly. If it was that painful for me, imagine what this little boy was going through having the walls around him collapse unexpectedly.

Ethan was very close to Doug and his mom. We were together 24/7, the four of us. Doug and I bathed Ethan every night. We read the Bible to him. We prayed with him. Doug did things with him every single day. His mom homeschooled him, so she spent even more time with him than most moms get to do with their children.

Suddenly, they were gone. And then I was taken away from him too.

Todd would not allow Ethan to talk to anyone. I felt it was critically important for him to express how he was feeling to someone neutral, someone who didn't know any of us and could help him process what he was going through. But Todd refused. He would say, "Oh, he's okay. He's very happy."

How can you say a kid is happy after what he went through? How can you say he's fine when he just lost the two people he loved most in the world, and then was yanked away from another person he's very close to? He was sad. He was hurting. But Todd didn't want to hear it, let alone acknowledge it.

I believe Todd didn't want Ethan to say what was really going on. He didn't hide anything, so Ethan knew what was being said and all the chicanery going on. And Ethan was clearly intimidated. I saw this little boy transform into someone who learned to manipulate for his survival and safety. I don't blame him, but it pains me. A child should be a child.

I remember during the initial court case when the court assigned an advocate for Ethan and she came to my house to interview him.

I said to her: "Aren't you supposed to interview Ethan away from the father?" Her response that he's going to be in another room was enough for me to know Ethan and I were cooked.

Anyway, Todd had to have been coached because when this advocate walked in, she walked into a "Norman Rockwell" scene. Father and son, sitting on the floor in the living room doing puzzles together. I think I threw up in my mouth when I saw this. She then tells the father to go into the next room so she can talk to Ethan away from any undue influence. Mind you, their bedroom was within earshot of the living room. Todd could hear the conversation and Ethan knew his father would be listening.

Today, Ethan still remembers what happened. Most of all, he remembers the good times—the happy moments with his mom and Papa. I show him videos. We talk about them. We send up balloons during holidays and birthdays. I talk about them as if they're still here because I don't want Ethan to forget them. I know he won't, but I still want to make sure he honors their memories and keeps them alive in his heart.

The First Weeks

It's been four years now, and the pain is still the same. There are days, even today, on a holiday or a weekend when I just cry. I miss them so much. But I know where they are, and I know that one day we're going to be together. My hope is in the Lord. He promised eternity with Him and with the people we love. This is what keeps Ethan and me going. This is what keeps us grounded—the hope of reunion for eternity. We know that our future is in Heaven with the people we love.

Warren Wiersbe reminds us: "**Faith is not believing in spite of evidence—it's obeying in spite of consequence.**" I had to choose faith even when I couldn't see the way forward.

The first weeks were horrible. I couldn't eat. I couldn't sleep. I lost 20 to 30 pounds. I looked horrid. Getting out of bed felt impossible. Functioning felt impossible. Breathing felt difficult.

But many people showed up for me. They came to talk, to pray, to help with the house and the things that needed to be done. That's one of the benefits of being in the family of God and of investing in your secular community too. You create bonds. You create relationships. You're there for them. You help. You give. You do. And they do the same thing—unexpectedly and without expecting anything in return.

Ghesi Stojanov, Ro Kendall, Case and Cindy Bennett, Lynda Bergh, Rose and John Trani, and so many others, they all showed up. They held me up when I couldn't stand on my own.

But there were also painful surprises. Some people I thought would be there weren't. My own siblings didn't come to the funeral. They didn't call. They didn't visit. They sent wilted flowers—and only because my mother forced them to. But that's a story I'll share in another chapter.

What Kept Me Going

What kept me going—and still keeps me going today—is Ethan. I was blessed to be a steward of this little one. Doug and I and Ethan's parents were blessed to be chosen as stewards of this beautiful boy, and that calling didn't end when Doug and Joanne went to Heaven.

As difficult as the days are to be juggling so much, I am happy and grateful to be able to be a huge part of Ethan's life today.

Ethan said to me recently, "Grandma, God left you here because He knew I needed you." That made my heart swell. He knows. He knows that God is the One who kept me here. So yes, I want to be here to help him become the man of God he was intended to be. God left me here for that purpose, and God is making all the provisions so I can do things for him. I can homeschool him. I can still work and live life and meet my obligations. I can provide what Ethan needs.

What got me through each day was the Lord, who said He is "Husband to the widow", I know this faithful God intimately, this all powerful Jesus, and I trust Him implicitly. His unfailing promises, the people He surrounded me with, His hands and feet, who encouraged and prayed. They prayed for me. They prayed with me. They prayed through everything and over everything with me.

You don't need a big community to feel safe and supported. When you invest in people around you, they will invest in you. We need our community. We need people we can trust, who care about us, and who we care for. It takes a village. This is what I always say—in everything, in all of life, it takes a village! That's how God created us: to fellowship, support and pray for each other, and to bear one another's burdens.

> **"Carry each other's burdens, and in this way you will fulfill the law of Christ." Galatians 6:2 NIV**

As Warren Wiersbe wrote, "**The will of God will never lead you where the grace of God cannot keep you.**" I held onto that truth through the darkest valley, and it sustained me.

Is It Possible to Normalize the Grief Experience?

There will never be a day when grief is normal for anyone, but it is a reality that will happen to everyone. Don't judge yourself harshly or rush through your emotions. In a world that often pressures us to "move on" or "get over" our losses, it's essential to recognize that feeling intense emotions is part of healing.

I find comfort and peace in God's promises. Perhaps you can, too.

> "**Fear not, for I am with you; Be not dismayed, for I am your God. I will strengthen you. Yes, I will help you, I will uphold you with My righteous right hand.**" Isaiah 41:10 NKJV.

Grief is a part of life. If you love or care for someone or something, you will experience grief. It's the price you pay. Allow yourself the grace and the time to grieve. It is essential.

It never entered my mind that I would lose my husband so early in life, but my forty-one-year-old daughter? I never expected, in my wildest dreams, that I would bury my child. I asked God, "Why, Lord? Doug, maybe, he has already lived his life somewhat at sixty-seven, but Joanne? She has a five-year-old son who needs her!" For the sake of Ethan, I would have gladly traded places with his mom. But in faith, I must rest on God's will for mine and Ethan's life. The fact is His will for us is greater than what we can imagine for ourselves.

> "But as it is written: 'Eye has not seen, nor ear heard, Nor have entered into the heart of man The things which God has prepared for those who love Him.'" 1 Corinthians 2:9

I know God didn't cause their deaths. They went to the hospital, and they never came home. Their story is just two of the hundreds of victims of greed. The world is evil, and it's filled with greedy people who will do anything, even sell their souls to Satan, for money.

COVID-19 was used to generate a lot of money. Corrupt and greedy doctors and hospitals all over the United States stole many lives between 2020 and 2022. Men, women, young and old. They went into the hospital trusting the men in the white coat, only to lose their lives! That is a book I will write one day when the wounds of my heart have fully healed.

Reflection Exercise

Journaling is a great way to express sorrow, regret, and disappointment. Start by praying. Tell God how you're feeling and ask Him to relieve the agony and physical pain of your broken heart. Ask Him to give you peace as you express your feelings about this unfair loss.

Then, seek comfort from His words in the Bible and the promises made to those who trust Him.

> "For I consider that the sufferings of this present time are not worthy to be compared with the glory which shall be revealed in us." Romans 8:18 NKJV

He lives up to His promises; He has never let me down.

> **"Commit your way to the Lord, Trust also in Him, And He shall bring it to pass." Psalms 37:5 NKJV**

Once you've read God's assurances and promises, pray and thank Him for giving you the fortitude and the courage to move forward with your life. With Jesus, you never walk alone.

> **"And the Lord, He is the One, who goes before you. He will be with you, and He will not leave you nor forsake you; do not fear nor be dismayed." Deuteronomy 31:8 NKJV.**

By recognizing and embracing your grief and the knowledge that you are not alone in it, you take your first steps toward healing.

> **"Cast your burden on the Lord, And He shall sustain you; He shall never permit the righteous to be moved." Psalms 55:22 NKJV.**

Emotional and Physical Symptoms of Grief

When you're engulfed in grief, the emotional turmoil isn't just something you feel in fleeting moments throughout your day. It's a constant presence, coloring and intensely influencing your entire world. Imagine carrying an invisible weight only you can feel, pulling at your heart with every step, affecting everything you do and how you relate to and respond to situations that arise.

Emotions like sadness, anger, guilt, and confusion don't just pass through like unwelcome guests; they move in, set up shop, and disrupt your life in unexpected ways.

Sadness might feel like a soft, persistent ache, a sorrow that deepens during quiet moments alone or when you pass by a restaurant you frequented with your loved one. Fury can surge up unexpectedly and fiercely, leaving you shaking or in tears. It's not just anger at the situation but a penetrating frustration that the world continues unchanged while your whole life has been turned upside down and spilled all over the floor.

Then there's guilt, a feeling that you could have done something different.

My grandson Ethan was only five years old when his dad told him that his mommy and papa went to Heaven. His words still ring in my ears and cause tears to rise and flow like a river. He said: "Grandma, I'm glad you didn't go to Heaven."

Watching Ethan suffer and not knowing exactly how deep the wounds of his loss were to his heart intensified my anger, knowing that loss is painful for me even though I understand it. How much worse is it for this little boy who doesn't? I questioned God. Grief is worse when others you love are suffering, too.

Ethan lost two important people to him in the blink of an eye. Ethan spent five years with his mommy, papa, and me. We worked at home and enjoyed flexibility in our day-to-day work activities so we could devote a lot of time to Ethan. His mom homeschooled him and taught him about Jesus.

Grief Can Be Destructive Physically

As if the emotional symptoms aren't challenging enough, nights plagued by restlessness or an overwhelming desire to sleep all the time as an escape. My appetite took a hit. I skipped meals without noticing. Then there's the sheer lack of energy—the feeling of having your internal batteries drained, leaving you listless, tired, and uninterested in activities that once brought joy.

The connection between the brain and the body is astounding regarding grief. Emotional pain triggers stress responses in the brain and dramatically affects the body. Stress hormones like cortisol can disrupt your systems, leading to physical symptoms like sleep deprivation, which can lead to medical issues.

Understanding this connection is pivotal because it underscores the importance of self-care—attending to the heart, mind, and body.

I did not know the extent of the damage grief caused me physically until I looked in the mirror. I was shocked to see how I looked in September 2021 after Doug and Joanne went home to be with Jesus. I couldn't sleep, I didn't eat nor hydrate appropriately, and I did nothing to help my body manage its ability to bear the burden of the destructive effects of grief and depression.

Make an Effort to Create a Routine

Coping with the symptoms and effects involves a gentle approach. Create small, manageable routines that help bring some order to your day:

- A regular bedtime routine to help combat sleep issues.
- Reminders to eat nutritious meals that can help stabilize your energy levels and drink plenty of water to hydrate the brain, cells, and tissues.
- Gentle physical activity, like walking, improves your mood, oxygenates your brain, and increases your energy levels. The goal isn't to "fix" yourself—it's providing your

body and mind the support they need to process your grief more healthily.

These are the first steps, laying the groundwork for deeper strategies you'll build as you heal. Each small step is part of a more extensive yet loving approach to caring for yourself during one of life's most challenging times.

In the following chapters, you will learn more about proper breathing, exercise, nutrition, supplements, and hydration. These activities will help you, along with your daily practice of praying, reading scriptures, or even meditating on quotes or information that have helped you in the past and complementing it with aromatherapy and face reflexology.

Grief Can Make You Question Your Faith

When life as you know it seems to unravel, it's not uncommon to find that your spiritual beliefs—whatever they may be—get stretched. Losing someone or something precious can shake the foundations of even the most devout faith. Questions like "Why me?" or "How could this happen?" might echo in your mind. These questions go beyond searching for answers; it's a spiritual earthquake, creating an unfamiliar environment that appears foreign and challenging to traverse.

During these periods of constant questioning, many find that their faith isn't just challenged—it's transformed. For some, this transformation means a deepening of faith. The loss becomes a gauntlet, an intense, fiery place where the trivial falls away, leaving only the most significant elements of their spiritual life.

Many report feeling a closer, more personal connection to God during this refining process. They find shelter in scriptures that once seemed distant or abstract, discovering a direct message of comfort and a source of unshakable strength.

> **"Seek the Lord and His strength; Seek His face evermore!" I Chronicles 16:11 NKJV.**

It is not easy or painless, but the struggle with questions and doubts can lead to a stronger and more grounded spiritual future.

Spirituality is as diverse as humanity, and so are the spiritual responses to grief. There is no right or wrong way. Some may step away from traditional practices, seeking assurance in nature or meditation rather than structured religion or relationship with God. Others might turn to new spiritual communities, like church or different faith traditions, looking for voices that resonate with their experiences of loss and renewal.

> **"You will keep him in perfect peace, Whose mind is stayed on You, Because he trusts in You." Isaiah 26:3 NKJV.**

In navigating these personal waters, tools for spiritual reflection can be invaluable.

An effective means of expressing to God is prayer. He is the One to whom you can communicate your deepest fears and hopes. In prayer, you can pour out your heart without fear of judgment or misunderstanding.

> **"I will lift up my eyes to the hills—from whence comes my help? My help comes from the Lord, Who made heaven and earth. He will not allow**

> your foot to [a]be moved; He who keeps you will not slumber." Psalm 121:1-3 NKJV.

Another powerful practice is the meditative reading of the Bible. But whether scripture, poetry, or other spiritual texts. This practice allows you to absorb and find personal meaning in comforting words.

These are not one-size-fits-all solutions; they offer a way to navigate the often-tumultuous grief journey with a sense of direction.

Accepting Grief as a Part of Life

Acceptance of grief often implies surrender, a final coming to terms with loss. However, in reality, acceptance is far more powerful and less about resignation than it is about integrating it with your "new life".

Acceptance doesn't mean forgetting or no longer feeling the pain. Instead, it's about acknowledging the loss and including this new reality in the details of your life. It involves moments of progress mixed with times of setback, where the pain feels as fresh as when it first struck.

It's important to understand that these setbacks are not failures but part of the natural process of healing.

One day, Ethan, my then-seven-year-old grandson, was with me. My friend, Melissa Esguerra, called to check on me and encourage me. We discussed grief, the various events in our lives, and how faith has been our anchor. After I hung up, Ethan asked, "Grandma, what's grief?" I explained that grief is the pain and sadness we are going through because of losing his papa (Doug) and his mommy.

Ethan's response was to the point and something I, as an adult, should learn to do. He said, "I hold my grief in one leg and my happiness in the other". At seven years of age, he was already aware of accepting his grief and had developed the ability to compartmentalize it.

> "The Lord is near to those who have a broken heart, and saves such as [a]have a contrite spirit." Psalm 34:18 NKJV

Acceptance is necessary in the healing process. It's the point where you see the possibility of a future, even if it's different from what you had planned. It's where the sharp edges of your pain dull, not because the loss matters less but because you've rebuilt yourself around it.

Each small step toward acceptance is a step toward reclaiming your life. Acceptance doesn't mean the absence of pain but the beginning of managing it in a way that allows you to function and eventually flourish.

Several practical strategies can ease the process of moving toward acceptance. One effective approach is to create rituals for remembrance, which can prevent beautiful memories from being overshadowed by sadness.

Some time ago, my friend from church, Krystin Tello, shared with me what she does with her nephew/adopted son, James, who lost his dad because of a heart attack recently. She buys a balloon for special occasions, and then James releases it to his dad in Heaven so he will always remember his dad.

I started doing the same with Ethan. We get balloons for birthdays and holidays, and Ethan sends Doug and Joanne a message of love.

He prays over the balloon and releases it to Heaven for his mommy, his papa, or both, depending on the occasion. He tells them he loves and misses them. Once, he even put some chocolates on the balloon to share it with his papa!

These acts of remembrance, which we repeat over time, offer comfort and a sense of continuity that is often lost in the aftermath of grief, making the grief tangible and manageable.

Another aspect of acceptance involves keeping a connection. I often talk to Doug or Joanne about what they might do in a certain situation. It's mostly the act of conversing as we used to. It's the same conversations I have with Jesus these days when I'm in a quandary over how to handle issues.

I habitually talk to Ethan about what we all used to do together, and we reminisce and laugh about the funny times, the activities he did with his papa, and the things he learned from him and his mommy. Through videos, he can see the moments of all of us together. This keeps him connected to them, just as it does me.

Share Your Story of Loss

Share your story of loss and how you conquer it daily. It's not only comforting to you, but it's also encouraging to others who need to hear it.

Sharing your story in a society where grief sometimes feels like a private or sensitive subject can be incredibly liberating. It can also provide support to others going through similar situations. Whether in a small group setting or with friends, sharing your journey can lighten your emotional load and provide a sense of community and understanding.

Ultimately, acceptance is about giving yourself grace. It's about understanding that some days will be more complicated than others and that healing is not about achieving a state of being okay all the time. It's about integrating the loss into your life in a way that allows you to appreciate the small blessings and find joy in them.

This doesn't mean the pain of loss is cured, but it becomes a bearable companion in the larger scope of your life. Acceptance is not an endpoint but a process, one that allows you to live fully and deeply with your loss as part of who you are.

As you move toward acceptance, remember that it's perfectly normal to feel you're progressing one day and regressing the next. Healing is not a straight path but a winding road with trials. Each step, each breath, each day is a part of the process—your process—of bringing the past into the present, the joy with the pain, the memories with new experiences.

As you read each chapter, keep the song "God Is In This Story" by Katy Nicholle and Big Daddy Weave in mind.

Visit the Resource page

CHAPTER 2

Faith and Healing

Embracing Faith in Times of Loss

There are days when, in the quiet moments of early morning, I open my eyes and crane my neck to listen for the noise of morning news on the TV in the den and the sounds of Ethan and Joanne making breakfast in the kitchen. Then I realize I am all alone, and sadness engulfs me.

The harsh realization that I will no longer hear the noise I've grown accustomed to or experience the daily assurance that Doug is just beyond the wall, sitting in the den, crushes me like a ton of bricks.

Many evenings, the weight of grief can feel overwhelming, and a deep hunger for my family comes up from the pit of my stomach and produces an unbearable pain in my heart. I miss every moment.

When Joanne, Todd, and Ethan moved in with us in October 2016, Ethan became the center of our lives. We bathed him every night and often got in trouble with his mom for letting him stay in the tub too long. After the bath, we read him Bible stories until he was ready for bed. Doug and I did this every night unless they were out of town. The gift of stewardship of this amazing little boy was a tremendous privilege, and we deeply relished every moment!

There are times when days and nights can be difficult. But it is in the stillness when the arms of my Savior envelop me, and I realize I am not alone. Regardless of the time it will take to be reunited with Doug and Joanne in Heaven, I'll never be alone.

It's during this time of brokenness, helplessness, sadness, and aloneness that I feel my Savior's presence more acutely. This truth strengthens and sustains me, allowing me to face the world and the lonely future ahead of me with courage and certainty.

> **"When you pass through the waters, I will be with you; And through the rivers, they shall not overflow you. When you walk through the fire, you shall not be burned, Nor shall the flame scorch you." Isaiah 43:2 NKJV.**

Embracing faith in times of loss isn't about ignoring the pain, masking the sadness, or pretending all is right. It's about allowing it to guide you through the storm.

The Power of Prayer and Meditation on Scripture

Prayer as a Communication Tool

> **"Prayer is simply a two-way communication between you and God." -Billy Graham**

Think of prayer as a heart-to-heart conversation with a "Friend" (even if you don't follow Jesus). He knows you better than anyone. This could be when you will experience the peace that passes all understanding only He can give. The time to open the door of your heart to Him and receive the blessing of His presence as He walks you through the "wilderness" in strength and victory.

> "Before I formed you in the womb, I knew you; Before you were born, I sanctified you." Jeremiah 1:5 NKJV.
>
> **"Prayer is the very link that connects us to Almighty God."** *-EM Bounds*

This "Friend" doesn't need you to hold back or put on a brave face. Express your deepest fears, your most significant pain, and moments of gratitude, no matter how small they may seem.

A hymn I loved to sing as a little girl in the choir at church is "What A Friend We Have In Jesus." Written by a preacher, Joseph M. Scrivner, originally as a poem to his mom in 1855. The song says it all.

The video and lyrics are on the Resource page.

Prayer is a lifeline in times of grief. It is a powerful conversation that helps you manage your emotions and seek comfort and strength from a Power bigger than you.

> **"We are to pray in times of adversity, lest we become faithless and unbelieving. We are to pray in times of prosperity, lest we become boastful and proud. We are to pray in times of danger, lest we become fearful and doubting. We are to pray in times of security, lest we become self-sufficient."** – Billy Graham

Prayer during grief can start as a whisper, a simple "help me" or "give me strength". It's perfectly okay if your prayers start this way. What's important is that you're opening a line of communication, setting the foundation for a deeper relationship with the Sovereign God.

Over time, as you become more comfortable, your prayers become less awkward and more intimate, incorporating praise in words and maybe even in songs, requests, thanksgiving, and gratitude. The transformation in your prayer life can reflect your healing journey—initially raw and tumultuous, gradually becoming more reflective, composed, and grateful.

Find a prayer partner. I found immense value in praying with another woman of God. If you feel inadequate or feel like you don't know how to pray or what to pray, find a partner to pray with. There's accountability when you commit to pray with someone. You will find there are many who would be happy to pray with you. Pray, talk to God. He is waiting for you to include Him in your life.

Jesus said:

> "Come to Me, all *you* who labor and are heavy laden, and I will give you rest. Take My yoke upon you and learn from Me, for I am gentle and lowly in heart, and you will find rest for your souls. For My yoke *is* easy and My burden is light." Matthew 11:28-30 NKJV.

Prayer as a Tool for Mindset Shifts

> "To be a Christian without prayer is no more possible than to be alive without breathing."- Martin Luther

Prayer can be incredibly transformative to your mindset. It allows you to express your deepest fears and hopes. Through prayer, you can lay down your burden at the foot of His Throne and begin to release and lighten the load.

> **"The effective, fervent prayer of a righteous man avails much." James 5:16b NKJV**

> **"My flesh and my heart fail, but God is the strength of my heart and my portion forever." Psalm 73:26 NKJV**

There's a tendency to pray only when everything else has been exhausted. But in reality, prayer should be your first step. Your first contact should be with the Creator of Heaven and earth—the One who created you and knows everything about you. Even if you haven't had an encounter with Jesus, when you approach God, He won't turn you away. Most often, your need for His help is a beckoning to go to Him. Jesus wants to help you carry your burden.

I was in desperate pain after Doug and Joanne died. My heart exploded into a million pieces. Seeing Ethan and knowing what he was feeling, burdened by the weight of his loss, I was a basket case. God was the only One who could lift this heavy load. I cried out to God, but I didn't raise my fist at Him. I sought His mercy and the relief that only He can give. I lived in prayer.

> **"Because he holds fast to me in love, I will deliver him; I will protect him, because he knows my name. When he calls to me, I will answer him; I will be with him in trouble; I will rescue him and honor him. With long life I will satisfy him and show him my salvation." Psalm 91:14-16 ESV**

When Ethan's father told me I would never see Ethan again, I was aghast, angry, and vengeful. How could this man be so calloused and evil that he would separate a grandson from his grandmother who practically was his second mom? The legal pursuit was a disappointment. But God! The court denied me, but God opened the door to bring Ethan and me together. God answers prayers. Don't you ever doubt that fact. He may say "yes," "no," or "wait—I have something better for you"—but He will answer.

When He answers "no," He is not punishing you or depriving you of something good. Remember, He is the only One who knows what is good for you. His will is greater than what you could imagine for yourself. When He says "no", it's because He knows it will not be good for you. Trust, believe and obey.

> **"For my thoughts are not your thoughts, neither are your ways my ways, declares the Lord." Isaiah 55:8 NIV**

Meditating on Scripture

While prayer allows you to speak to God, meditating on scriptures is listening to Him. It's digesting His words, pondering their meanings, and letting them saturate your heart and spirit. He is telling you something to comfort you and give you peace.

Scriptures can provide immense comfort and guidance, especially when the words speak directly to your heart, addressing your pain and offering hope.

> **"Now may the God of hope fill you with all joy and peace in believing, that you may abound in hope by the power of the Holy Spirit." Romans 15:13 NKJV**

Select a scripture that resonates with your situation or how you are feeling. For instance, those in grief find the Psalms incredibly relatable as they express cries for help and gratitude for victory through a relationship with and trust in God.

Read the scripture slowly, perhaps even out loud, letting the words sink in. Focus on a verse that strikes a chord, repeating it softly, letting its message of comfort or guidance wash over you.

As you meditate, reflect on what the scripture means to you personally. Does it challenge you? Comfort you? Give you peace? The key is to let the scripture interact with your innermost thoughts, allowing it to touch the parts of your heart that most need healing.

Scripture for Grieving Hearts

Here are a few scriptures that I have found comforting in times of grief:

- **Matthew 5:4: "Blessed are those who mourn, for they will be comforted."**
- **Revelation 21:4: "He will wipe every tear from their eyes. There will be no more death or mourning or crying or pain, for the old order of things has passed away."**
- **John 16:22: "Therefore you now have sorrow, but I will see you again, and your heart will rejoice, and your joy no one will take from you."**
- **Deuteronomy 31:8: "It is the Lord who goes before you. He will be with you; He will not leave you or forsake you. Do not fear or be dismayed."**

These verses can be a good starting point for your scripture meditation. They acknowledge the reality of pain and promise comfort, hope, and help from the Sovereign God.

Use of Psalms and Scriptural Prayers

The Psalms offer a treasure trove of emotional expressions that can resonate deeply during grief. These ancient songs and prayers articulate a spectrum of human feelings—from despair to joy, abandonment to redemption. Engaging with the Psalms can be like finding words for emotions you haven't quite been able to articulate yourself.

Try reading through some Psalms and notice which lines speak to you. Many find comfort in Psalms 23, 34, or 91. Use these Scriptures as a springboard for your prayers.

> **Psalm 23:1-3:" The Lord *is* my shepherd; I shall not want. He makes me to lie down in green pastures; He leads me beside the still waters. He restores my soul; He leads me on the paths of righteousness For His name's sake."**

> **Psalm 34:4: "I sought the Lord, and He heard me, And delivered me from all my fears."**

> **Psalm 91-2: "He who dwells in the secret place of the Most High Shall abide under the shadow of the Almighty. I will say of the Lord, '*He is* my refuge and my fortress; My God, in Him I will trust.'"**

David wrote many of the Psalms as a young shepherd boy and as an adult. You can read about him in the Bible, first and second Samuel, first Kings, and first Chronicles. He is sinful and less than perfect; yet, he is referred to as "a man after God's heart." I believe a repentant heart, a heart whose desire it is to please God and the awareness of his deep need for God, kept him continually seeking God, as reflected in the Psalms he wrote.

Scriptural prayers aren't just about seeking comfort. They invite you to wrestle with your beliefs, ask hard questions, and seek deeper truths, all within the safety of God's presence. Engaging with scripture can transform your prayer life into a dynamic conversation that can sustain and nourish you through your grief.

I love Matthew Henry's method of prayer, which uses scriptures to express to God. Here are two:

Prayer for God's Grace to Fortify Against Evil

"I draw near to the throne of grace, that I may receive not only mercy to pardon, but grace to help in every time of need: **Hebrews 4:16(ESV)** grace for seasonable help. From the fullness that is in Jesus Christ (in whom all the fullness of God was pleased to dwell), **Colossians 1:19(ESV)** let me receive grace upon grace. **John 1:16(ESV)**"

Prayer for Faith

"Lord, let it be granted to me to believe; **Philippians 1:29(ESV)** for the faith by which I am saved is not my own doing, it is the gift of God. **Ephesians 2:8(ESV)** Lord, increase my faith, **Luke 17:5(ESV)** and supply what is lacking in it, **1 Thessalonians 3:10(ESV)** that I may grow strong in faith, as I give glory to God. **Romans 4:20(ESV)** Lord, give me so to be crucified with Christ, as that the life I may now live in the flesh, I may live by faith in the Son of God, who loved me and gave himself for me; **Galatians 2:20(ESV)** and so to carry in me continually the death of Jesus, as that the life also of Jesus may be manifested in my mortal body.

2 Corinthians 4:10(ESV) As I have received Christ Jesus the Lord, enable me so also to walk in him, rooted and built up in him and established in the faith, just as I was taught, abounding in thanksgiving. **Colossians 2:6-7(ESV)** Let every word of yours benefit me, being united by faith, **Hebrews 4:2(ESV)** by which I receive your testimony and set my seal to this: that God is true. **John 3:33(ESV)** I beg you, work in me that faith which is the assurance of things hoped for and the conviction of things not seen, **Hebrews 11:1(ESV)** by which I may look above the things that are seen, that are transient, and may look at the things that are unseen, that are eternal. **2 Corinthians 4:18(ESV)** Enable me by faith to set the LORD always before me, **Psalm 16:8(ESV)** and to have my eyes ever toward him, **Psalm 25:15(ESV)** that I may act in everything, as seeing him who is invisible and may look to the reward. **Hebrews 11:26-27(ESV)** Let my heart be cleansed by faith, **Acts 15:9(ESV)** and let it be my victory to overcome the world; **1 John 5:4(ESV)** and let me be kept from fainting by believing that I shall look upon the goodness of the LORD in the land of the living. **Psalm 27:13(ESV)**"

Matthew Henry wove the Scriptures together and made them into prayers to God. You can talk to Him using His own words and promises. This would be like holding Him to His own words and expressing your trust in them in faith.

Prayer Journals

Keeping a prayer journal is an enriching way to track your spiritual journey and see your growth. It can be a place to pour out your feelings, document your prayers, and celebrate answered prayers or moments of insight.

Journaling can be a means of worship—a reflective practice that helps process your emotions and experiences and express your gratitude. Looking back over your journal over time can offer valuable insights into how your relationship with God has sustained and transformed you. It's a physical testament to your resilience, the steadfastness of your faith, and the work God has done in your life through your grief.

Create a Time for Daily Devotion

Incorporating prayer and scripture meditation into your daily life can help establish spiritual nourishment and emotional release, which are important for healing. Deliberately set aside a specific time each day, perhaps in the morning when the house is quiet or in the evening as part of your wind-down routine. Create a comfortable space where you won't be disturbed, such as a corner of your bedroom, a favorite chair by the window, or anywhere that feels peaceful.

Begin with a simple prayer, open your heart to God, then read and meditate on a chosen scripture. Allow yourself the grace to sit with the words and feel their impact without rushing. Conclude with a prayer that reflects your thoughts and feelings, asking for strength for the day or peace for the night. This routine doesn't have to be lengthy; even a few minutes daily can make a significant difference.

The regularity of time devoted to praying and reading scriptures creates an opportunity for spiritual support, offering anchors of hope and strength as you deal with the circumstances of the day brought on by grief.

Engaging with Scriptures for Deep Comfort

On days when your emotions feel most turbulent, start your day with a prayer of praise and thanksgiving. Remind Him of His promises in scripture, like:

> **"He heals the brokenhearted and binds up their wounds." Psalm 147:3** or this promise: **"Have I not commanded you? Be strong and of good courage; do not be afraid, nor be dismayed, for the Lord your God *is* with you wherever you go." Joshua 1:9**

Grief can manifest in myriad ways—anger, loneliness, despair, or even numbness. Scriptures can speak to each of these emotions, offering understanding and perspective.

For instance, if you're feeling abandoned or alone, **Psalm 27:10** assures, **"Though my father and mother forsake me, the Lord will receive me."** In moments of despair, **Lamentations 3:22-23** reminds us of hope: **"Because of the Lord's great love, we are not consumed, for His compassions never fail. They are new every morning; great is Your faithfulness."** If anger is part of your grief, consider **Ephesians 4:26-27, "In your anger do not sin: Do not let the sun go down while you are still angry, and do not give the devil a foothold."** These Scriptures do not provide a quick fix but offer a means to process your emotions.

Finding Comfort in Biblical Promises

Promises made by God give the hope and assurance that can light your darkest days. These promises are not just ancient words; they are living, breathing declarations breathed from the mouth of God that offer comfort and healing to hearts broken by grief.

When the night seems too silent and the path ahead too daunting, these biblical promises can be like stars in the sky, guiding you and reminding you of the love and security that comes from trusting in God.

Promises of Comfort and Healing

The Bible is rich with verses that speak directly to the weary and the wounded.

Matthew 5:4 offers a powerful reassurance: **"Blessed are those who mourn, For they shall be comforted."** In moments of loneliness or despair, this promise can be a gentle reminder that you are not alone; a Divine and powerful strength is there to hold you up and see you through your pain.

Similarly, **Psalm 147:3** declares, **"He heals the brokenhearted and binds up their wounds."** This verse acknowledges the reality of heartbreak and promises tender care and restoration.

During times of grief, drawing on these promises can provide a peace that passes all understanding. They serve as a reminder that God Himself sees your pain and knows your heartache—not just by those around you. They assure you that your grief does not show abandonment but rather a season in which you can witness God's faithful hand in your life. It's a refining, a strengthening, a building of character for greater use.

Trust in God's Plan

Understanding and accepting God's plan, especially when it involves loss and suffering, can be one of the most challenging aspects of faith. The question of "Why?" often lingers without a satisfying answer. Yet, faith invites you to trust in a plan beyond your understanding to believe there is a purpose in the pain, even if it is not immediately clear.

> **"And the Lord will guide you continually and satisfy your desire in scorched places and make your bones strong; and you shall be like a watered garden, like a spring of water, whose waters do not fail." Isaiah 58:11 ESV**

This verse doesn't diminish the reality of suffering but frames it with an immense promise of hope and restoration. Embracing this trust isn't about finding all the answers; it's about holding on to the belief that there is a bigger picture, one painted with broad strokes of love and redemption. It's about letting this trust anchor you, allowing it to be the firm ground you stand on when everything else feels like shifting sand.

> **"For we walk by faith, not by sight." 2 Corinthians 5:7 ESV**

These aren't merely words, these are promises made by a faithful God, the Creator of Heaven and earth and everything in it. Knowing and assured that you never walk alone if you believe and trust in the One who made the promise. My friends, Krystyn and Tom Tello are in this valley right now. Tom was recently diagnosed with a rare cancer called chromophobe renal cell carcinoma. They have eight little kids going through this heartache watching their dad suffering. The Tellos grieve as a family but are steadfast in their faith that no matter what happens, they are certain, they are in the hands of a loving, gracious and merciful God, who is faithful!

I saw them at church recently, Tom looks great. Krystyn seemed tired, but they are in church to praise and worship our Lord and Savior; to hear the comforting words of our faithful Father to His people.

Renewing Faith Through Promises

These promises of hope and a future have the potential to renew and deepen your faith. They are not just words to be read but to be lived. As you cling to these promises, you allow them to reshape your understanding of God and His role in your life. They become personal in what you've lost and what you are being led toward.

Incorporating these promises into your life can transform them from abstract concepts into pillars of truth that support and sustain you. They become the truths you tell yourself when grief feels overwhelming, the script you rely on when your words fail. This active engagement with God's promises can turn them from a source of comfort into a source of strength.

Faith and Gratitude

Gratitude is a powerful practice. It might seem hard to find things to be grateful for when you are in the depths of grief, but acknowledging even the smallest blessings can shift your perspective and lighten your heart.

Each morning or evening, jot down three things you are thankful for. They can be as simple as a sunny day, a friend's comforting message, the blessing of provision, or the peace you find in a moment of prayer. This practice can slowly transform your outlook, helping you to see the light at the end of the tunnel in the shadow of your loss.

I've practiced gratitude since having gone through the challenges in my adult life after the Lord rescued me in 1993 from my prodigal life. It has transformed my faith and my life in ways I never expected. It brought to life the truth in the words: ***"He makes all things work together for good to those who love Him and are the called according to His purpose." Romans 8:28 NKJV***

Songs and Hymns of Comfort

Music is unique in touching the soul, and hymns and spiritual songs can be exceptionally comforting during grief. Songs like "It Is Well With My Soul" or "Love Lifted Me" carry messages of hope and resilience that can lift your spirits.

The story of Horatio Gates Spafford is very inspiring because, similar to Job in the Old Testament of the Bible, Spafford suffered significant losses. First, four-year-old Horatio Jr. died of scarlet fever. A year later, a massive fire destroyed their properties.

And if that wasn't enough, two years later, in 1873, Spafford took his family on a vacation to England to see his friend Dwight L. Moody preach. Because of business, Horatio delayed his trip and sent his wife and four daughters—eleven-year-old Anna, nine-year-old Margaret Lee, five-year-old Elizabeth, and two-year-old Tanetta—ahead.

While crossing the Atlantic on the steamship Ville du Havre, on November 22, 1873, an iron sailing ship struck the vessel. All four of Horatio's daughters perished with two hundred other people. Anna, his wife, was the only survivor.

GRACE RICHARDSON

The Resource page has the lyrics to the song "It Is Well With My Soul," which Spafford wrote in response to his losses.

Create a playlist of hymns and spiritual songs that speak to your heart. Listen to it during your morning routine, in moments of distress, or as you wind down for the night. The lyrics and melodies can soothe your pain and remind you of the enduring presence of God's comfort and grace.

Here are a few songs that you will find the links on the Resource page:

- "The Goodness of God," Ed Cash, Brian Johnson, Jason Ingram 2019 CeCe Winans
- "Come, Jesus Come" by Stephen McWhirter, Hank Bentley, Bryan Christopher Fowler, Tara McWhirter 2020
- "I Trust In God," by Christopher Joel Brown, Steven Furtick, Brandon Lake, Mitch Wong, 2023 Elevation
- "God Is In This Story" by Katy Nichole 2022
- "What A Friend We Have In Jesus" by Joseph M. Schriven (1855) Glen Campbell
- "In The Garden" by C Austin Miles (1912) Anne Murray
- "Softly And Tenderly" by Will L. Thompson (1880) Anne Murray
- "Why Me, Lord?" by Kris Kristofferson, 1972
- "Together" by Chris Tomlin, Russell Dickerson, Corey Justin Crowder, Bryan Kelley, Tyler Reed Hubbard 2020
- "Knowing What I Know About Heaven" William D. Austin, Charles David Robbins, 2010, Guy Penrod and Sarah Darling
- "Scars In Heaven" Matthew West, Joh Mark Hall 2022, Casting Crowns

Faith Reminders

Physical reminders of your faith can serve as tangible sources of comfort. For example, you could carry a scripture card in your pocket. When you feel overwhelmed, you can read it, using it as a focal point for a moment of prayer or meditation. You might also place verses around your home—on your bathroom mirror, kitchen sink, or nightstand. These comforting verses can gently prompt you to refocus on your faith when sorrow seems to cloud everything else.

Memorization for Quick Access

There's a unique comfort in carrying words of hope wherever you go. Memorizing scriptures can be a powerful way to keep them close, especially when you might not have a Bible. Think of the verse that corresponds with how you're feeling at that moment. Let it address the cry of your heart.

Then, commit it to memory and recite it whenever you feel overwhelmed or lost. This can be a powerful affirmation of your faith and a reminder that you are not alone in your struggles.

Recitation can also be meditative, helping to center and calm your mind during moments of acute grief. Ethan's favorite is *"At the right time, I, the Lord, will make it happen." Isaiah 60:22b NLT.*

Many Bible verses remind me of God's nearness and involvement in the details of my life. Ethan memorized these verses because they comforted him:

> **"But as it is written: Eye has not seen, nor ear heard, Nor have entered into the heart of man.**

The things which God has prepared for those who love Him." 2 Corinthians 2:9 NKJV.

"The Lord *is* good to all, And His tender mercies *are* over all His works." Psalm 145:9.

Visit the Resource page

CHAPTER 3

Faith and Community

The Value of a Supportive Community

I was sitting on the floor of Doug's office, surrounded by boxes of his legal files, completely overwhelmed. I didn't know where to start. I just sat there and cried, wondering how to deal with all of it.

Then my doorbell rang. It was Ghesi.

She didn't ask what I needed. She didn't offer suggestions. She just said, "I'm here to help. Show me the boxes."

For the next six weeks, she came over three days a week and organized everything, from labeling folders, to sorting documents, creating order out of chaos. She didn't give it one thought. She just did it.

That's what community does. It shows up. It doesn't wait to be asked. It sees the need and meets it.

There are going to be many days ahead when the pain of grief will be relentless and without mercy. The role of a strong and supportive community is essential to overcoming.

This is especially true for someone going through it alone, as I was. The companionship of a supportive community is like joining hands with someone who holds you up and keeps you steady, who says without words, "You don't have to walk this path alone."

This is the essence of community during times of sorrow: hearts and hands holding the weight of individual pains, transforming the journey into one marked by shared encouragement and understanding.

It was a blessing to have both a faith and a business community—a small group with strong ties. Doug, Joanne and I believed in the power of relationship building. The funny part is that we all had the same love language: giving to and doing for others. People knew us for our generosity.

Relationship building was easy for us. It was energizing and fulfilling to have a tight-knit community of people whose beliefs and values are similar to yours. The goal of each person in the relationship or community is more geared to benefit the whole. It becomes a source of comfort and shared stories and is mutually uplifting and encouraging.

The Importance of Community

When you are in the throes of grief, isolation may seem like the easiest path. The world moves jarringly fast when loss throws your inner life into a sudden stop. Communities provide spiritual support and a social framework that can help reduce feelings of loneliness and isolation.

Community members can find common ground, strength, and mutual compassion. Each interaction, whether through a shared prayer, a comforting hug, or a knowing glance, gently affirms that "we see your pain", "we acknowledge your loss," and "we value your presence."

Someone once said, "God puts people in our lives for a reason, a season, or forever." I believe this because I've seen it happen in my life. You help people in your beloved community, not expecting anything in return, but assured that they will be there to lean on one day if the need arises.

Treasured Friendships

> **"Every good gift and every perfect gift is from above and comes down from the Father of lights, with whom there is no variation or shadow of turning." James 1:17 NKJV.**

Doug and I met Case Bennett in 2004 when we moved into our new home in Anaheim, California. We needed a new air conditioning system. We all laugh when we reminisce about the first time we met Case.

He was young then, but we took to him right away. We saw his honesty and a certain joy emanated from Case. It was on his face and in his smile.

We quickly became close friends. It was easy. Case is very generous, caring, loving, and funny. It's his nature, even more so toward the people he loves. Doug was the same, so they meshed well together.

One day, Case told Doug that the previous company he worked for was suing him for damages in the millions of dollars. Doug immediately took on the legal case. Case was just starting out, and the lawsuit would have jeopardized his new business. His new company, Sirius Mechanical, would not be financially equipped to defend against an already established enterprise.

With Doug's help, Case prevailed and, praise God, has a thriving business today. Case's success in his business did not surprise us. He is hardworking and very smart, and he and his wife Cindy are excellent businesspeople. They care about their employees and provide excellent work to all their customers.

Doug and I weren't as close to Cindy as we were with Case because our interactions with her were mostly during social events. When Cindy got extremely sick, Case was so distraught. He would come by to visit, and together, we would pray for Cindy. This was a comfort to him.

I believe men aren't as open about their feelings, so having us pray with him for his beloved wife gave Case a certain peace and assurance. It's been twenty years since we first met Case.

I will never forget how Cindy took the reins and sprang into action, taking care of every detail of Doug's celebration of life. I am overcome with emotion and gratitude whenever I think of what she did. Cindy did everything from arranging Doug's celebration of life to ordering the cards and the pictures that were needed, along with the reception afterward. Cindy arranged and paid for everything! I felt so loved and cared for and thankful to God for her. She was my rock and my angel when I needed one!

While I was grieving my losses, Case also lost his dad, Herman, who was a unique man. He was full of stories and could make you laugh all day. They don't make men like Herman anymore. I miss him, too.

There are no words good enough to express my gratitude and love for Case and Cindy, who continue to support me and make sacrifices on my behalf. They are truly a blessing.

God Sends People to Help Us in Unexpected Ways

I met Joseph Newsome some fourteen years ago through his business, which provides training, certification, and continuing education classes related to medical businesses, including, but not limited to, medical record auditing, medical coding, and billing.

Over time, I got to know Joe, his wife Allison, son Ryan, and daughter Holly. MCHC is a well-established, family-owned small business that provides quality and affordable online, virtual, and in-person training for medical professionals.

Through the years, our friendship grew. Before the pandemic, Joe held annual conferences in Anaheim, California. He allowed Joanne and me to have a doTERRA table to share essential oils with attendees at the events.

When Joe heard about Doug and Joanne, his immediate response was to give me two options for help: 1) Send him all the work that needs to be done for Doug's medical business clients, or 2) He would fly to California from Florida and stay here to take care of the business until I'm back on my feet.

I was stunned by the offer. With his own business and family in Florida, it would have been an enormous sacrifice. I couldn't accept it, but I was grateful to Joe for his willingness to sacrifice on my behalf and to God for giving me this friend. Like Case and Cindy, Joe and Allison continue to support me.

I'm So Blessed That God Gave Me Such Faithful Friends

To have people step up as God's instruments of love and commitment without hesitation, I was so floored. God is fulfilling His promise never to leave or forsake me.

Ghesi Stojanov and I hadn't known each other long, so her role in my victory over grief overwhelmed me. You will learn more about her in chapter 12.

Doug had an office in the garage for his law practice and medical business services, which I helped him with. Doug's clients were long-term clients, and the new ones were referrals, so he didn't need an office. There were no filing cabinets, only boxes. His central filing system was his brain, with documents sorted on his massive mixture of desks. He knew exactly where everything was.

The sight overwhelmed me, as I knew nothing about real estate or business law. But not Ghesi! She told me she needed to organize everything in folders and boxes. Ghesi wasted no time and started working as soon as the supplies arrived—labeling folders, packing boxes, and sorting documents by property address and year. She came over three days a week for hours. In six weeks, she completed the task without giving it one thought. I was so relieved and so grateful. It would have taken me a lifetime to do what she did in such a short time. I was and still am grateful beyond words.

Grow Your Community by Networking

Whether for business or to meet people, networking may seem like an unlikely place to find genuine friends. But when God brings someone into your life, He doesn't choose where they will come from; He sends them. I met the best people in my life through networking!

After our losses, Todd, in anger, complained to my friend Ro Kendall that in the past, I used events like birthday celebrations at my house for business because I invited people I met while networking. But isn't that what networking is for: meeting people you can become friends with? One of the best ways to build friendships is to invite them to important life event celebrations!

From where I stand, I see a number of people I met through business events who have become treasured friends who stepped up when I needed help. Unlike Todd, I didn't have to lie to them about the truth to help me get through my tragedies!

For example, I met Ro Kendall at a networking event. Like the others above, we had one glaring thing in common: our faith in God and His Son, Jesus. Over time, we forged a close relationship as sisters-in-Christ. She loved Joanne, and when Ethan came along, she was G3 (Grandma #3) to Ethan, as Joanne called her.

In January 2022, I heard about an organization called Former Feds. This group, organized by Carolyn Seay Blakeman, supported families that lost loved ones in hospitals from 2020 through 2022 because of a hospital killing protocol put into action by corrupt hospitals, doctors, and pharmaceutical companies to get money from the government.

Carolyn is a Godsend to many of us who have received help from the resources and encouragement provided by Former Feds. She has given many of us hope to get justice for our loved ones who were taken from us. Gail Seiler, another instrument of God, is the one who interviewed me. She is a survivor of the hospital killing protocol. Her husband, Brad, and their daughter were able to get her out of the hospital before the doctors could carry out their evil deed.

The organization would interview the victim's wife, husband, child, or parent. They then document in writing and on video the details of the medical records and what their loved ones could communicate to them in hospitals nationwide. They gathered approximately 500 law firms nationwide to represent the families with claims against the hospitals and doctors.

By God's grace, I learned I could file a lawsuit in California. Two law firms in Fresno did a press conference after they took on the representation of fourteen families in Northern California against hospitals and doctors in that area. I contacted them, but they were so busy they said they wouldn't even be able to look at Doug's medical records for two months. I couldn't wait because the clock was running on Doug's possible wrongful death claim by the time I learned about available legal recourse.

I had difficulty finding an attorney in Orange County and Los Angeles. I believe no one wanted to take on the government who protected the pharmaceutical companies, hospitals and doctors. Finally, on the eve of the ninety-day extension to sue, I found Matthew Tyson, who represented approximately fifty families in Southern California of victims who lost their lives in the hospitals.

I had a problem, though. I received Doug's medical records at the beginning of 2022, but for months, I couldn't bring myself to look at them, let alone read them. Ro Kendall came to the rescue!

She came over and picked up the box containing hundreds of pages. She painstakingly reviewed every page, noting all the questionable prescriptions and actions taken or not taken by the doctors.

When Ro was done, we understood what Doug went through. I sent the copies to Mr. Tyson, and shortly after that, he and Mr. Garrie filed a lawsuit on my behalf. As of January 2, 2025, the case had to be dropped.

I received a call from Mr. Tyson that of the fifty cases they filed, only two may be strong enough to keep going, and even then, these two cases may not be strong enough against the power they're up against. He recommended that I agree to drop the case because if we lose the opposing attorneys could make me pay costs in the thousands of dollars!

So, it seems justice is denied. But God. There is a God who will even the score in this life or the next. This is what His promise says: **"Beloved, do not avenge yourselves, but rather give place to wrath; for it is written, " Vengeance is Mine, I will repay," says the Lord."** *Romans 12:19 NKJV*

Ro came over to help me and encourage me. She would come nearly every day and get angry over what was happening with Ethan and how Todd was treating me. I will always be grateful for the support from Ro and indirectly from her husband, Greg. He put up with the time she was dedicating to me with no complaints.

There's No Such Thing as Coincidence with God

I met Yvette Kronick at a networking event in late 2021 during the early part of my loss. We met but didn't have an opportunity to talk, if at all. It was much later, after I first met her, that we saw each other again. I'm unsure when, why, or how we connected heart-wise, but I believe it was because of our faith in Jesus. We found out later that we went to the same church, Calvary Chapel Chino Hills.

I don't remember what made Yvette want to come and help me organize the house. It must be her compassionate heart and faithfulness as a servant of God. A close friendship between us formed at once. I believe this is true for followers of Jesus who share the same values and beliefs and want to live according to "What would Jesus do?"

Yvette started coming over and spent several hours helping me put stuff away. There's still much to be done, but the house looks better organized. I'm grateful for her help. She continues to come over when time allows. I appreciate her so much as my friend, sister-in-Christ and prayer partner.

Chris Blum, our mail carrier since 2004, is a faithful follower of Jesus, with whom we have become friends. After Doug and Joanne went home to be with Jesus, he became my prayer partner. The time he spent praying with me during the dark days has yielded so much strength and uplifting. We still pray together for my Ethan, my concerns, his ministry, and his kids, Josh and Amanda. I'm so grateful that when I'm down, Chris always makes the time to stop and pray over me.

Peggy and Gus McAulay were our Bible study teachers. She lost Gus in December 2020, the year before Doug and Joanne. Peggy and Gus watched their children battle health issues, but they stayed faithful to God. It was their trust in Him, and they would not allow the circumstances of life to interfere with it.

Peggy became my spiritual mentor and friend when Gus went home to be with Jesus. She could relate to my pain and sorrow; it was helpful and comforting. We prayed and reminisced together about the wonderful husbands God gave us. She knew Doug well and comforted me by recalling what made him unique and how much he loved me.

Genevieve Dobiesz is G2 (Grandma #2), as Joanne referred to her. She loved Joanne. I met Genevieve and her sisters, Rebekah, Rachel, and Naomi, in 2006 at our old church Cornerstone in Anaheim Hills, California.

When I was going through the grandparent's rights case, Genevieve would come over to pray with me and reminisce about Joanne and Doug. Genevieve and her sister Rachel are prayer warriors. They prayed with and for me and continue to do so today.

Doctors diagnosed Genevieve's sister, Rebekah, with esophageal cancer during my ordeal. Within a few weeks, she went home to be with the Lord as well. This was devastating for the family. The sisters were and are extremely close, so this loss was an enormous blow to them and their families. Rebekah is missed by numerous friends and clients, especially by her kids, Joaquin, who has recently married, Alejandra has found her niche in the medical industry and August, who, having followed his mom's footsteps, remain to be the best hairdresser this side of the equator. Their faith and the strength of the family relationships held them together.

George Gutierrez and Raul Mendez have been friends of ours for over 30 years. We're close, like family. They live in Miami, Florida, but if I need anything, they are just a phone call away. This verse describes them both to a tee. "….. **But there is a friend friend who sticks closer than a brother."** *Proverbs 18:24b*

I've known Eunice Choi, acupuncturist and chiropractor, since 2006. She lost her dad in March 2021 through poor medical care at a nursing facility in Tustin, California. We've become very close in the past eighteen years. Being constantly present is emotionally challenging for her, but she tries to spend time with me as often as work allows. I am blessed to reminisce about the wonderful and funny memories of her father, Doug, and Joanne with her. And because she and her mom are both believers, I have received powerful prayer coverage in everything I've gone through.

We saw each other often, so Eunice had a more intimate relationship with the family. She knew all our family issues in a much deeper sense. So when we recalled moments, especially about the quirks each showed, it was a lot of laughing and some crying.

Dr. Anastasia Lander is a constant support and prayer warrior. She was one of the many in my community who wrote letters on my behalf in the Grandparents' rights case. Joanne and I attended and took part in many events at her clinic over the years. She has experienced her grief, such as the recent loss of her mom. Her faith keeps her tethered to the One and only faithful Lord Jesus. Her husband, Dr. James, is my chiropractor. Doug and I see him weekly, so it's a comfort today when I go in and am reminded of Doug. Dr. James is also a praying man; I know he prays for me and Ethan.

I met Eunice Montes Hamaguchi at a pregnant women's event that Joanne and I attended in 2017. When God brings people into your life, you never know why and how they will affect you and your life, or vice versa. We became so close that I referred to Eunice as my second daughter. These days, she and her husband, Heath, visit me with their daughters, or invite me to their home on special occasions and holidays.

Todd hates Eunice still today for helping me exercise the temporary custody order by the judge in the probate case filed by the first attorney. The exigent or pressing circumstances prompted the judge to grant me temporary custody of Ethan.

For this reason, Ethan has not been allowed to see Eunice and her daughters, Kyra and Shiloh. Joanne loved Eunice and her family and was close to Eunice. This prohibition against her son seeing those who love him would disappoint her.

Todd continues to prevent people who helped me in the legal case from seeing Ethan. I pray he will release and forgive them for his sake. Unforgiveness is a barrier between him and God, and he is only hurting his relationship with God.

This little "community" bloomed into a close-knit family of God and became strong because we are bound by the friendship created through the bond of faith in Jesus Christ. These are just a few examples of the importance of building a close community, whether church or local.

Finding a Faith Community

> "As each one has received a gift, minister it to one another as good stewards of the manifold grace of God." I Peter 4:10 NKJV

If you already go to a church you have found comfort and support in, get involved, join ministries of interest to serve in. Immediately after Doug and Joanne, I did three things I believe increased my ability to push grief forward and used the pain of my broken heart to light the fire in me, share my testimony with others and help them in their grief.

First, I befriended the door ushers in my church near the area where Doug and I sat during service and church events. Anthony Macias and Rigo Jacobo treated me kindly and with love and compassion. They adopted me at once when I started inserting myself to usher with them before the 10:30 am service started on Sunday mornings. Mitch Haynam, the supervising head usher, didn't stop me even when I had not gone through the administrative process required to serve in the ministry.

I greet, welcome, and acknowledge the good I notice to make people smile and feel recognized. I have always believed that sincerely affirming something good about people, no matter how small, and making them feel seen and valued is important. Many live obscure lives these days, grieving, for one reason or another, so to be seen and heard is a boon to their emotional state.

The smiles, appreciation, and gratitude made me happy when I wished them a blessed week after the service. I found comfort, satisfaction, and happiness in greeting attendees, so I joined the usher team. My only regret is that Doug and I didn't serve together.

I am so grateful to the 10:30 a.m. usher team—Anthony, Rigo, Fran, Linda, Edwin, Jane, Scott, Dave, Karen, and Michael—for inspiring me to serve.

Find a faith community that corresponds with your spiritual needs, beliefs, and doctrine and understands your grief journey; it can enhance your healing process.

I am encouraged when I get cards and flowers with kind sentiments of appreciation and hugs. People have come up to me just to say how much they appreciate that I greet them with joy and wish them a "blessed week" every Sunday. I don't miss church, so they see me every week.

Meeting special people like Jim and Julie Boswell and their son, Brody, Andrea Ortiz, Peter and Lisa Mouzakis and their daughter, Bella, Mitch, Wendy and their daughter, Shelby, Andre Kolchev, Glenn and Kathy Linde, Dawn Carpenter, who has become a friend and a prayer partner, and many others confirmed God has me where He wants me to serve for now.

Some people who come to church may be facing tough challenges. The words "Have a blessed week," "God is good," or "He is faithful" encourage and remind them He is near to the brokenhearted.

Pastor Rob Harston oversees the usher ministry, so I met his wife, Monique. We often talk when she comes to church, so we got to know each other. She's kind and sweet and easy to talk to. She said I'm one of her favorite ushers. Don't get me wrong—this is not about ego and is not a brag. It's reassuring that God placed me in a ministry where I can be a light to many people.

Starting From Zero

Maybe you're reading this chapter and thinking, "That's great for you, but I don't have anyone."

I understand. Grief can be isolating even when you have people around you. And if you've moved to a new city, lost the person who was your main connection to others, or simply never built a strong community before your loss—starting from zero feels impossible.

But here's what I've learned: community doesn't happen by accident. It's built one conversation at a time.

Start small:

- Attend one church service and introduce yourself to one person
- Join a small group or Bible study or a women's group
- Say yes to one invitation, even when you don't feel like it
- Ask one person to pray with you
- Attend a networking event to get introduced to people in your community

You don't need a hundred friends. You need one or two people who will show up. And often, those people come from unexpected places, a networking event, a neighbor, a mail person who becomes a prayer partner.

God sees your isolation. He knows your need. Ask Him to bring the right people into your life, and then be willing to receive them when they come.

> "Two are better than one, because they have a good reward for their labor. For if they fall, one will lift up his companion. But woe to him who is alone when he falls, for he has no one to help him up." Ecclesiastes 4:9-10 NKJV

"The Know Like and Trust" Principle

Building Community Through Know, Like, and Trust

I'm a relationship builder by nature. In business, in ministry, and in personal life, I've learned that everything comes down to one fundamental principle: know, like, and trust.

This principle isn't just for business—it's for every meaningful relationship in your life.

Know: People need to know who you are. Not just your name, but your story, your heart, your struggles. You can't build community if you remain a stranger. Show up. Be present. Let people see the real you. And get to know one person. Go for coffee or lunch, open yourself up a little bit at a time.

When Doug and Joanne died, the people who showed up for me were the people who knew me. They knew my story. They knew my heart. They knew what I was going through because I had been transparent with them.

Like: People invest in people they like. This doesn't mean you have to be perfect or put together. It means you have to be genuine, kind, and consistent. It means you show up for others before you need them to show up for you.

I had invested in Ghesi, Cindy, Case, Ro, and so many others long before I needed them. I prayed for them. I helped them when needed. I celebrated their wins and cried with them in their losses. When my darkest hour came, they didn't hesitate to show up for me.

Trust: This is the foundation of every lasting relationship. Trust is built over time through consistency, integrity, and follow-through. When you say you'll do something, you do it no matter the cost to you. When someone shares their heart with you, you honor it. When someone needs you, you show up.

Trust is what allows you to be vulnerable. Trust is what allows you to ask for help. Trust is what allow others to step into your pain and carry you when you can't walk.

When you invest time and emotion into relationships, you're building something that will sustain you through the hardest seasons of your life. You're creating a safety net of people who will catch you when you fall.

But here's the key: you have to invest before you need it.

You can't wait until you're in crisis to start building community. You can't expect people to show up for you if you've never shown up for them. Community and friendships and are built in the ordinary days, so it's there for you in the extraordinary ones.

This is why I tell business owners: know, like, and trust isn't just a marketing principle, it's a life principle. The strategies that build an enduring and thriving business are the same for building an enduring and a thriving life.

Show up. Be consistent. Be genuine. Be trustworthy. Invest in others. And when your world falls apart, you won't be alone.

> "A man who has friends must himself be friendly, but there is a friend who sticks closer than a brother." Proverbs 18:24 NKJV

The Blessing of Engaging in Your Church and Local Community

> "Bear one another's burdens, and so fulfill the law of Christ." Galatians 6:2 NKJV

A healing pathway that a faith community offers is the opportunity to give back through volunteering. To engage and serve in areas within your church or other secular organizations can be extremely therapeutic. It shifts your focus from your grief to the needs of others and fosters a sense of purpose and connection.

Volunteering can contribute to healing. Organizing community meals, joining outreach programs, or helping clean up group meeting areas. It helps not only those you serve but also rebuilds your sense of self-worth, which is often eroded by grief.

I joined The Call, a ministry at my church, at the loving urging of friends Eddie and Elissa Kim. The ministry teaches people how to disciple others and evangelize the Gospel of Jesus Christ. It was exciting to have a foundation, a simple tool that I could use to share the saving grace of Jesus Christ. Although I have been a believer for a long time, I didn't have an easy-to-follow guide to relate Jesus' redeeming sacrifice on the cross to others. I continue to be part of The Call today while I occupy until He comes.

I had just lost Doug and Joanne and was going through the fight for Ethan; I was still crying a lot. When I joined The Call ministry, I was like a fish out of water. What a blessing! I got Phil Hart as my small group leader. He encouraged and comforted me during my first ten-week session. I felt so welcomed and supported.

I also learned so much, even the one time I could go out in the field and knock on doors with Phil. When I met him, I knew he was a person I wanted to have in my life as a friend. He just had a way about him; he loved the Lord and wanted to share that with us. Today, he and his wife, Sandy, are my friends!

The Call ministry trains us to share Jesus with strangers simply and clearly. After the small group lessons, we would go out, knock on the doors of homes, or lovingly approach people at shopping malls. It was nerve-wracking but satisfying. You never knew how people would respond. We prayed before we went and asked the Holy Spirit to lead us. Some doors opened, but many didn't.

A Secular Community: An Opportunity to Share Your Faith

Although I'm a closet introvert, I enjoy networking in a secular environment. It's a great place to share your faith. You realize you're not the only one going through grief; you make yourself available to others who may not be holding up as well because they don't have a faith community that prays for them.

I belong to two groups, EWomen and Heartlink, in Orange County. Both groups include women of faith and those unaware of the power of Jesus' presence in their lives.

I met Misty Loreto at EWomen, a woman of faith. Grief strikes us in different ways; it affects us differently and one's grief is no less significant than another. Her parents live with her and her family. If you or someone you know is caring for a parent with dementia, you understand Misty's and her dad's grief of watching her mom suffer as she slowly deteriorates. They know the day will come when she will no longer recognize them, which is painful.

Through Misty's faith, the support of her husband, Jim, and the prayers of people in their faith community, they're able to comfort and support her dad in managing the daily emotional challenges of caring for her mom.

Diana Sabatino, a small business owner and managing director of EWomen Network, Orange County Chapter, and a constant support of mine these past three years through prayers and encouragement, wrote the foreword for this book. As she is doing so, she is in grief because of her health and the physical pain she is going through.

Diana has become fatigued by heavy bleeding for several weeks now and the emotional impact of a cancer scare, based upon what happened to beloved family members. But she hasn't let her personal difficulties deter her from inspiring women in the business community. Her strength comes from her faith in God and the knowledge that people are praying for her, lifting her up to the Great Physician for healing and restoration.

While in the depths of my legal issues related to Ethan, I met Lynda Bergh. Her business as a private investigator helped me learn things pertinent to the case that I wouldn't have otherwise known. We are close friends today, and we continue to support each other.

At the time we met, Lynda was in remission from colon cancer. Recently, she also suffered the loss of her dad. Recently, her colon cancer returned, and she's in chemotherapy treatment again. Lynda stays positive, as she continues to work hard on her business and commit to speaking engagements to raise funds on behalf of Million Kids, a sex trafficking prevention organization.

Despite the threat that cancer poses, Lynda keeps going. I admire her tenacity; if you met her, you wouldn't think she has cancer. She doesn't wallow in grief. Instead, she funnels her energy to educate parents and grandparents on how to protect and safeguard their children.

Cancer is a devastating diagnosis. Being told you have cancer is like being given a death sentence. Even if chemotherapy and radiation therapies are available, it's never a certainty that the body can withstand these treatments. As I watch Lynda blast her way through colon cancer and the harshness of the treatment protocol, I am inspired. I want to be like her when I grow up.

Here's what I believe. Attitude and gratitude are 99 percent of overcoming, bolstered by faith. Only God knows when each of us will leave this earth, regardless of the diagnosis and what the doctor says. God numbers our days!

If you're seeking a deeper, more structured way to relieve the daily triggers of unbearable grief, faith-based retreats and workshops designed specifically for individuals in mourning can offer valuable respite and renewal. These get togethers often provide in-depth study of the Bible, personal reflection time, and group share sessions, all set in environments that encourage peace and reflection.

The activities might include meditations on the Scriptures, praying, worshipping with songs, therapeutic art sessions, and group discussions, all facilitated by leaders trained in grief counseling and spiritual care. The immersive nature of these retreats can help you escape the routine pressures of daily life, sadness, and painful memories, providing a secure space to process your grief and find spiritual nourishment.

Community faith activities—whether regular worship services, small group meetings, volunteer opportunities, or specialized gatherings—play an important role in healing. They remind you that while your grief is personal; you are not going through it alone. You are part of a group of people who care for you, will support you, and walk with you. This realization can be a powerful antidote to isolation, often accompanying grief.

I am fortunate to have established incredibly supportive relationships within my church and local community, albeit small ones. These people were and are a source of support through prayers and friendship. Many gave of their time and expected nothing in return. They helped me through the tough days after my losses, and some continue to do so.

Intercessory Prayer

I was in awe and filled with gratitude for all the prayers poured over me and the hands and arms extended towards me after my losses and during my fight for my grandson, Ethan. Between my faith and the secular community, there was no way but victory. It showed through the many miracles that happened.

I met Elissa and Eddie Kim when Joanne and I attended mommy events a lifetime ago; it seems. I did not know they were followers of Jesus. One day, they expressed their dissatisfaction with their church because they said it went the way of the world after the 2020 pandemic. I invited them to my church, and they were hooked. They've become very involved in The Call ministry. Once I got into The Call ministry, Elissa became my prayer partner.

Having a prayer warrior beside me during a battle with the supernatural was a huge blessing. Miracle after miracle came from our prayers and the prayers of many other faithful and righteous men and women of God. Elissa even had her little girls, Nadia and Lydia, pray for Ethan.

This is a couple who truly obey God, fight for children's welfare in the Orange County school district, and share the Gospel. Elissa told me they're going to start The Call ministry at Calvary Chapel Old Town Orange. I'm excited to see the impact this relentless couple will make in that community!

Here's a miracle I'll share that you will agree is by the hand of God.

When Todd told me I would never see Ethan again, I was angry and vowed it would never happen. My mistake is not consulting God in prayer first to ask for godly wisdom, discernment, guidance, and direction about what to do.

I sought legal help at once—man's solution. Finding two-three law firms, I interviewed each one and settled on one in Beverly Hills. Of course, it's always the one with the best pitch, a hope-filled pitch. Long story short, the lawyer roped me in. He told me I could file in probate court. Then, he put me in the care of a junior attorney.

I was relieved when I got the temporary court order for custody of Ethan after we told the judge that he wasn't getting sufficient care. Todd would leave him unattended in the car with the engine running while he ran back into the house because he forgot something. This was a daily occurrence, at least a half a dozen times a day. Todd is forgetful. He also did this when he went to Starbucks. Lynda Bergh, my friend and private investigator, was keeping track of Todd's activities.

But to prevent me from taking temporary custody of Ethan, Todd stopped going to work to keep Ethan away from me. I couldn't get into the house and cook food; I couldn't do my laundry. I was afraid to be around Todd because he would create a story that reflected me as a crazy, evil, confrontational person and his lawyer would submit an exaggerated statement to court.

When forced to return to work, Todd had his mother come to my house to keep Ethan away from me. I called the police, and she was told that what she and Todd were doing was against the court order and that she had to leave. When she told Todd, he rushed home to take Ethan away from me.

The junior attorney accomplished little except for the temporary custody, which I never got to use and he didn't fight to enforce. The attorney did nothing to fight what Todd was doing, so I was back to square one. I had a horrible time, and my stress level was overwhelming. Only by God's grace and mercy could I endure and live through it.

When my friend Ro Kendall came over, she expressed her disappointment that I was allowing Todd to hurt me and affect my life in the way he was doing. I would tell her it was for the love of a grandson.

It was six months before Todd moved Ethan out in the "cloak of darkness". No goodbyes, nothing. Having accomplished nothing, I fired the law firm. Once that happened, I received an invoice for $28,526.70.

I quickly sent an email to the managing partner. I contested the invoice and complained about the poor handling of the case. I had already paid them thousands, they accomplished nothing, and now they want more money. Well, I want a discount, a big one!

I received an email response defending their actions. At first, my reaction was to give him a piece of my mind, but I believe the Holy Spirit stopped me. God knew I was too dense to understand that I needed to involve Him in the matter, so the Holy Spirit had to act.

> **"Be anxious for nothing, but in everything by prayer and supplication, with thanksgiving, let your requests be made known to God; and the peace of God, which surpasses all understanding, will guard your hearts and minds through Christ Jesus." Philippians 4:6-7 NKJV**

I obeyed, so I didn't respond. Three weeks passed, and it was Valentine's Day. I was in front of my computer, missing my family. Suddenly, I felt the Holy Spirit nudge me. "Email the managing partner again. Ask him for a line-by-line description of what was done and the result of every charge on the invoice." I did as I was told.

Thirty minutes passed when I received an email from the managing partner, Eli, who said, "I've instructed Erin Kelly to waive your entire balance of $28,526.70". I was stunned, still thinking, "I want a big discount!" I couldn't believe it. To be sure, I asked for a copy of the invoice showing zero balance due. I attached a copy on the Resource page.

I hired a new law firm in Orange County. Lori Klein was compassionate and honest. She was able to get me time with Ethan, albeit monitored by a service. It was an hour and a half short, but a win for me—praise God! I think the family court system has many cutthroat attorneys just by the nature of the beast.

In July 2023, we were in the courtroom, and I hoped the judge would schedule a trial date so my witnesses and I could testify. The judge asked Lori if I would agree to skip the trial; he was ready to rule. Of course, I said yes. It would save me a lot in legal costs and relieve the burden for the witnesses.

I have to say, it's dangerous when you pray and ask for God's will to be done. You have to be ready for the response and the consequences that may come from it. His will won't necessarily coincide with yours. Remember His words in **Isaiah 55:9**?

> **"For as the heavens are higher than the earth, so are my ways higher than your ways and my thoughts than your thoughts."**

The judge turned to me and asked if everything I said about Todd was true. I said, "Yes". He asked Todd the same question, and Todd answered, "Yes". Turning to me and Lori, he said, "Denied!". He denied my rights as a grandparent even though I met all the requirements. The other attorneys in the courtroom couldn't believe it!

Ms. Klein jumped up and said adamantly, "But, your honor, we have witnesses—we want a trial!". The judge responded, "No, you can appeal my decision." I should have been crying my eyes out, but I didn't shed a tear. What I heard was God saying, "Grace, I want you to handle this My way, not man's way." Once again, I obeyed.

In Lori's conversation with Todd's attorney earlier that morning, he said I don't go to Todd's church to see Ethan. I didn't know I could do that, so I started going on Saturdays. Even if I only got five minutes out of the several hours I would spend at the church, I was grateful to the Lord.

Humble pie much? Let me tell you how unpleasant the taste is. A friend told me: "Grace, you know you would swim with the sharks for Ethan!" She was right. God rewarded my obedience. I saw Ethan more, and Todd allowed him to stay with me overnight and on weekends. My relationship with Todd improved slowly. I'm sure he would rather not let Ethan spend time with me. But God.

Why Intercede for Others?

Did you know Jesus intercedes to God the Father on our behalf? Here's a portion of Jesus' prayer—the complete prayer is in John 17—to show you He intercedes for us.

> **"I pray for them. I am not praying for the world but for those You have given me, for they are Yours. All I have is Yours, and all You have is Mine. And glory has come to Me through them. I will remain in the world no longer, but they are still in the world, and I am coming to You. Holy Father, protect them by the power of Your name, the name You gave Me, so that they may be one as We are one." John 17:9-11 NIV**

Never underestimate intercessory prayer. Nothing is impossible for God. Lift each other's needs to God in the power of Jesus' name. He answers the prayers of those who love Him. It may be "Yes," "No," or "Wait, I have something better for you."

In my stupidity, I didn't involve God in the details prior to the lawsuit. He still listened to my prayers and the prayers of so many on my behalf. He came to my rescue.

I don't doubt that Doug, an attorney, also interceded with the Father on my behalf regarding the huge legal invoice since he has direct communication with the Father in Heaven himself.

Praying for the needs of others can be a healing practice, especially when you're engulfed in grief. It shifts your focus outward, raises your empathy level, and may bring perspective to your struggles. Something about bringing someone else's needs before God is interesting, especially when you're acutely aware of your own vulnerabilities.

Intercessory prayer can reinforce your connection to others and God, a reminder that you are not alone in your struggles—that you are part of a larger community of faith where mutual support and love are abundant. Praying for others can solidify your purpose, it can affirm that even in your grief, you have the power to offer something valuable to others—your prayers.

I was grateful to many people for my healing and the many victories through their prayers. It was no surprise that I would become an intercessor myself, knowing what it's done for me. I started a prayer list to take my focus off myself and redirect it to others going through trials and challenges of every form, even worse than what I was going through.

I asked random people I met at church, the supermarket, or the gym if they needed prayer for anything—even strangers who seemed to need encouragement. I put all the requests on my list to lift up to God during my daily prayer time. As of December 23, 2024, I have been praying for 428 requests! Most of the time, I will pray right then and there. I want them to know that I really pray for people when I say I will.

I believe in the power of prayer! When our beloved Pastor Jack Hibbs announced that all services on Sunday, October 13, 2024, would be a prayer meeting instead of a focused study of the Bible, I rejoiced. It is important to intercede for the many needs in the lives of people around us. I lived on prayer. I prayed, and many others prayed for me and Ethan.

Sharing Scriptures in the Community

While personal meditation on scriptures is powerful, sharing these words within a community can amplify their impact. Breaking down scriptures with others, whether in a Bible study group or online forum, can provide new insights. How others relate to the same verses will strengthen your understanding and sense of connection.

This group engagement with scripture can be an exceptional comfort. It reminds you that others have walked paths of grief before you; lean into the exact same words for strength and consolation. Share your thoughts and listen to the interpretations of others to reaffirm that while your grief is personal, you do not have to bear it in isolation.

> "Anxiety in the heart of man causes depression, but a good word makes it glad." Proverbs 12:25 NKJV.

As you continue to navigate the challenges of loss, your community, whether faith-based or secular, stands as a pillar of support. It illuminates your path and reminds you of the strength of shared faith and fellowship. While still paved with challenges, the journey ahead may feel lighter, assured that you do not walk alone.

Visit the Resource page

CHAPTER 4

The Impact of Grief on Health and Beauty

Grief is more than just an emotion. Its impact on the entire body is both an emotional experience and a physiological phenomenon. There is a spectrum of responses to loss, from sadness to anger, and these emotions manifest physically.

The psychological impact of grief has cognitive effects, memory issues, and decision-making difficulties; this is why grief feels all-consuming. I experienced "widow brain," which I had no idea was real.

Intense emotions can lead to physical symptoms, such as fatigue, hair loss, weight fluctuations, and a weakened immune system.

The Devastating Impact of Stress

What Is Stress?

The book Aromatherapy for Healthcare Professionals states: "There's no definitive, accepted definition of stress". One definition is that stress is an influence that disturbs the natural balance of a person's body or mind, including physical injury, diseases, deprivation, and emotional disturbance (Lazarus 1998, Wingate & Wingate 1996).

Anxiety (a state of apprehension) and worry (an over-anxious state of mind) are often the forerunners of both stressful and depressive states. The first stage of stress can be because of a reaction to a potentially harmful situation or an ongoing life event.

Here is the list of the top ten stress-causing events and their scores:

- Death of a spouse: 100
- Divorce: 73
- Separation: 65
- Jail term: 63
- Death of a close family member: 63
- Personal injury or illness: 53
- Marriage: 50
- Fired from work: 47
- Marital reconciliation: 45
- Retirement: 45

Stressors are adverse life events that happen to everyone. Even something as minute as being stuck in traffic or being late for work produces a physical and emotional response. It is a natural human reaction. The body learns to cope with stress, but if the stress is ongoing without the ability to relax, it can become a problem.

According to the Cleveland Clinic, there are three types of stress:

1) Acute stress is short-term, comes and goes quickly, and can be positive or negative. For example, if a family member fails to bring out the steaks you want to barbecue for dinner because you have a guest coming, dinner will be delayed, and you'll be stressed. Everyone experiences this.
2) Episodic stress is acute stress that occurs regularly and does not allow the body to return to a calm or relaxed state. This stress affects healthcare professionals.

3) Chronic stress is long-term stress that lasts weeks or months. Marriage, work, or financial issues can cause it. Managing chronic stress is important to avoid becoming ill.

When you have chronic stress, your autonomic nervous system, which controls your heart rate, breathing, and more, is your built-in stressor response, referred to as the "fight or flight" response, which helps your body face stressful situations.

Chronic stress, which continually activates the stress response, causes wear and tear on the body, which may lead to physical, psychological, or behavioral symptoms.

Some of the resulting health issues are exhaustion, headaches, dizziness, shaking, high blood pressure, digestive problems, chest pain, muscle tension, aches and pains, anxiety or irritability, depression, panic attacks, sadness, and a weakened immune system. These could lead to more severe and chronic illnesses like heart disease, diabetes, and a whole long list.

Extreme distress may bring on behavioral symptoms to cope that can become habit-forming:

- Overeating or developing an eating disorder
- Participating in addictive activities like gambling or drinking
- Smoking
- Substance abuse

I'm grateful that I didn't get into these habit-forming behaviors. They are used to drown out the pain and despair, but they are temporary and more physically and emotionally destructive.

> **"Cast your burden on the Lord, And He shall sustain you; He shall never permit the righteous to be moved." Psalms 55:22 NKJV.**

I believed in relying on my faith through prayer and the Holy Scriptures, community support, and holistic solutions as simple as proper breathing, exercise, nutritional support, aromatherapy, and face reflexology for comfort, restoration, and rejuvenation. I didn't have the time nor the inclination to get swallowed up by these addictive "solutions" to ease my pain.

Stress Insinuates Itself into Your Body Systems and Organs Slowly and with Deadly Effects

Have you noticed that your skin is more dehydrated and wrinkled these days? You're wondering what's causing the red blotches? Have you been experiencing digestive issues like stomach pain, diarrhea, or constipation? Extreme jaw pain? Severe emotional stress can make you clench your jaw, raise your blood pressure, have sallow skin, and even lose hair.

Just as grief can affect you emotionally, it also deals a heavy blow to your physical health. Life-altering loss from the death of a loved one, the end of a marriage, losing a meaningful relationship, or a terminal disease diagnosis can jar one's existence, which leads to unbelievable stress on the body.

When you're going through a trauma, the last thing you concern yourself with is your appearance. I know I didn't care how I looked to others (I still don't care; the man I want to look beautiful for is not here!). The emotional upheaval caused by grief can be so burdensome that the physical symptoms go unnoticed.

The extent of damage grief can do to the body will differ from person to person, and the ability to cope will be different. The degree of grief or pain from loss can vary depending on the importance of the loss and its effects, based on coping mechanisms employed by each person.

Three Stages of the Body's Response to Stress

Here are the three stages of the body's response to stress (Selye 1956):

1) The initial direct response of the body exposed to the stressor brings about the alarm stage: temporary cessation of digestive juices occurs. Respiratory and heart rates increase. Extra oxygen is transported to the brain and the muscles (to prepare for strenuous action or emotional strength). Energy is released quickly by stored fats and sugars. Extra adrenaline is produced. The immune system shuts down.

2) The second resistant stage involves using these extra resources, where the extra oxygen, energy, and adrenaline enable the body to cope with unacceptable situations. Lacking relief from the situation, the response in the first stage continues as the body tries to adapt and reach a balanced state. The body reaches the third stage if the stress level becomes chronic and continues without help.

3) With the excess build-up of stress, stage three begins, and true (clinical) stress is experienced. This can occur because of an emotional disturbance like the above, severe physical injury, illness, or work overload. There is exhaustion, which eventually results in health problems. These may manifest as headaches, insomnia, digestive issues, skin disorders, and susceptibility to infection

owing to the gradual closing down of immune responses (Price & Price, 2007).

I Was a Mess

I am no stranger to loss. However, losing people I loved was something I never expected to happen to me. But isn't that the way it is? Tragedy seems to happen when it's least expected. The damage to my physical health was drastic. I was shocked when I looked in the mirror and saw the old, wrinkled, and sagging face staring back at me.

Thin and fragile, eyes sunken and sad, I was exhausted from lack of sleep, although I continued to work. I didn't nourish my body; I stopped taking my supplements, and I didn't exercise. Besides, I only did it because I wanted Doug to exercise for his heart health.

The stress my body was under manifested in difficulty sleeping, body pain, headaches, digestive problems like stomach aches and nausea, and, worst of all, a weakened immune system that made me get sick easily. Because of a compromised immune system, I easily caught a cold or full-blown flu. The health of the digestive system is a massive indicator of the condition of the immune system.

Negative emotions release adrenaline and cortisol, two chemical messengers that influence the immune system to switch off in the face of sudden and long-term stress. I was not surprised at the impact on my health and appearance. Stress is a substantial endocrine disruptor that interferes with hormone production.

I couldn't believe the damage negative emotions did to my physical health in a short period of time!

Having learned more about how stress permeates one's very being, I am not surprised I looked like I aged twenty years. My thoughts continually flooded with the pain and sadness at the loss of my husband and daughter four days apart and the threat that I would not see my grandson Ethan again. You can imagine the anger that came up inside of me as I went through each day.

My heart was broken and continues to be shredded into pieces, one painful slice at a time at the thought of living the rest of my life on this earth without this precious little boy in it. It was a nightmare that I prayed I could wake up from. The prospect that this wonderful boy that I've loved so much was going to be yanked out of my life permanently and forever?

Todd told a friend, "She will regret every word she said to Joanne!" He bad-mouthed me to Ethan. I was sad to see what Todd was putting Ethan through. A five-year-old toddler should not be made to take part in all the anger and hatred that his father has in his heart against me.

Joanne went to the hospital the week before Doug. They both complained of difficulty breathing and trusted they could get relief in the hospital. While Joanne was in the hospital, Todd texted and complained to Joanne about Doug being in the den trying to breathe with the oxygen tank, which he claimed prevented him from watching TV. Doug said that when Todd came out of their room and saw him in the den, Todd would run back to their room and slam the door in anger.

I was infuriated. It's my husband, and it's our house!

This was disappointing because while they lived with us, they had no financial burden except expenses for their personal necessities. Doug and I carried the load of running the household for two families. Todd was able to go to school and get his EMT certification. He had no pressure to work or pay rent and utilities. Joanne worked with me, so she had the income to meet their obligations.

Doug and I paid for the car they drove, their car insurance, and their cell phones. This isn't a complaint; we were happy to have them with us, especially Ethan. It was a heavy undertaking that we gladly took on. I don't believe too many parents out there would do what we did for Todd and Joanne. There wasn't a hint of gratitude in Todd at all.

So much of Todd's animosity toward us came out. All the grudges and resentments he held against Doug and me accumulated over time. Everything was reflected in the legal papers his lawyer filed in court.

To be honest, I don't know how I survived the emotional beating that I endured. It was vile. The things written about me and submitted to the court were so disheartening. I was told by someone who makes a living in the family court system, "Unless there's blood on the floor, they keep the children with the parents."

I met a grandma at a church event who told me her grandson was being sexually molested by his father. It took them four years to get the boy away from the father. While they fought in court, they were abused by the people in charge and even threatened with jail time.

I was only asking for time with Ethan.

But God.

> **"Blessed is the man who remains steadfast under trial, for when he has stood the test, he**

will receive the crown of life, which God has promised to those who love Him." James 1:12 ESV.

Persevere—it is a challenge you can win.

"If you faint in the day of adversity, your strength is small." Proverbs 24:10 ESV

Needless to say, I survived the ordeal. With the help of friends and the prayers poured upon me, I slowly rebuilt a semblance of normalcy in my daily life once Todd moved out. I knew I would miss Ethan a lot, but the peace of not being around Todd was necessary for my recovery. I would not be any good to Ethan if I were sick.

Emotional Turmoil and the Skin

In Chapter 1, I described my appearance in September 2021: haggard and tired, with sagging, dry, old-looking skin, a weary, depressed expression, and eyes without a glint of joy. That's the product of emotional turmoil, which starts from the inside out—the gut-brain connection.

Stress and the Skin Connection

Emotional stress can worsen skin conditions, acne, eczema, and even skin issues that come from autoimmune diseases like rosacea and psoriasis. Stress is a massive trigger of autoimmune disease that results in skin disorders.

This is why, even though this is a book on grief, I have included beauty. When I saw my ugly old mug looking back at me, I knew rejuvenation was part of recovery and healing. Looking good is a big part of feeling good and regaining self-confidence.

Don't Give Up: Be Proactive, You Can Restore and Rejuvenate

Praise God for the strength of my spiritual foundation. I continued to lean on Jesus, talking to Him through prayer and listening to His voice in His Holy Scriptures.

Over the years, I gained skills and tools to coach women on their graceful aging journey. Combining the powerful, unique, and excellent benefits of Clinical Aromatherapy and Face Reflexology, I created a "unique-to-you" method called AromaReflex Healing™.

There's no such thing as a one-size-fits-all. We're all made different, and medical issues vary from person to person based upon the "root cause" of the manifestations on the skin, the body's largest organ.

In ancient times, traditional Chinese or Ayurvedic medicines relied on the outward manifestation of disease to diagnose the problem and recommend a healing protocol. The root cause must be addressed first; otherwise, external solutions are either temporary or ineffective. I figure out the "root cause" by "reading the face."

The face is like a roadmap. Wrinkles, fine lines, red blotches, acne, and many other skin concerns manifest on the face. The location of the marks on the skin allows me to determine the internal issue. Once I understand what's going on internally, I can create an individual, unique-to-you plan to use pure essential oils and face reflex points. You can learn to do the same.

The AromaReflex Healing™ method is a three-step plan I created for individual needs. However, for the purpose of this book and considering the many aspects of and means to recover from the harmful effects of grief, I decided to expand the steps by adding

Step 4 to discuss mindful breathing and exercise and Step 5 for nutrition, hydration, and supplementation. These were essential to my recovery and will also be to yours.

I want this book to provide a complete guide to holistic healing strategies for women suffering from grief-induced stress. These strategies include combining faith in God, aromatherapy, face reflexology, mindful breathing, exercise, and adequately nourishing and hydrating the body to restore health, rejuvenate beauty, and overcome the ravages of stress.

I pray you will be encouraged and empowered as you read and progress to the following chapters. You CAN take an active role in your healing process. Your journey may present challenges, but the book's goal is to be a supportive guide every step of the way.

Clinical psychologist Regina Josell, PsyD, gives this analogy: "If you think of life as a house, the foundation of your house is taking care of your body and mind. Without a solid base, the house isn't going to hold up."

Surely, you have others around you, kids, grandkids, parents, or siblings who love you and want you to recover and be around. If not for you, do it for them.

Get into this guide and use the tools that I have provided you. Others in your family affected by the loss can also use the tools here. Going through the recovery together may create a deeper bond and a faster healing for everyone.

Visit the Resource page

CHAPTER 5

AromaReflex Healing™ Method – Step 1: Essential Mindset™ Cultivating a Positive Mindset Through Faith

Do you remember when they used to say mind over matter? It's a positive mind that will help you get past the darkness and let you see the light, the sun shining, the flowers blooming.

A positive mindset (a state of being) is important to overcoming grief and conquering pain, sadness, and sorrow. As I've said, this is not to get rid of grief, because grief stays with you. It's about your ability to manage it and move forward with your life for the good of others who will be inspired by seeing you rise from your pain and suffering.

Faith is a mindset. It's the choice to put your life and future in the hands of the One who created you. It isn't just about attending church on Wednesdays and Sundays or reciting prayers—it's a lifeline, particularly when the seas of life get stormy, and you need a "rope" to hang on to and avoid drowning.

Do you remember when Jesus was in the boat, and the storm came and frightened the disciples? They were so scared that they woke Jesus up frantically.

> "Now, when He got into a boat, His disciples followed Him. And suddenly, a great tempest arose on the sea so that the boat was covered with the waves. But He was asleep. Then His disciples came to Him and awoke Him, saying, "Lord, save us! We are perishing!" But He said to them, "Why are you fearful, O you of little faith?" Then He arose and rebuked the winds and the sea, and there was a great calm."
> Matthew 8:23-26 NKJV

Faith in God is the anchor that keeps the boat steady, even in the most turbulent waters. But how exactly does faith fit into the healing equation when it comes to grief?

Let's dive deep into understanding this amazing mindset-correcting process and explore how faith supports and actively propels your attitude toward a successful recovery journey.

Faith as a Foundation for Healing the Mindset

Imagine for a moment that your life is a building affected by the seismic waves of loss. Faith is the deep, underlying bedrock—it doesn't prevent the shaking, but it keeps the structure from collapsing. It provides a solid base you can rebuild, even in the face of devastating loss. Faith instills a sense of hope and purpose when everything feels transient and fragile. It assures you that your story will play an important role in someone else's life and be used to glorify God.

Faith assures a sense of community and belonging and comforts and encourages. It elevates your desire to help others going through grief, bringing your focus to someone other than yourself. Sharing stories or praying with and for each other reinforces you are not alone in your struggles and can benefit lives. This aspect of faith can be emotionally healing.

Using Faith to Frame the Grief Experience and Improve Your Mindset

Understanding your grief through the framework of your faith can provide a deeper sense of meaning and peace. Recognize that grief is not just a path of pain but also spiritual growth, cleansing, and refining. If you follow Jesus, He is readying you for something He wants you to do.

If you're not yet a follower of Jesus, reflect on the lessons you're learning, such as the value of a faith-filled life, the importance of relationships, or the strength of your spirit. See your grief as the road to the saving grace of an intimate relationship with Jesus Christ. Gain godly wisdom and empathy to transform how you experience your sorrow and create a testimony of victory from it. Look around you and see who God wants you to help or speak to using the trials you overcame.

Biblical Examples of the Power of Mindset to Triumph Over Grief

The Bible isn't just a book of teachings; it's a testimonial about real people with stories overflowing with grief, resilience, and recovery. Consider Job, who lost everything—wealth, health, and children. Yet, his response is of incredible faith and patience, providing a powerful example of enduring belief amid suffering and a mindset that he is not alone.

> "Then his wife said to him, 'Do you still hold fast to your integrity? Curse God and die!' But he said to her, 'You speak as one of the foolish women speaks. Shall we indeed accept good from God, and shall we not accept adversity?' In all this Job did not sin with his lips." Job 2:9-10 NKJV.

There's also David, who experienced deep woes and sorrows as a man chosen to be king over Israel, even in his imperfection. With Goliath, the first giant he faced, David looked to the Power greater than him. His faith in God firmly influenced his mindset. Here's what he said:

> "Then David said to the Philistine, 'You come to me with a sword and with a spear and with a javelin, but I come to you in the name of the Lord of hosts, the God of the armies of Israel, whom you have defied. This day the Lord will deliver you into my hand, and I will strike you down and cut off your head. And I will give the dead bodies of the host of the Philistines this day to the birds of the air and to the wild beasts of the earth, that all the earth may know that there is a God in Israel and that all this assembly may know that the Lord saves not with sword and spear. For the battle is the Lord's, and He will give you into our hand.'" 1 Samuel 17:45-47 ESV

You, too, can win over your "giant." Look to the One who can and will deliver you if you put your trust in Him.

> "And those who know Your name will put their trust in You; For You, Lord, have not forsaken those who seek You." Psalms 9:10 NKJV.

These stories offer more than historical accounts; they encourage you to lean into your faith, draw strength from the stories of resilience, and see them as mirrors reflecting your capacity to strengthen your mindset through faith.

Case Studies

Consider the story of Elizabeth Oliver, who struggled with unbearable guilt after her husband passed away within five days of receiving the COVID-19 vaccine. The vaccine interacted with various pre-existing health issues that she knew would hasten his death, yet she didn't stop her daughter from insisting her dad get the vaccine. She allowed it to happen, so she blamed herself.

After that trauma, Elizabeth's sister invited her to move in with them in Las Vegas, Nevada, so they could "help" her through her loss. Instead, they took $300,000 from her and bought property in Mexico under their name.

Elizabeth had the faith to hold her up and keep her on steady footing despite the unbelievable and shameless treatment of her own family. She also found respite in aromatherapy and face reflexology after I taught her how to adopt the practices into her daily routine, even incorporating them into her prayer and scripture meditation time.

See the video clip on the Resource page. Elizabeth gives a brief story of what she went through and how her faith in God, aromatherapy, and face reflexology have helped address many pent-up emotions that kept her angry these past several years.

An Essentially Essential Mindset Is Key

An essential mindset is the first step in healing the mind and body. One must address the state of mind first to begin healing. Mindset, a state of being, is a starting point for building a solid foundation to keep your feet on the ground no matter how much shaking you experience daily.

When prayers, scriptures, and community are combined and incorporated into your daily routine, there is a greater chance of conquering the emotions that can hinder your ability to move forward despite the overwhelming grief that can easily drown you without these supportive and powerful activities and engagements.

The tools are great, but unless the mindset is improved first, and I don't mean you stop being sad or crying, grief doesn't leave. It stays and takes up residence in your mind and heart. It's a matter of learning how to manage it.

The key to fixing the mindset is to put grief on the shelf and bring it out when it's safe to remember. No matter how painful, you will want to be reminded because it is part of staying connected to what you lost.

As my grandson Ethan said in the earlier chapter, once he learned what grief is, "Grandma, I put my grief on one leg and happiness on the other leg!" At age seven, he has learned to compartmentalize, which I believe helps him cope with his sadness and maybe even anger.

In earlier chapters, I wrote about the importance of faith in God. Not everyone who reads this book will be a follower of Jesus. However, I pray that once non-Christians read the scriptures and connect with the stories of the real people presented here through the videos—people whose lives were helped by overcoming grief through faith in God—it will stir their hearts toward seeking Jesus Christ's saving grace.

This is what the scriptures say in **Isaiah 26:3 NKJV:**

> **"You will keep him in perfect peace whose mind is stayed on You."**

> **"The Lord is good, A stronghold in the day of trouble, And He knows those who take refuge in Him." Nahum 1:7 NKJV**

Overcoming Common Mental Blockades to Healing the Mindset

When you're wading through the deep waters of grief, it can sometimes feel like you're also dragging chains of guilt, anger, or denial. These big blockades can stall your healing, making every day feel like a struggle against the current.

Understand these blockades, recognize their presence in your life, and learn how to get through them through faith and a holistic approach. Conquering grief physically and emotionally can transform your healing process.

Identifying Blockades

The first step to overcoming these mental obstacles is recognizing them.

- Guilt often poses a haunting question: "Did I do enough?" Whether it's guilt over things said or not said or actions taken or not taken, it can make you feel as if you're carrying a heavy burden long after your loss.
- Anger can be fiery and loud or cold and simmering. You might find yourself angry at the unfairness of your loss, at others who don't seem to understand your pain, or even at the one who left you behind.
- Disappointment, sadness, or displeasure can be caused by the non-fulfillment of one's hope or expectation.
- Denial, on the other hand, can be trickier to pinpoint. It might manifest as disbelief in the reality of the loss, a persistent feeling that things will soon "go back to normal," or an avoidance of any reminders of the truth.

Evan and Melissa Esguerra, a young couple I've known since 2015, were disappointed to have gone through three rounds of in vitro fertilization (IVF) and three IUIs (Intrauterine Insemination) unsuccessfully. They want a child. In between these heartbreaking disappointments, they lost their cat, whom they loved dearly.

Their faith in God redirected their mindset to adopt instead to fill the need for a baby God intended for Evan and Melissa to have. To a Christian, disappointment is merely a delay and an indicator that God has something better in store. He's not saying no; He is saying, "Wait, I have something better for you."

> "'For My thoughts are not your thoughts, Nor are your ways My ways,' says the Lord. 'For as

> **the heavens are higher than the earth, So are My ways higher than your ways, And My thoughts than your thoughts.'" Isaiah 55:8-9 NKJV.**

Our childhood experiences and emotions can affect our lives, as well as how we handle grief and other circumstances that cross our paths. Unfortunately, what we grow up with can affect even the tiniest detail of our lives and influence how we live, relate to others, and make decisions.

My friend, Shannon Eggleston, said she couldn't cry when she lost her parents. She had to force herself to cry. She didn't know why. Perhaps the reason is an experience in her youth. Sometimes, even something so minor can affect how we respond to sad or shocking things that happen to us.

I'm a crier, so I can't imagine not being able to cry and release the floodgate of pain and suffering. I don't know why Shannon couldn't cry, but it's a blessing that she can now.

Today, Shannon is a Naturopath and Clinical Master of Nutrition Response Testing at the Natural Healing Center in Newport Beach. Her clients come in with a variety of issues, many of which are stress-related and some of which are grief-induced. Having dealt with her difficulty with grief, she's able to coach and direct her clients on the path of healing. Check out Shannon's video on the Resource page.

More Blockages to a Healthy Mindset

These are just a few of the many negative influences that sabotage discipline and affect one's ability to improve one's mindset to ease and support the emotional manifestations of grief.

Many things can hinder discipline:

- Procrastination
- Bad habits
- Impatience
- Lack of motivation
- Hopelessness
- Overwhelm

Improving the mindset is a commitment that many people find hard to do because it requires many changes to daily habits and routines:

- Want immediate gratification
- Belief
- Lack of credible information
- Insecurity
- Mistrust

Consistency is another factor in improving the mindset. Consistency is a big one; many hindrances affect one's ability to be consistent:

- Lack of motivation
- Impatience
- Insufficient information
- Laziness
- Belief
- Overwhelm

Notice the similarities in hindrances to a healthy mindset through discipline, commitment, and consistency. Each one plays a huge role. These factors interconnect and influence one another. One must observe and overcome all three. A positive mindset is a significant ingredient to achieving goals.

Essential Oils for a Healthy Mindset

Let's look at some essential oils you can play with to improve and balance your mood, the foundation of a healthy mindset.

Basil

Basil is referred to as the "oil of renewal."

Negative emotions addressed:

- Anxiety
- Overwhelm
- Exhaustion
- Addictive tendencies
- Negative habits

Positive emotions produced:

- Renewal
- Rejuvenation
- Energy
- Rest
- Strengthening
- Hope and optimism
- Mental stimulation
- Stress management

Cypress

Cypress is the "oil of motion and flow."

Negative emotions addressed:

- Need to control
- Fearfulness

- Rigidity
- Feeling of being stuck
- Tenseness
- Perfectionism
- Overwhelm

Positive emotions produced:

- Flexibility
- Trust
- Flow with life
- Adaptability
- Confidence
- Diminishes guilt
- Aid in difficult transitions
- Combating grief and trauma
- A sense of security

Fennel

Fennel is "the oil of responsibility."

Negative emotions addressed:

- Lack of desire
- Unwillingness to take responsibility
- Shamefulness
- Weak sense of self

Positive emotions produced:

- Responsibility
- Energy
- Self-confidence

- Reduction of anxiety
- Promotes balanced emotions

Strategies for Overcoming Blockades

Recognizing these feelings isn't about judging yourself. It's perfectly normal to experience these emotions, and it's the first step toward recovery.

Forgiveness is not for the forgiven but for the forgiver. Unforgiveness affects your relationship with God. It is a poison that will affect you. Forgiveness releases you from anger toward the person or circumstance that may have caused you pain.

Marianne Williamson wrote, "Unforgiveness is like drinking poison yourself and waiting for the other person to die." There's nothing more toxic than the poison to the heart that comes through a grudge, and no other poison could be subtler.

> **Mark 11:25: "And whenever you stand praying, if you have anything against anyone, forgive him, that your Father in Heaven may also forgive you your trespasses."**

Accept the loss and look instead to the benefit of the refining and the strengthening, then use the fire created within you to fulfill God's plan and purpose for what you went through.

> **As He said in Romans 8:28, "And we know that all things work together for good to those who love God, to those who are the called according to *His* purpose."**

Look to God; He is your shield. Pray and ask Him for clarity, wisdom, and discernment.

> "Do not be afraid or discouraged, for the Lord will personally go ahead of you. He will be with you; He will neither fail you nor abandon you." Deuteronomy 31:8 NLT

> "The name of the Lord *is* a strong tower; The righteous run to it and are [a]safe." Proverbs 18:10 NKJV.

Aromatherapy is not just about smelling essential oils. Imagine a powerful scent that can bring peace, calm, and healing. This is the essence of aromatherapy—an ancient practice that harnesses the transformative power of pure essential oils to heal, soothe, restore, and rejuvenate the body and soul.

Aromatherapy offers a gentle yet tremendous way to find balance and comfort as you sail through the tumultuous waters of grief. This chapter will explore how these fragrant oils can become essential to your healing toolkit, provide a respite from the acute pain of loss, and provide a way to deeper emotional healing.

What Is Aromatherapy?

Aromatherapy involves using essential oils and concentrated extracts derived from the flowers, leaves, roots, or seeds of plants, fruits, and trees. Each oil has its unique chemical makeup and aroma, which can influence both your body and mind.

The way scent affects the brain's limbic system, the area controlling emotions and memories, underpins the science of aromatherapy.

When you inhale an essential oil, its molecules enter your nostrils and interact with sensory receptors, sending signals directly to your limbic system. This can trigger emotional responses, such as calm or uplifting, and affect physiological reactions, like reduced heart rate or lowered blood pressure.

Ancient cultures in China, India, and Egypt have used aromatherapy for thousands of years, incorporating aromatic plant components in resins, balms, and oils. Ancient cultures used these natural substances for medicinal and religious purposes. They were known to have both physical and psychological benefits.

Some well-known uses include:

- Soothing inflamed areas
- Balancing, grounding, or uplifting emotions
- Healing or soothing skin conditions
- Boosting immunity
- Supporting healthy digestion
- Rejuvenating and nourishing the skin
- Purifying infections
- Cleaning and disinfecting
- Reducing stress
- Improving sleep

Keep in mind that even though essential oils offer many helpful benefits, they should be seen as complementary treatments to medical care.

What Are Essential Oils?

You have heard of essential oils, right? Did you know they are all around us? They are in the zest of lemons, the needles of pine trees, the petals of roses, and the resin of trees. Essential oils are extracted from plants, trees, flowers, seeds, stems, roots, resin, and fruits.

Plant materials are harvested and processed to release chemical compounds through steam distilling, cold pressing, CO^2 extraction, or solvent extraction.

If you are wondering why they are called "essential" oils, they are essential to plants because they protect them from external things like bugs and other annoyances or hazards. Unlike humans, they can't run into the house to escape the hazard, so the essential oils protect them.

Fun Facts

- It takes seventy-five lemons to make a 15 ml or ½ ounce of essential oils.
- It takes four to five pounds of lavender flowers to produce 15 ml or ½ ounce of lavender essential oil.
- To produce a 5 ml pure therapeutic rose essential oil, you need 255,000 petals or 10,000 roses. Rose is an expensive essential oil because of this.

As you incorporate aromatherapy into your recovery process, remember that this practice is as much an art as a science. Each drop of essential oil holds a spectrum of therapeutic potential, ready to support you as you heal from grief.

Two Ways Essential Oils Can Support Emotional Healing

Inhalation

The first way essential oils can support emotional healing is inhalation. When you inhale essential oils, they interact with your olfactory system, the sense of smell, and quickly stimulate your brain. Then, the essential oil molecules travel to the lungs and enter the body through the respiratory system.

The inhalation of essential oils also affects the system through receptors that influence the limbic system. The limbic system is the seat of emotions; it controls the heartbeat, blood pressure, breathing, memory, stress levels, and hormones.

Diffusing involves using a device to disperse the oil molecules into the air, to allow for easy inhalation. It's effective for creating a calming environment or uplifting your spirits.

Simply breathing in these concentrated, naturally occurring chemicals can impact the systems quickly and in multiple ways. Put a drop on your hands, rub them together, bring them close to your nose, and inhale deeply two or three times.

Please note that quality matters. Buy the essential oils from a trusted source. The word "organic" does not show quality or purity. Disclaimer: I only recommend doTERRA essential oils for purity and efficacy. If you need guidance, please let me know via email at www.gracefulwellnessco@gmail.com.

Topical Application

When essential oil is applied to the skin, it enters the system by absorption. The skin is semi-permeable, allowing small molecules or ions to travel into the body. Seventy percent of what touches the skin stays on it, enters the system, and penetrates the cells and tissues. Therefore, you must use only essential oils from a trusted source to avoid allergic reactions and endocrine disruption from toxins.

> Please note that essential oils are potent, so diluting them with a carrier oil like fractionated coconut oil (FCO) is best. Doing a patch test before putting them on the skin is also a good idea.

From a holistic perspective, aromatherapy is more than just a tool to manage symptoms—it's a form of therapy that integrates and heals the mind, body, and spirit. It acknowledges the connection between scent and memory, between our olfactory senses and our emotional center; it offers a way to access and alleviate grief at its deepest layers.

Whether it's the calming scent of lavender that helps you find peace before sleep or the refreshing aroma of wild orange that boosts your mood in the morning, each essential oil offers a unique key to balancing your emotional state.

I hope this explains essential oils in a new light. Each has myriad uses. Having just a few different types in your bathroom and kitchen can bolster your recovery and support your health and beauty.

Safety First

While natural, essential oils are potent and must be used with care. Here are some key safety guidelines:

- **Dilution**: Essential oils should be diluted in a carrier oil like coconut, jojoba, or almond oil before being applied to the skin. This prevents irritation and sensitization. A general rule of thumb for topical applications is to maintain a dilution rate of 1 to 2 percent, which translates to about one to two drops of essential oil per teaspoon of carrier oil.
- **Skin Patch Test**: Before using a new essential oil, perform a skin patch test. Apply a small amount of the diluted oil to the inside of your elbow and cover it with a bandage. Wait twenty-four hours to see if there is any adverse reaction.
- **Diffusion**: One of the safest methods of using essential oils is to use a diffuser to disperse them into the air. However, it's important to follow the manufacturer's guidelines regarding the amount of oil to use and to ensure the room is well-ventilated.
- **Ingestion**: Generally, you should avoid ingesting essential oils unless under the guidance of a qualified professional. I don't suggest this unless I am coaching the person, whether in person or online.

Selecting Essential Oils for Emotional Support

With their rich, aromatic essences, essential oils can touch the raw and aching parts of us, providing comfort when words often fall short. As you start to explore the world of aromatherapy for emotional and physical healing, knowing which oils are particularly supportive during grief can be immensely helpful.

The following essential oils, each with unique properties, can soothe the heart, calm the mind, and aid in improving the mindset.

Lavender

Lavender is the oil of "communication and calm." It is a great oil to use at the beginning of your journey, especially during emotional turmoil. Renowned for its calming and sedating properties, lavender can help ease anxiety and insomnia, familiar companions of grief. Some of the favorable properties of lavender are peace of mind, open communication, and a feeling of calm and security. It is a sedative and antidepressant, encourages a restful night's sleep, and combats frustration.

Lavender is also immune-supportive, helps lower blood pressure, and aids detoxification, which is beneficial for ridding the body of toxins accumulated from stress.

Frankincense

Frankincense, the oil of "truth" with its deep, resinous aroma, is another powerful ally. It is often used to deepen breathing and bring about a sense of peace, making it invaluable when grief feels like a physical weight on your chest. Additionally, Frankincense is known to relieve negative emotions like abandonment, spiritual disconnectedness, and grief, encouraging emotional healing. Some physical benefits include anticancer properties, improved digestion, pain relief, and anti-inflammatory effects.

Rose

Rose, the oil of "divine love," is often associated with the heart. It has a profound ability to help heal emotional wounds, restore a sense of well-being, release traumatic memories, calm and soothe

the nerves, encourage restful sleep, relieve deep despair and grief, and combat anger.

Rose balances heart function and female hormones. Stress dramatically affects these functions.

Bergamot

Bergamot, the oil of "self-acceptance," relieves despair, self-judgment, and low self-esteem. It cleanses stagnant feelings and limiting belief systems and promotes optimism, self-acceptance, hope, and confidence. It encourages a restful night's sleep, relieves anxiety, is uplifting, helps release suppressed negative emotions, combats aggression, reduces mood swings, and is an antidepressant.

Bergamot promotes physical health by supporting endothelial and cardiovascular function. It also has anticancer properties, stimulates hormone release, provides pain relief, aids digestion, and reduces inflammation.

Cedarwood

Cedarwood, the oil of "continuity," promotes emotional connectedness, belonging, and community. It is grounding and uplifting and helps with morale and courage.

Cedarwood supports balanced blood sugar levels, brain function, circulation, and digestion.

Peppermint

Peppermint, the oil of the "buoyant heart," addresses negative emotions like unbearable anguish, intense despair, sadness, heavy-heartedness, and pessimism. It calms anger, encourages self-confidence, aids concentration, combats fatigue, invigorates, calms and soothes the nerves.

You can also use peppermint to relieve headaches, aid digestion, support the immune system, and stimulate the liver and the gallbladder.

Lemon

Lemon, the oil of "focus," promotes mental clarity, alertness, and focus; acts as an antidepressant; combats frustration and nightmares; has sedative properties; and encourages restful sleep.

Lemon also supports the immune system, helps lower blood pressure, and aids digestion.

Eucalyptus

Eucalyptus, the oil of "wellness," calms and soothes the nerves, stimulates, invigorates, and refreshes. It aids concentration, combats negative emotions, and relieves mental exhaustion.

Please note that the benefits listed above for each essential oil are not exhaustive. They target the ravages of grief, stress, and despair on the body and the mind.

When these oils are blended, their benefits can be enhanced. To make a blend, start with a carrier oil base—like sweet almond or jojoba—and add one or two drops of each essential oil. Remember, the blend is not just about the oils; it's about what you need now. Trust your instincts and nose—often, they will guide you to the combination that will serve you best.

Click the video on the Resource page to watch a demonstration of blending and using essential oils. Enjoy the recipes that you will find there as well.

Daily Aromatherapy Routines to Ease Grief

These can be simple additions to your daily routines: Diffuse essential oils like lavender. Make a roller you carry, like a blend of peppermint and lemon. Replace your perfume with a rose roller that you can apply on your wrists and the back of your ears as often as you want without the toxicity of synthetic fragrance, which affects brain function.

Wild orange, the oil of "abundance", is one of my favorite oils. It reduces anxiety, combats pessimism, helps reduce perfectionism, and is anti-depressant and uplifting. It blends well with peppermint and floral oils like lavender.

Wild orange essential oil has various benefits for the body. It aids digestion, supports lymph drainage, has anticancer properties, and reduces inflammation. I use it for cleaning because it is also a disinfectant.

Integrate aromatherapy into your morning routine and set a nurturing tone for your entire day, especially when going through the tender times of grief. Start your day with the sweet aroma of wild orange, it provides an energetic boost that can help lift the morning fog of sadness.

Consider using a diffuser set on a timer so the fragrance fills your space just before you wake up. Take deep, intentional breaths as you inhale the aroma to help center your thoughts and prepare you for your time of prayer and scripture meditation.

As the day unfolds, moments of heightened grief or sudden stress may arise unpredictably. If you expect a stressful day, keep a small, portable bottle of essential oil or a rollerball bottle with a specific blend that helps calm you, handy.

Oils like frankincense, known for its grounding effects, or peppermint, are revitalizing and can help clear your mind. Apply the oil to pulse points such as the wrists or temples, or simply open the bottle and breathe in deeply for instant relief. The key here is immediate accessibility. Having these oils readily available means you can address your emotional needs on the spot, wherever you are.

In the evenings, create a wind-down time with soothing scents that can significantly enhance your ability to relax and induce restorative sleep. Consider lavender, renowned for its relaxing properties, stress relief, and sleep-inducing properties.

When my grandson Ethan spends the night, he loves to take a long, warm bath. He's got a routine: bubble bath, a handful of Himalayan Sea salt, and drops of lavender. At bedtime, depending on the size of the room, I put five drops in a diffuser in the bedroom then I apply diluted lavender to his chest and the bottoms of his feet.

Inhale essential oils and oil blends to achieve calming benefits. Drop a drop or two on the palm of your hands, rub them together, cup your hands to your face, and inhale two to three times as deeply as possible.

The beauty of these routines is their ease of use and flexibility. Grief is not a static experience; it unfolds, shifts, and changes daily, sometimes moment by moment. As such, vary your activities according to your needs. Pray the scriptures over the pain or sadness you're feeling while inhaling your essential oils and breathing in deeply.

As you continue to incorporate these practices into your routine, remember that this isn't just about smelling pleasant aromas or rubbing your face; it's what they represent to you. They restore your peace and calm and help you heal grief.

Watch the videos in the Resource page to connect you to real people who overcame their grief, just like I did and just like you will. They strengthened their faith and used a mixture of the holistic tools presented here.

Visit the Resource page

CHAPTER 6

AromaReflex Healing™ – Step 2: Essential Beauty™

Aromatherapy for Physical Healing

"You are what you eat!" It is accurate and applies to our skin, too.

In Chapter 5, you read about how important a positive mindset is to achieving your goal of healing grief and overcoming its manifestations. Unless you overcome the hindrances and create a positive attitude that motivates you to make the changes, anything else you do becomes an exercise in futility.

Looking good may be the last thing on your mind as grief feels like you're being swallowed up by sadness, pain, misery, and hopelessness, but looking good has a lot to do with feeling good about yourself.

How you feel about yourself is a big part of recovery. With that in mind, I will dedicate this chapter to improving your health, fortifying your body, and rejuvenating your appearance using aromatherapy blends you can create independently. In this chapter, you will learn which essential oils give you the benefits needed to heal internally and emotionally to restore your physical health and beauty.

Did you know that 70+ percent of what you put on your skin gets "eaten" by your skin and distributed throughout your body through your cells and tissues? When I say you are what you eat, I mean what you feed your body and skin. Everything we ingest, whether through our mouth, skin, or brain (through inhalation), ends up in our gut, and the liver processes all that out of our bodies. The digestive system controls the immune system.

I don't want to get too technical and overwhelm you with scientific terminology, but the digestive system houses 70 plus percent of the immune cells. They live in the digestive system's lining, which filters nutrients and prevents toxins from entering the bloodstream.

So, maintaining a healthy digestive system with nutritious food, supplements, vitamins, and proper hydration is essential to a healthy immune system. Limiting and eliminating toxic products is also important to maintaining a healthy gut.

But how does one do this? From stress caused by grief to toxic products like skincare, makeup, body products, home products, and so much more, it seems we can't avoid it.

Toxins in products you use daily penetrate your skin, cells, and tissue and accumulate in your liver. Dangerous chemicals fill commercial products, like laundry detergent, shampoo, body wash, perfume, commercial skincare products, makeup, and fragrances. If you don't diligently read ingredients and research sustainable products, supermarkets and department stores will sell you products filled with toxic chemicals.

Using products with toxic chemicals has many negative implications. "Endocrine disruptors" disrupt the proper function of the endocrine system, affecting hormone production and regulation. They Impact sleep quality, the ability to lose weight, libido, and the immune system.

Fragrance Is in Everything

Here's what the National Institute of Health says about the toxicity of fragrance chemicals and the synthetic chemicals in perfumes, colognes, body lotions, and detergents, to name a few: "The negative impact of fragrance chemicals on human health includes cutaneous, respiratory, and systemic effects (e.g., headaches, asthma attacks, breathing difficulties, cardiovascular and neurological problems) and distress in workplaces."

The label "organic" does not always mean a "clean" or toxin-free product. The label shows the company can afford to pay for the privilege of using the word "organic" on their products.

When I consider a product, I look at its ingredients. There should be no more than five ingredients, all of which are pronounceable. Even products labeled "clean" may not be toxin-free. These are from companies called "greenwashers". They refer to their products as "clean," but when you look at the ingredients, you will see dirty chemicals.

To take the mystery out of what you can do to help yourself, the following pages with recipes will show you how to make your own skincare and body products to help you minimize the amount of toxins your body ingests daily. This approach will be easy to do and inexpensive to keep. It can lead to learning many other ways to use beneficial essential oils to support the body and mind and guide you to recovery and a graceful aging journey despite the grief you carry and the pain and sadness that comes upon you at certain moments of your day.

I call this step "beauty from the outside in" because using pure and efficacious essential oils on the skin promotes physical and emotional healing as they penetrate the skin and support the cells, tissues, and organs.

Defy Nature: Build Up Your Collagen, Naturally!

Why is stimulating the production of collagen so important? Collagen is one of the biggest buzzwords in the beauty industry today. Countless products offer "collagen-boosting" effects designed to improve the appearance of your skin to keep that youthful glow. From reducing wrinkles to improving skin texture and hydration, collagen helps us look younger and longer.

Collagen accounts for 30 percent of your body's protein, making it one of the most essential substances in our body. It provides structure, support, or strength to your skin, muscles, bones, and connective tissues. As we age, collagen production decreases. Collagen exists in almost every body part, from hair to nails, bones to organs, and joints.

Collagen Decreases After a Certain Age

Most often, starting at age thirty, the amount of collagen in your body will decrease by about 1 or 2 percent per year. This reduction is the body's response to aging and is a natural part of aging.

Lifestyle choices or habits, such as exposure to UV rays, smoking, and even pollution, can increase this reduction. Several noticeable effects of less collagen in the body are a reduction of elasticity in the skin, dull and sagging skin, wrinkles, and scarring on the skin from acne or injury because the body doesn't have the same capacity to heal.

Therefore, rejuvenating essential oils is vital to your daily beauty and health routine.

Rejuvenating Essential Oils for Your Beauty and Health Routine

Here are a few that I recommend to boost collagen production, hydrate, repair, rejuvenate, restore, beautify the skin, and fortify physical health.

Even natural products like essential oils may interfere with prescription medications. Exercise caution if you are taking medication.

Geranium

- Boosts collagen production in the skin
- Contains powerful antioxidants that can safeguard the skin from damaging free radicals
- Keeps premature signs of aging at bay
- Stimulates lymph flow and drainage
- Anti-inflammatory
- Regenerates cells
- Wound healing
- Reduces the appearance of scars and blemishes
- Astringent

Sandalwood

- Promotes collagen production and helps skin attain a youthful glow

- Possesses the ability to encourage the regeneration of skin cells, fighting off various signs of aging
- Astringent
- Antibacterial
- Anti-inflammatory
- Relieves skin conditions (especially those that involve inflammation)
- Anti-tumor
- Stimulates lymph drainage
- Nourishes and softens skin

Rose

- Refreshing fragrance
- A rich source of collagen-boosting compounds that can combat signs of aging like wrinkles and fine lines
- Replete with astringent properties that stimulate elastin production and help skin become firm
- Reduces the appearance of blemishes, stretch marks, and scars
- Nourishes and moistens skin
- Anti-inflammatory
- Antiviral

Frankincense

- Slows down the skin's aging process by boosting collagen production
- Improves skin elasticity and prevents problems like sagging skin
- Anti-cancer
- Anti-tumor
- Anti-aging
- Encourages cellular regeneration and a healthy cell cycle

- Reduces the appearance of scars and blemishes
- Wound healing

Myrrh

- Relieves chronic skin conditions
- Cell rejuvenator
- Anti-tumor
- Astringent
- Anti-fungal
- Anti-inflammatory
- Antiseptic
- Wound healing

Patchouli

- Nourishes and moisturizes the skin
- Soothes skin conditions
- Regenerative
- Protects skin from UV radiation damage
- Reduces the appearance of blemishes
- Antiseptic
- Anti-fungal

Thyme

- Reduces the appearance of scars and blemishes
- Wound healing
- Anti-inflammatory

Lavender

- Skin healing
- Relieves burns and sunburns
- Anti-inflammatory

- Anti-fungal
- Reduces the appearance of scars and blemishes
- Helps bruises and boils heal

Roman Chamomile

- Soothes redness
- Fights acne
- Reduces signs of aging
- Treats weather-related redness and dryness
- Wound healing
- Anti-inflammatory
- Helps with eczema
- Reduces hyperpigmentation and free radical damage

Why Dilute and What Is the Role of Carrier Oils?

The term "carrier" implies that the oil is mixed with essential oil, carrying the essential oil through the skin. Essential oils evaporate quickly, but when combined with carrier oils, the skin can absorb them better, providing more benefits.

Carrier oils are plant oils, such as coconut, almond, and avocado. You most likely have seen these oils and their applications in the cosmetic industry, but they do not have the label of carrier oils.

I usually recommend coconut oil. Here are its benefits and uses:

- Contains essential fatty acids and polyphenols
- Has antimicrobial properties that can help protect against harmful microorganisms
- Known for reducing inflammation on the skin, which can also lead to reducing the appearance of acne

Hydrate and Rejuvenate

The first step to a hydrating and relaxing regimen is aromatherapy.

Blend a drop of each recommended oil, or one or two, with fractionated coconut oil (FCO). Rub your hands together and apply to the face and neck. If you don't have essential oils, please use FCO.

Apply the oil(s) on your face and spread them all over your neck and chest. As you spread the oil, use your knuckles and stimulate first on the left side, going in a circular motion all over the face slowly and firmly for about one or two minutes. Enjoy the feel of your smooth skin as the oil penetrates and hydrates your skin. Make sure you stimulate slowly, gently, and firmly. Please don't rush through it. You will start to feel relaxed as you awaken your skin.

When you stimulate the skin firmly, the blood flows, and the lymphatic system delivers lymph fluids, providing disease-fighting cells and removing toxins. The energy flow opens up, and the body stimulates collagen production. You will feel relaxed and notice your skin is bright and glowing after.

Look to Your Skin to Tell You What's Going On

The choice of oil can depend significantly on your skin type and the specific skin issues you're dealing with internally and emotionally. To rejuvenate the skin, the body's biggest organ, one must first address the "root cause." For instance, if your skin has become dry and flaky from the endless stress and sleepless nights, add lavender, known for its hydrating and soothing properties.

Application Techniques for Maximum Benefit

Use essential oils correctly and routinely to unlock their full therapeutic potential. For skin application, always dilute essential oils with a carrier oil, such as jojoba, coconut, or almond oil, to avoid irritation. A general guideline is to keep a ratio of one to two drops of essential oil per teaspoon of carrier oil.

To set up a routine, start simple and deal with one concern at a time. If it's stress, focus on reducing it to balance your emotions and improve sleep to recharge your brain.

The first step to an effective routine is inhaling the essential oil. See the video on the Resource page, where I show you the simple steps you can adopt in your daily morning and evening routine. If you haven't been following one since going through your loss, this will be an excellent place to start.

Emotional and Physical Connection

How you care for your skin can reflect and influence your feelings. It's a visible organ, one that shows signs of stress but also signs of care and attention. Improve the appearance of your skin and send a message to yourself about your worth and capacity for recovery.

Each time you see a fresh glow, a softness, or even a slight improvement in how your skin looks and feels, it's a reminder that healing is happening, not just on the surface, but deep within.

This connection between emotional and physical well-being is deep. It teaches that self-care is a necessity instead of an indulgence, especially in times of emotional stress. By taking care of your skin and dedicating those few minutes each day to stimulate the face and breathe in the scents of essential oils, you're also caring for your emotional self. It's a minor act of kindness to yourself, a way to nurture the body.

When you embrace this ritual of beauty and self-care, you take active steps toward healing your skin and soothing your grief. Each oil application, each moment spent caring for yourself, is a step toward healing—a gentle, loving reminder you deserve care and attention and possess the strength to heal from the inside out and the outside in.

Routine for Morning and Night

Establish a daily skincare routine, incorporate aromatherapy and face reflexology to turn personal care into an effective self-healing ritual. In the morning, after a night that might have been restless, wash your face and then apply lavender diluted with jojoba to hydrate your skin and soothe your nerves.

Then, follow it up with a blend of oils like peppermint and wild orange on the palm of your hands to inhale and invigorate the senses, wake up the brain, and prepare you for the day ahead. This combination is uplifting and packed with antioxidants that protect from environmental stressors.

At night, your skincare routine can signal your body that it's time to wind down. After cleansing your skin, take one-two drops of a calming oil like Roman chamomile to help soothe the skin and relax the mind. Dilute with coconut oil or jojoba, then gently massage it onto your face, neck, and other areas that need attention.

Then, take your knuckles and move upward with circular strokes to boost circulation and lift the spirits. Stimulate firmly but gently, allowing the oils to penetrate and nourish your skin. Let it be a reminder that you are caring for yourself and, despite the grief, bringing restoration and peace into your life.

Essential Oils for a Restful Sleep

Restful nights can seem elusive when your heart is heavy with sadness and loneliness. In the stillness of the night, when memories flood your mind, overpowering emotions can prevent sleep. During these times, the gentle power of essential oils can help bring calm, offer a natural, soothing touch to ease your mind, and guide you into a peaceful slumber.

Many people admire oils like lavender, Roman chamomile, and frankincense for their delightful scents, natural soothing properties, and ability to calm the nervous system and promote tranquility.

Widely recognized for enhancing relaxation and sleep quality, lavender is a true gem in essential oils. Components like linalool and linalool acetate, which researchers have studied for their practical, calming, and soothing effects, contribute to the sweet floral scent of lavender.

Roman chamomile is just a little behind in its sleep-promoting qualities. It also has compounds that help reduce anxiety and settle the mind, making it easier to slip into restorative sleep.

Consider a lavender and Roman chamomile blend for nights when sleep seems stubborn. Mix these oils to enhance their effectiveness and create a powerful duo that supports deeper sleep. To make this blend, combine equal parts of each oil in a small bottle, shake gently to mix, and use a few drops in your diffuser or dilute with a carrier oil like coconut for topical use on your chest and the bottoms of your feet. This blend combines and complements the individual strengths of each oil.

Frankincense is one of the gifts Jesus received from the three wise men, and it's no wonder. Its excellent value for many uses includes shrinking tumors and helps the entire body and the mind. It's an invaluable oil when you're drowning in grief and struggling to breathe; it offers a lifeline, emotional release, clarity, and calm.

Create a bedtime ritual and incorporate these oils to transform your nights from restless to restful. Set a consistent bedtime to help regulate your body's clock and start winding down from the day's activities. Dim the lights in your bedroom, switch off electronic devices, and take a few moments to write any lingering thoughts or worries in a journal. Transferring your thoughts onto paper is a great way to let go of your fears, allowing you to clear your mind.

Create a haven for sleep. Ensure your bedding is comfortable and the temperature is cool. Add a few drops of lavender to a diffuser and let it fill your room with its calming scent. The soothing aroma will envelop you as you lie down, setting a peaceful tone for sleep.

As you settle into bed, try a gentle relaxation exercise. Close your eyes and take slow, deep breaths, inhaling the calming scent of the oils. With each exhale, imagine releasing the day's tensions.

Pray and recite your favorite scripture to yourself; it is incredibly helpful in lifting your worries away. You can enhance this relaxation by applying a small amount of diluted lavender oil to your temples and your wrists. Use light, circular motions upward and clockwise to massage the oil into your skin to benefit your skin and deepen your sense of relaxation

When you embrace these nightly rituals, you promote better sleep and cultivate a space of peace where you can shelve the day's troubles and enjoy the quiet and comfort of the night as a cocoon of rest and healing.

Beautifying Self-Care Rituals with Oils

When the weight of sorrow and grief feels like it's pressing down on every inch of your being, transform your bathroom into a sanctuary for self-care with the addition of a diffuser and turn it into a daily haven. Whether diffusing essential oils while you get ready for the day or preparing for bed at night, it's a beautiful space to lift the spirits and nurture the body. Imagine stepping into your paradise, where you can let go of all the angst of the day and enjoy tranquility.

Smell the soothing scent of eucalyptus or the refreshing aroma of wild orange. Each breath is a reminder that you are here to care for yourself, to soothe the pains that linger both on the surface and deep within.

Bath and Body Care

Enhance your bath with essential oils that cleanse and nourish the body and soothe the soul. Fill your tub with warm water, then add a handful of Himalayan Sea salt mixed with essential oils like lavender for relaxation, rosemary for mental clarity, or both. As the room fills with steam, the oils evaporate and create a fragrant sanctuary that hugs you, easing the tension in your muscles and the clutter in your mind.

Need a more invigorating bath? Add two drops of peppermint or wild orange oil to your bath. These scents energize the senses and help lift your mood. As you soak, let the warmth of the water and the benefits of the oils coax your body into relaxation, washing away the worries and stresses that accumulated in the wake of your loss. This ritual of renewal and purification is a physical and emotional cleansing that prepares you to face the world anew.

My grandson Ethan loves sea salt soaked in essential oils!

Beautifying Facial Care Routines

Start a nontoxic skincare routine, incorporate pure, therapeutic oils, and address skin issues worsened by unbearable grief, such as dryness or dullness. Start your morning with a gentle cleanser you created yourself, followed by a toner to balance the skin's pH. Then, apply a serum or oil blend customized for your skin's needs as your moisturizer. A simple blend of jojoba oil, rich in vitamins B and E, with a drop each of lavender, Roman chamomile, frankincense, and cypress, is excellent for revitalizing tired, lackluster skin.

An evening routine can be just as simple but more focused on repair and rejuvenation. After cleansing, apply an oil blend using myrrh, frankincense, and cedarwood diluted with more decadent carrier oils like rosehip or evening primrose, known for their deep moisturizing properties and ability to improve skin elasticity.

Face Stimulation Techniques

Incorporate face stimulation into your skincare routine to enhance the effectiveness of the oils and provide healing benefits, as described in Chapter 7. It is an easy technique that involves gently massaging the oil into your face using your knuckles in a clockwise circular motion, starting from the center and moving outward. This helps wake up circulation and aids in lymphatic drainage, reducing puffiness, boosting skin health, and promoting internal healing.

These Rituals Have a Power to Ease

Rituals like bathing in scented waters, caring for your skin with aromatic oils, and massaging tension away from your body—are all combined, intending to heal grief and the pain it brings. When so much can feel like it's been taken from you, it's a way of reminding yourself that amid the chaos of loss, you still have the power to nurture and nourish your own body.

Moments spent caring for your body are not just about aesthetics or vanity—they are foundational acts that fortify your emotional resilience. They remind you that you are still here, capable of giving and receiving love, and can still find moments of beauty amid pain.

Visit the Resource page

A Note from Grace

Dear Reader,

Thank you for joining me on this healing journey through grief. As you've reached this pivotal point in "Thrive in Grief," I hope the Essential Steps™ system has already begun to provide you with practical tools for navigation through life's challenges.

Your experience with these first chapters matter deeply – not just to me, but to others walking similar paths. Would you take a moment to share your thoughts on Amazon? Your honest review could help someone else decide if this book might be their next step toward healing.

To leave a review:

1. Visit Amazon.com/do/[INSERT BOOK ID]
2. Click on "Write a customer review"
3. Share your experience so far, even if you haven't finished the book
4. Select your rating

Every review makes a difference in helping this message reach those who need it most. Thank you for being part of this supportive community of healing.

With gratitude,

Grace Richardson

P.S. Feel free to update your review once you've completed the book – your journey matters at every stage.

CHAPTER 7

AromaReflex Healing™ – Step 3: Essential Stimulation™

Face stimulation promotes internal and emotional healing, ultimately manifesting as a healthy mind and body and beautiful, younger-looking skin.

You can imagine how excited I am to show you how the combination of aromatherapy and face stimulation packs a powerful punch in giving the body the natural means to heal and support your grief journey. And to think, you can do this on your own, without expensive trips to health experts! When you have control of your healing process, you can heal faster because you aren't relying on someone else.

Stimulating the points and zones on the face with your knuckles or other specific tools is a treatment protocol that relaxes the face muscles and nerves, activates the connections to the areas of internal and emotional concern reflected on the skin, and promotes faster healing results.

I use the tools to make it easier to stimulate the face and cover a more extensive area when I'm pressed for time. However, using your knuckles, you can stimulate your skin easily during the day when you're on the phone, watching TV, or even while reading this book.

My grandson, Ethan, loves to play with the special tools I have for rubbing his face. You can do this as a game with your kids or grandkids! Teach the littles how to care for themselves naturally and independently; it is an excellent way to create a fun response to attending to medical concerns like a cold or stomachache your little one is going through.

Interesting Facts

- Similar to the principles supporting acupuncture, face reflexology focuses on manipulating hundreds of points and reflex zones in the face to support internal and emotional healing.
- Stimulate the points and zones on the face with the knuckles, fingertips, or specific tools to help ease neck and back pain and other discomforts.
- Young children can learn and apply this treatment protocol to promote self-care at home. It revives the areas of concern reflected on the face, encourages faster results, and promotes and supports a quicker way to heal while minimizing pain and discomfort.

Some of the Benefits of Face Reflexology

- Instant relief of tension on the face, neck, scalp, and brain
- Works with the entire body system to address specific internal and external issues
- Works to firm the facial muscles, reduces and prevents fine lines and wrinkles
- Stimulation increases blood circulation and activates lymphatic drainage for the removal of toxins from the body and to achieve a naturally glowing complexion

- Enhances the skin tone
- Enhances hydration and cell regeneration
- Reduces stress and improves sleep

Beauty marks, moles, wrinkles, dimples, and spots on the face reflect a potential, existing, or ongoing internal imbalance and show present or past weaknesses.

Observe tone, brightness, and texture; the face is an essential source of information about the general internal state of the body and is an excellent indicator of health.

It makes perfect sense! When we overeat sugar, pimples pop up. Or when we don't drink enough water, our skin starts to feel and look dehydrated.

Bumps found in areas of the face during stimulation and the marks mentioned above enable us to see the origin of the imbalance. Tenderness or sensitivity in the areas of the face can be indicators that require attention.

The reason I love face reflexology is the by-product of beautiful skin. Restoring or rejuvenating your looks might be far from your mind right now, but I want to discuss it in this book and show you the "how-to" when you realize your need to rejuvenate and restore confidence in how you look and feel.

It makes sense that you look good when you feel good! "Beauty from the outside in." Beauty is not only skin deep; it's "within" deep.

How Face Reflexology Works

A firm touch and gentle manipulation of the face restore energy, sending the message to the brain to balance blocked areas. Face stimulation is powerful because it has the shortest pathways for the nerve cells to connect to the brain stem and release chemicals called endorphins.

Face reflexology or stimulation sends a message to the Central Nervous System (CNS) to direct energy to specific organs and glands, regulating blood flow, hormone production, and most importantly, boosting the immune system. It is also an essential workout for the face, which can help it look younger and healthier.

Reflexology tools and application techniques help the skin absorb essential oils and nontoxic plant-based skin care products more readily.

From a medical point of view, the tools I use have a purely mechanical action on the skin. They regulate the circulatory and peripheral nervous systems, stimulate the secretion of lymphatic fluids to strengthen the immune system, and encourage collagen production.

Basics of Face Reflexology for Healing

Imagine your face not just as a mirror reflecting your emotions, but as a map of reflex points that, when pressed or touched, can lead to healing and rejuvenation. This is the heart of face reflexology—a practice where each point on your face connects to your body's systems, the pathways to emotional and physical wellness.

As we explore these delicate connections, I invite you to consider face reflexology not just as a technique but to create intimacy with yourself as you get to know how God made you, how much power He has given you, and how excellent the tools are that He gave in nature to care for yourself in situations like grief and loss.

Understanding Reflexology Points

According to reflexology, different points on your face correspond to different parts of your body, organs, and emotions. For instance, the area beneath your eyes reflects your kidneys, organs that, in many healing traditions, are associated with fear and stress—emotions you may be all too familiar with. By gently stimulating these points, you can influence the corresponding areas in your body, helping to soothe and balance your emotions and physical responses to grief.

Before I start my face reflexology session, I always apply essential oils. In Chapters 5 and 6, I recommend essential oils that rejuvenate the skin and calm the mind.

If you don't have essential oils now, please don't use just any essential oil brand unless you are sure it is from a trusted source. You can start with fractionated coconut oil, liquid, or solid coconut oil; both will work.

Put a little on your hands; stroke it all over your face and neck slowly and leisurely. Close your eyes, breathe deeply, and enjoy the comforting touch of your fingers on your face. Feel the calming effects of your touch. Continue to do that for about two minutes. I have a video link here that you can follow.

Okay, now let's map these points together. Use your knuckles and rub in a circular motion, starting with the eyebrows. These points connect to your liver, an organ processing toxins and emotions, and easing anger or frustration.

Move to the temples; gentle circular motions here can help ease the mental pressure that often accompanies deep sadness. As you trace your knuckles down to the sides of your nose, you're engaging points connected to your sinuses and emotional pathways that might help rational feelings of confusion or overwhelm.

The technique is simple but requires mindfulness. Using either your fingertips or your knuckles, you can also apply gentle and firm pressure, as you can tolerate, to each point for about thirty seconds, always remembering to breathe deeply as you do so. The pressure should be firm but not painful. It's about making a connection, not causing discomfort. In circular motions, stimulate each point, paying attention to the sensations and emotions that arise.

I encourage you to do this daily as part of your beauty routine, even for two to three minutes. It's a great way to start or end the day, centered and focused.

Benefits Beyond Grief

While the primary target here is to soothe the emotional turmoil of grief, the benefits of face reflexology extend further. My goal is to show you that regular stimulation of the reflex points on your face has many internal benefits, including improving circulation, sleep, energy, organ function, and external pain relief. This brings more oxygen and nutrients to your skin, enhancing its health and glow. It's a natural boost to your complexion, helping you look and feel rejuvenated.

The practice of face reflexology can significantly reduce stress. Stress creates cortisol, which causes many problems in the body. The pressure on the points helps calm the nervous system, slow breathing, and invites a sense of deep relaxation. As your body relaxes, so will your mind, even amid the turmoil of grief.

Let's Recap with Emphasis on Ease

You can start simply by applying a diluted blend of essential oils. In Chapters 5 and 6, I talk about a few of my favorite essential oils I recommend. Use one, two, or even three and dilute it with fractionated coconut oil (FCO) or jojoba oil. Drop essential oils and FCO on your hands, then rub your hands together. Ensure you inhale deeply while cupping your hands to your face, and then breathe out two to three times. Apply liberally on your face and neck.

Then, use your knuckles in a circular motion for about three minutes, gently but firmly and slowly, enjoying it. You can also focus on one or two points that resonate with you, the temples are a perfect area to rub if you're experiencing a lot of mental chatter or beneath the eyes if you feel weighed down by emotional stress. Spend two-three minutes each day gently stimulating these points, integrating this practice into your morning or evening routine.

Key Reflex Points for Alleviating Grief

On your face, there are specific points that, when gently pressed or stimulated, can unlock deep-seated emotions, helping to ease the burden of grief. Think of your face as a roadmap where specific locations hold the potential to release emotional pressures that build up during times of sorrow. These points are not random; they are gateways to healing and offer a way to engage and process sorrow physically.

Targeted Points for Grief

One of the most significant points to address grief is at the inner corners of your eyebrows. This area, often associated with emotional and mental stress, can be a powerful spot to relieve sadness and deep emotional blockages. Apply gentle pressure with your fingertips to help release the tension that often accumulates in this area, allowing for a clearer mind and a lighter heart.

Move down the face and find another essential point along the crease of your nostrils, aligned with the edge of your eyes. Many traditional healing practices believe this point powerfully connects to your heart and lungs, which hold grief. Stimulate this area to help ease the heaviness of heartache, promote a sense of relief, and produce endorphins, hormones that help relieve pain, reduce stress, and improve mood.

Now look straight ahead and find the third key point directly below the pupils, approximately one finger-width under the cheekbones. This region helps to balance the energy circulating the face and, when massaged, can soothe and calm the spirit. It is a gentle reminder to your body that letting go of the emotions that might overwhelm you is okay.

Frequency and Duration

For the best results, integrate the stimulation of these points into your daily routine. Morning and evening are ideal times; allow yourself to start and end your day with a moment of self-care. Spend one to two minutes on each point, using either firm pressing on the reflex point or a slow, circular massage. The pressure should be firm but not painful.

If you're going through a tough day, repeating this process as needed is perfectly fine. Sometimes, midday sessions can be beneficial, especially if your emotions are overwhelming. These moments of pause and care can be significant anchors, helping you navigate the day more efficiently and gracefully.

Combining Breathing Techniques

To enhance reflexology's calming effects, always use aromatherapy first, then incorporate breathing exercises into your routine. As you press each point, take slow, deep breaths. Inhale through your nose, imagine warm and healing energy entering your body, and exhale through your mouth. Imagine grief and sadness leaving your body with each breath.

A specific breathing technique that complements face reflexology is the 4-7-8 method. Here's how you do it: Press on a reflex point, breathe quietly through your nose to a mental count of four, hold your breath for seven, and then exhale completely through your mouth, making a whoosh sound to a count of eight. This helps reduce emotional stress and brings a deeper level of relaxation to your entire body.

Personal Anecdotes

Many have found face reflexology to be a transformative tool in managing grief. For instance, you read about my friend and client in an earlier chapter, Elizabeth Oliver, a recent widow, who shared how she integrated reflexology into her daily routine to help her cope with the intense waves of sadness. She would spend a few minutes massaging the points under her eyebrows and along her nostrils every morning.

Over time, she noticed a significant decrease in her morning anxiety levels, which had been exceptionally high since her husband's passing. Touching these points gave her a tangible way to deal with her emotions, making them more manageable.

There's a tendency to relate grief to just the loss of a human loved one, but loss happens every day in the most unexpected way. Some time ago, my friend, Donnis Hiskett, lost her beloved cat and experienced grief and a very deep sadness. Essential oils and reflexology are tools she takes everywhere when she travels for business.

These stories highlight the deep effects of face reflexology on dealing with grief. Beyond the physical act of pressing points, it's about connecting with and processing your emotions in a way that respects your body's need for a gentle, healing touch. As you explore these techniques, remember that each small step is a part of your path toward healing—a path that honors both your pain and your resilience.

When sadness and pain well up while you're in an unlikely place, your "tools" give you the confidence to keep going. This book's handy guide to prayer, scriptures, essential oils, reflexology, and breathing are available wherever you are, whatever situation may arise.

Integrating Reflexology into Your Daily Routine

Incorporate reflexology into your daily life for a soothing ritual, a gentle reminder each morning and evening that you are taking active steps toward healing. Think of these practices that ground you in the morning and unwind you in the evening.

Even before the coffee brews, a simple AromaReflex Healing™ routine can help set a calm tone and intention for the hours ahead. Apply the serum you created on your face and neck. Use your knuckles to massage critical areas on your face, like the gentle area just beneath your eyebrows, the spot just below each cheekbone, or your whole face. This can stimulate your body's natural energy to clear mental fog and start your day with clarity.

This morning routine doesn't need to be lengthy. Just a few minutes can have an amazing effect. As part of your wake-up routine, perform this gentle practice after stretching or while waiting for your morning tea to steep. It's about waking up your body gently, cradling it with kindness after a night's rest.

In the evening, this practice can serve as a soothing transition into the night. After a challenging day, focus on the reflex points on your face to signal your body that it's time to slow down. This can be wonderfully comforting if you find your grief feels heavier at night, as many do. The rhythmic, gentle pressing on points around your eyes or along your jawline can ease tension, helping you to let go of the day's emotional load and prepare for rest.

Knowing how to stimulate the face is valuable when grief spikes or stress feels overwhelming throughout the day, after a tough phone call, or just before a challenging task at work. Set aside a few minutes to apply diluted essential oil and stimulate applicable reflex points to make a significant difference.

You might keep the complimentary PDF workbook that has all the tools you need and carry it with you in your purse as a guide or at your desk to help you any moment grief strikes.

Just a minute or two of firmly rubbing your face while taking deep, intentional breaths can reset your emotional outlook, making facing the rest of your day easier. You can also focus on the point between your thumb and index finger, a spot known for alleviating stress.

Track your progress and feelings before and after each session to get a perspective. Keep a simple journal where you note which points you stimulated and how you felt afterward to help you see patterns. Did specific points consistently bring relief? Did one or two sessions leave you feeling more energized or calmer?

This record-keeping isn't just about monitoring your progress—it's about a deeper connection to your body and its responses. It can teach you so much about how your body holds and releases emotions and heals.

Whether it's a morning ritual that helps you face the day with steadiness, a quick midday reset, or an evening routine that prepares you for restful sleep, face reflexology enhances the benefits of aromatherapy.

Combining Aromatherapy with Reflexology to Enhance Healing

Face reflexology is a necessary part of aromatherapy. When you blend the therapeutic touch of reflexology with the enormous healing power of aromatherapy, you create a symphony that echoes deeply within your body and spirit.

This harmonious combination amplifies the therapeutic effects of each practice, turning your healing sessions into an incredibly nurturing experience. As you explore this integrated approach, imagine each element—touch and scent—working to soothe your grief, calm your mind, and rejuvenate your body.

Synergistic Effects

Aromatherapy and reflexology create synergy and enhance each other's healing properties. While stimulating focuses on releasing tension and restoring energy flow through specific reflex points on your face, aromatherapy adds an extra layer of relaxation, mood enhancement, and rejuvenation through its fragrant therapeutic oils. This combination multiplies the calming effects and deepens your emotional release, making it easier to process grief.

For instance, while massaging pressure points on your temples might relieve mental stress, add a soothing scent like lavender to significantly boost this effect, helping you achieve a deeper state of relaxation.

Think of it this way: As you press on a reflex point associated with emotional health, the scent of essential oils like rose or bergamot can heighten your sense of peace, making the stimulation technique more effective.

This dual olfactory stimulation engages multiple senses and encourages your body to respond more deeply. The oils can improve skin contact during knuckle stimulation, reducing friction and enhancing the smoothness of each stroke, which further contributes to the overall soothing experience.

Incorporate essential oils into your reflexology practice to enhance the physical benefits and deepen emotional healing. It provides a multi-sensory experience that can support you through your grief. Each session becomes a moment of personal retreat, a space where scent and touch work together to soothe, heal, and restore your spirit.

I hope this chapter has helped you understand as you experienced even just one point to stimulate on your face, along with combining aromatherapy through the video demonstrations. These powerful and unique benefits can get you through tough times as they occur throughout the day. Through the thoughtful choice and application of essential oils and the strategic stimulation of the reflex points on your face, you possess a powerful toolkit to aid your emotional and physical healing journey.

Visit the Resource page

CHAPTER 8

AromaReflex Healing™ – Step 4A: Essential Breathing and Exercise

Have you ever paid attention to how you breathe? Did you know that many of us take shallow breaths throughout the day? I didn't realize that I breathed shallowly until I listened to a presentation by a breathing coach.

What Is Proper Breathing?

This prompted me to examine breathing and its impact on the physical, emotional, and spiritual foundation. Breathing poorly worsens the effects of grief.

How do I know I'm breathing shallowly?

Let's start by answering this question: You're breathing shallowly when your breath is not engaging your diaphragm. What you think is a deep breath is not; the air you breathe doesn't get far.

Here's what I mean. Taking a big breath into your upper chest doesn't reach the air sacs in the lungs (called the alveoli). The result is that the lungs cannot access the oxygen in that air sac, and you feel breathless no matter how much air you breathe in.

Shallow breathing is also fast breathing. When breathing is too fast, there is not enough time for air to reach the deepest part of the lungs, and the lungs cannot extract sufficient oxygen from the air.

Fast breathing also results in the loss of too much carbon dioxide, which can cause feelings of breathlessness by reducing breathing efficiency and oxygen uptake. A person having a panic attack and breathing fast can experience shortness of breath.

Why don't we pay more attention to our breathing?

Isn't it strange that breath symbolizes life, yet we don't even consider if we are breathing correctly? Lack of breath signifies the end of life. Breathing should get our focus and attention.

> **"Then the Lord God formed the man of dust from the ground and breathed into his nostrils the breath of life, and the man became a living creature." Genesis 2:7 NKJV.**

This means that we became alive because of the breath of life that God breathed into our nostrils. So, how essential is breathing?

Breathing is the focus of attention only when a person suffers from respiratory issues like chronic obstructive pulmonary disease (COPD) or asthma.

Some Dangers to Shallow Breathing

- Reduced oxygen impairs thinking. A study by Northwestern University found a connection between breathing and cognitive function. Shallow breathing disrupts the balance of oxygen and carbon dioxide

- Increased blood pressure leads to increased stress hormone cortisol, known to speed up aging, among other adverse effects.
- Prevents the body from using the respiratory muscles. Many people equated this to reduced physical ability, leading to less endurance and becoming winded faster. This often led many people to equate it with reduced physical ability, resulting in less endurance and a faster onset of fatigue
- Sleep issues complicate fatigue due to not breathing effectively with respiratory muscles, exacerbating pain, like headaches and pain in the neck and upper back because of the disengagement of the diaphragm
- Causes pain in the lower back and neck
- Leaves the brain feeling foggy and muddled
- Chronic stress, poor posture, and inadequate oxygenation inhibit the immune system. Long-term stress can make the body more vulnerable to illness and make it take longer to recover and heal if it gets sick
- Increases fatigue and the flare-up of respiratory symptoms in people with asthma and rhinitis or during exercise
- Acts as a vital risk factor for cardiovascular disease over the long term
- Triggers anxiety, considered purely a psychological disorder, and there is a strong link between levels of blood carbon dioxide and susceptibility to panic attacks

How Serious Is Shallow Breathing?

I can't believe shallow breathing harms our health. Why has no one ever said anything about this? I am in my sixties and just now learning about it. I believe most of us take shallow breaths.

Shallow breathing affects the way you sleep. Dysfunctional breathing during the day can lead to insomnia, snoring, and even sleep apnea, a serious condition in which breathing stops periodically through the night, disrupting the body's ability to deliver adequate oxygen to the blood.

Breathing and Chronic Stress?

In Chapter 4, I talked about stress. Let's talk a little more about it here and how shallow breathing causes stress. Scientifically defined, stress is a physiological reaction to undesired physical or emotional situations. First, the body triggers a "fight or flight" response, which hormones, including adrenaline, mediate.

When stress becomes chronic and lasts long, the stressed body responds with physical and physiological changes. It gets used to unfavorable conditions, negatively affecting the immune system and how the brain governs the interaction between the nervous system and the hormones. Stress is a common risk factor in 75 to 90 percent of all human diseases. Stress accounts for 70+ percent of doctor visits.

Many scientific studies support the assumption that the development of chronic stress can be because of an increase in oxidative stress. Oxidative stress may also contribute to rheumatoid arthritis, high blood pressure, heart disease, Alzheimer's disease, Parkinson's disease, and aging.

So What Do We Do?

Deep breathing, or breathing from the diaphragm, is a way to reduce oxidative stress and prevent the increased levels of cortisol, the primary stress hormone. We can also avoid the effects of shallow breathing on the muscles, which can cause tension and headaches, jaw pain, neck and back pain, and other chronic symptoms.

Researching this topic made me pay attention; the question is, will I breathe better? I talked to the breathing coaches I know and sought their help because after seeing how shallowly I breathed for two days, I realized that shallow breathing had become second nature. To improve, I need to learn how to be aware of how I breathe to correct myself.

It's important to learn to distinguish between shallow or upper chest breaths and breathing that prevents disease and stress.

Deep breathing from the diaphragm is the correct way. The advantages of deep breathing include better lung health (great for skin health), a more relaxed mind (supports emotional health), and stress reduction.

Breathing is more efficient when it is slower. This is because the air spends more time in the lungs and has more time to reach the alveoli (the small air sacs), where the exchange of oxygen and carbon dioxide takes place.

In one research study done by scientists showed that breathing at six breaths per minute is 20 percent more efficient in blood oxygenation. Breathing more slowly (and therefore deeply) gets more oxygen to your cells and organs, including your brain. (2021 NIH Min You, Sylvain Laborde, Nina Zammit, Masa Iskra, Ulrassu Borges, Fabrice Dosseville)

Benefits of Deep Breathing

Physical Benefits to Health

When you breathe gently and slowly from your diaphragm, you experience the following benefits of deep breathing:

- Promotes the habit of slow respiration
- Draws air deep into the lungs
- Improves the exchange of oxygen and carbon dioxide for maximum breathing efficiency
- Generates intra-abdominal pressure (IAP) for postural control and spinal stabilization
- Supports functional breathing for functional movement
- Enhances heart rate variability
- Improves heart-breath coherence
- Increases resilience and adaptability of blood pressure
- Enhances oxygenation of tissues and organs
- Supports a healthy cardiovascular system
- Improves lung health
- Maintains optimum levels of carbon dioxide in the arterial blood

Scientific studies have found therapeutic applications for diaphragm breathing in conditions including:

- Depression, including comorbid depression in people with conditions like bipolar disorder, affects individuals who cannot take antidepressants because of conditions like bipolar disorder.
- Emotional/mood regulation
- Blood sugar control in diabetes
- Seizure frequency in epilepsy or people with non-epileptic seizures (hyperventilation is a known trigger for seizures)

- Core strength and balance, less risk of injury
- Back and neck pain

Emotional/Mental Health Benefits:

- Promotes mental calmness and resilience
- Calms your mind and enjoy a more incredible feeling of relaxation
- Regulates the relaxation response
- Activates the parasympathetic nervous system partly because of its influence on the vagus nerve, allowing your body to slow down, rest, and heal.
- Stimulates the vagus nerve to secrete acetylcholine, a neurotransmitter (a chemical messenger) that slows the heart rate, triggers relaxation, and supports physical and mental resilience
- Boosts focus, concentration, memory, and learning ability; prevents or reduces cognitive decline in elderly people; and supports mental health.

Spiritual Benefit

We must recognize who gives us breath every day. Above every other blessing, we have breath in our lungs, not through anything or anyone, not by mistake, not by luck, not by our choosing or doing, but by the grace of God.

I remember the song "Great Are You, Lord," about whose breath is in our lungs. Please listen to it. The link is on the Resource page for Chapter 8. It will confirm that you can trust this God who created the heavens, the earth, and everything in it because He created you and gave you breath!

Honoring God and praising Him for His gift of breath through song and prayer brings us closer to Him. As a follower of Jesus, I strive to grow and nurture my intimate relationship with Him daily. Acknowledging and thanking God is not for the benefit of God; it's for our spiritual growth and health and for nurturing our relationship with Him.

When your spiritual foundation is strong, you can more easily "weather the storm". You know you are safe and will be victorious in any circumstance because God is going through it with you.

Remember: Breath in the body means life. Take care that you breathe well to support a long and healthy life.

- **Psalm 150:6 "Let everything that has breath praise the LORD. Praise the LORD!"**
- **Job 33:4: "The Spirit of God has made me, And the breath of the Almighty gives me life."**
- **John 20:22 "And when He had said this, He breathed on them and said to them, 'Receive the Holy Spirit.'**
- **Job 27:3: "As long as my breath is in me, and the spirit of God is in my nostrils,"**
- **Ezekiel 37:9 "Then he said to me, 'Prophesy to the breath; prophesy, son of man, and say to the breath,' Thus says the Lord God: 'Come from the four winds, O breath, and breathe on these slain, that they may live.'"**

My Recommendations to Support Breathing

Breathe Essential Oil Blend

I recommend Breathe, the oil of "breath" for the emotional cause of shallow breathing. It addresses the inability to let go of grief and pain. Individuals who struggle to breathe can feel suffocated by sadness. Stress, fear, pain, and despair affect breathing.

Breathe benefits people who have asthma, cough, pneumonia, bronchitis, and many other respiratory issues that affect breathing.

It is a great blend to diffuse and apply to the bottoms of the feet and chest. My best recommendation is to put a drop on your hand, rub your hands together, make it like an inhaler with both hands, and inhale deeply.

Eucalyptus

Eucalyptus, the oil of "wellness," has a solid menthol-like aroma and powerful physical and emotional effects. It supports those who face constant immune-compromising situations. Eucalyptus addresses unresolved emotional pain in the heart center and specifically in the lungs. It is excellent for fever, sore throat, earaches, bronchitis, and other respiratory concerns. Dilute with fractionated coconut oil and apply to the chest and the bottoms of the feet.

Face Reflexology

Face reflexology or face stimulation on the area of the cheeks below the cheekbones for a minute or two on both sides, one side after another, or at once.

AromaReflex Healing™ - Step 4B: Exercise

To be honest, I hate exercising! I only exercised to ensure Doug did, too, so I stopped altogether when he and Joanne went to heaven. Between poor nourishment, poor sleep, and lack of activity, my health deteriorated quickly.

This is what the National Library says about exercise and grief:

> "Grief is a natural outcome. Physical activity can help improve the anxiety and depression that people may identify as outcomes of grief after experiencing a bereavement.
>
> The goal of this review was to determine from the existing literature if physical activity can improve grief outcomes in individuals who have experienced bereavement.
>
> From 1,299 studies screened, twenty-five met the inclusion criteria, detailing eight types of grief: parental ($n = 5$), spousal ($n = 6$), patient ($n = 4$), pre-natal ($n = 3$), later life ($n = 1$), caregiver ($n = 1$), multiple ($n = 4$) and non-defined ($n = 1$).
>
> Researchers found that engaging in activities like running, walking, and martial arts provided benefits. Physical activity allowed a sense of freedom to express emotions, provided a distraction and an escape from grief, while enhancing social support."

Doug and I walked to exercise. Because of complex knee tears and a 3mm herniated disc, it was challenging to find a suitable exercise that would not worsen the injuries or induce post-workout pain.

When I tried Barre, it was painful. I could walk to exercise again, but I didn't want to walk alone. I also didn't want to start with LA Fitness because it was not an environment conducive to working out.

I accidentally found the Smartfit Method in Yorba Linda. The ultramodern equipment was impressive, as it adapted to the body's ability to perform exercise. The trainers are extremely professional and friendly, and they clean the machines after each use.

Simone LeCompte, the owner and a certified nutritional coach who has also become a friend, understands the needs of people like me—those with injuries who must exercise to prevent weight gain, which can worsen pain and negatively impact recovery. Irreparable injuries cause emotional trauma and result in grief.

The state-of-the-art equipment tracks the body's ability to perform the exercise. It measures the force the body can safely execute each exercise without straining the muscles or worsening the injuries.

Check out Simone's video as she describes the machine and how they help the body get stronger without punishing it with heavy weights, long sessions on a treadmill, or knee-pounding jumping jacks.

Exercise may be the furthest thing from your mind right now, and that's okay. But even a tiny amount of physical activity or movement can help support your well-being.

We include breathing and exercise in Step 4 because they work together to alleviate grief's effects on the body and the brain.

Make time to move around the house. Play worship music or sing praises to the God who is with you. Pray and give thanks. Recite the Scriptures you've learned that have given you peace. Think of the strength and confidence you've gained and the future God has planned for you.

Visit the Resource page

CHAPTER 9

AromaReflex Healing™ – Step 5 - Essential Nutrition/ Hydration/Supplementation

Nutritional Support for Skin and Body

When we talk about healing, especially from grief, it's important to recognize that what we nourish our bodies with can directly influence how we heal, both emotionally and physically.

Imagine your body as a garden. What you plant in it, how you water it, and how you care for it can determine the health of the fruits you produce, if any. Your body needs various nutrients to flourish, particularly during emotional stress, which can damage your physical and mental health.

Holistic Approach to Nutrition

The connection between diet, skin health, and emotional well-being is deep. Foods rich in vitamins, minerals, and antioxidants can do wonders for your skin, helping it to repair itself, support elasticity, and even reduce the visibility of stress marks and wrinkles. But the benefits aren't just skin deep; they're within deep.

These nutrients play a necessary role in modulating mood and mental health. For instance, omega-3 fatty acids found in fish, like salmon, and seeds like flaxseed have known anti-inflammatory properties and play an important role in brain health, which can be helpful when traversing the fog of grief.

Incorporating a variety of whole, nutrient-rich foods into your diet can be a game-changer. Leafy greens, berries, nuts, and lean proteins fuel your body and provide the nutrients needed to support your emotional resilience.

Create meals that taste good and provide comfort and nourishment on all levels. For example, a smoothie made with spinach, blueberries, and a touch of ginger can be both refreshing and healing.

Essential Oils in Cooking

While essential oils are commonly used in aromatherapy, certain oils can also be used in cooking to enhance your food's flavor and therapeutic properties. However, it's important to use food-grade oils that are safe for consumption and to use them sparingly due to their potency.

For instance, adding a drop of lemon essential oil to a salad dressing brightens the flavor and provides detoxifying benefits. Similarly, a drop of peppermint oil in a chocolate dessert can aid digestion and elevate your mood.

When using essential oils in cooking, always remember to dilute them properly and integrate them into fats or oils since they are fat-soluble. This ensures that the flavor disperses evenly and that you reap the maximum health benefits. It's a delightful way to infuse your meals with an extra layer of nurturing care, turning everyday dishes into therapeutic treats. doTERRA essential oils are the only oils I recommend for oral intake, whether for cooking or taking orally in veggie caps.

Hydration and Essential Oils

Staying hydrated is necessary for supporting healthy skin and overall health, especially during stress when your body's demand for water increases. Consider infusing your water with essential oils to make hydration more appealing and beneficial.

Add a drop of lemon or wild orange essential oil to your water to transform a simple glass into a refreshing, alkalizing, uplifting beverage that encourages you to drink more throughout the day. Just make sure you know the source of the essential oil and how it is processed and tested for purity and safety, especially for internal use.

Hydration isn't just about drinking water; it's ensuring your cells, tissues, and organs are properly hydrated for function and maintenance. Carrying a water bottle infused with aromatic essences is a great habit to set up to keep up with your body's needs. Sip throughout the day and breathe deeply for internal and emotional health.

Supplemental Support

While a balanced diet is the cornerstone of good health, supplements can play a supportive role, especially when your body's needs are increased by stress or grief. Supplements like vitamin C, vitamin E, and collagen can be particularly beneficial for skin health, helping repair damage and enhance resilience. For emotional well-being, B vitamins, magnesium, and omega-3 fatty acids can help manage stress and maintain brain health.

It's important to approach supplements with care. Before starting any new supplement regimen, consult a functional medicine provider who can guide you to the best products to ensure they are right for your specific health needs and conditions. This is especially important during times of grief when your body is already managing significant stress.

Embrace a holistic approach to nutrition, integrate essential oils into your cooking, stay hydrated with oil-infused waters, and consider supplemental support, to take active steps toward healing your body and soul. Each meal, each sip, and each supplement can be a part of your healing process, a way to nurture yourself deeply and wholly during this tender time.

As we wrap up this chapter on nourishing your skin, body organs, and systems, remember that each choice you make at the table, each flavor you savor, and each glass of water you drink can be part of your healing journey.

These nutritional practices are about enriching your path to recovery with every bite, every sip, and every drop of oil. As we move forward, let these practices be your companions, sustaining and comforting you as you navigate your healing process.

Visit the Resource page

CHAPTER 10

Embracing Life from a Fresh Perspective

Look to each morning as a fresh canvas—a new opportunity to paint your healing journey with strokes of faith, dashes of aromatherapy, and gentle reflexology point stimulations.

In this chapter, we'll explore how to embrace this new life and maintain your daily routine seamlessly. This will enhance your spiritual and physical wellness and provide a comforting structure as you go through the ebbs and flows of grief. Transform everyday routines into a process of healing and hope.

My dear friend Caprice Crebar, Certified Health Coach and CEO of Heartlink Worldwide Network has a great perspective on loss, grief, honoring memories, faith, community, and self-care. Let's take a look.

Healthy Grief

I don't claim to be an expert in the stages of grief. If you are reading this and have experienced painful loss, mourning, walked through the stages of grief (denial, bargaining, anger, depression, acceptance) and healed or are still healing, I honor you. I imagine I could learn a few things about navigating grief from you as well.

As a fifty-five-year-old woman, I think back to my younger years when loved ones dying were the furthest thought from my mind. And now, here I am in this season of life when it seems everyone I know is experiencing the loss of parents, pets, siblings, aunts, and uncles. It's best to accept rather than worry about its eventuality.

When people leave this earth far earlier than expected, grief can feel insurmountable. Yet, healing is available to everyone.

I feel for and have the utmost respect for those of you who have experienced tragic and premature losses. The author of this book, Grace Richardson, is an outstanding example of strength after the insurmountable loss of her husband and daughter in the same week. She has shown me the strength she draws from the Lord Jesus and the knowledge that she will see Joanne and Doug again in Heaven one day. Grace allows herself to have those bad days and reaches out to her close friends when she needs prayer as she continues to process and live beyond her losses with gratitude in her heart. I'm fortunate to be among her prayer partners. **"For where two or three gather in my name, there am I with them." - Matthew 18:20**

Grieving My Father, Keeping His Legacy Alive

In April 2024, I lost my dad, Robert David Barnes. I helped care for him as his body began to deteriorate in multiple ways, all of which developed over time and accelerated over the last year: kidney failure, bone-on-bone hip pain, diabetes, pneumonia, skin cancer, declining eyesight, and hearing. He finally ended up in the hospital for over a month after a serious fall. Despite all that ailed him, my dad loved his life and family so much and still expected to get well enough to go home and live a little longer. God had different plans for him, though, and there was only so much pain this strong man and former special agent could take. He finally succumbed to the reality that his time had come for us to let him go, to which we sadly agreed.

Some of my favorite memories with Dad were the times when I got to hear him sing. These treasured moments started when he sang to my brothers and me when we were young and in his sunset years when, on several karaoke nights, he was happy to sing along with some of his musical heroes, such as Johnny Cash and John Denver.

As frail as he was, he could still carry a tune with his deep, handsome, beloved voice, even from his wheelchair with a mic in hand. His love for gathering around music has left an indelible mark on our family, and we continue his legacy with the many musical people in our family, including my son, a professional singer.

The good news is, we got to have my dad for eighty-four years! I realize what a tremendous blessing and gift that is. My dad was an investigator reliant on facts, so he had difficulty with faith. Grace knows about many of my conversations with him, attempting to share biblical evidence. Dad's hospice nurse assured me that in her conversations with him, he had accepted Jesus Christ as his Lord and Savior (a debate he finally surrendered to, thankfully).

Mourning Our Beloved Pet

Shortly after Dad celebrated life, our family dog Rosco, who seemed to be declining in a similar fashion, also passed away. He almost made it to seventeen years old, so I'm grateful for longevity and hope there's a doggy Heaven.

Rosco was more than a pet; he was a cherished member of our family. We loved his expressive eyes, his pose for photos, the mischievous ways he had of finding food, his snuggling in our son Gary's neck, and how he brought joy, laughter, and lots of cuddles to our lives. Losing him so soon after my dad was incredibly painful, though remembering the happiness Rosco brought us helps ease the sorrow.

I believe our bodies are temples created by God to give us the opportunity to serve our unique purpose, serve others, and carry us through to eternal life after we pass (all of which glorify God in the process). When I watched both my dad and Rosco take their last breath, I became certain that earth is left with our empty shell after our spirit immediately enters Heaven, a place the Bible describes as a place of eternal joy, peace, and the presence of God.

Recognize and Honor Your Loved Ones and Your Grief

One key to healing is allowing yourself to experience the full range of emotions that come with grief. This includes feelings of sadness, anger and moments of happiness and laughter. It's okay to find joy in life again, even while grieving. These moments of joy don't diminish your loss; they are a testament to your resilience and capacity for healing.

I've honored my grief by scouring through every photo of both my dad (and Rosco) that made me smile. Our family agreed to keep his office intact, covered with his favorite photos, quotes, many awards and acknowledgments, and memories of what was important to him.

When I work in his office, I feel his spirit near me, pulling for my success like he always did. Even when it became difficult to climb the stairs to get there, he made it enough time to get all of his affairs in order and to complete a book of poetry he presented to my mom on Valentine's Day 2024, two months before he passed.

Dad was an avid gardener and had to let the garden plot go after he couldn't tend to it anymore. The week of his service, we prepared the soil, and the day after, our family re-planted the garden in his honor. His garden will still feed us, and thoughts of Dad will forever bloom.

We cherish our visits to his favorite bench by the waterfront in the town where my parents raised us. We fondly call it "Dad's Bench." He and Mom used to love to sit on it and gaze over the water at the hillsides and the Carquinez bridge.

Through my grief, I have found new purposes in advocating for hospice care and peaceful passing for pets and also supporting a non-profit that was important to Dad. These causes allow me to honor both my dad and Rosco while making a positive impact in the world.

My mom, brothers, and I took turns caring for Dad. Each of us brought our own unique strengths and perspectives, and together, we formed a support system that carried us through the toughest times. Their grief, like mine, is a testament to the deep love and bond we shared with Dad that we can now be grateful for.

These tangible connections help me process my emotions and feel close to Dad and Rosco, even in their absence.

The Importance of Self-Care

Just as self-care is important to live your best life and age gracefully, it's important when facing difficult times such as the passing of a loved one. It's easy to neglect your physical health when you are overwhelmed with emotional pain, but maintaining healthy habits can support your overall well-being and help you navigate your grief more effectively. Good nutrition, regular exercise, and adequate sleep are foundational to physical and emotional health.

For instance, focusing on a balanced diet can help stabilize your mood and energy levels. Incorporating fruits, vegetables, whole grains, and lean proteins into your meals can provide the nutrients your body needs to cope with stress.

Regular exercise, even a daily walk, can also be incredibly beneficial. Physical activity releases endorphins, which can improve your mood and help you manage stress. When you are feeling down, being physically and mentally strong can help you feel better and manage grief more easily.

When you have the opportunity to watch someone live long enough to experience illness and decline, it's simultaneously difficult and a blessing.

As a certified health coach who has spent her life helping others stay well and age gracefully, I have also learned that the natural course of aging can be more joy-filled and less challenging when healthy habits and accepting support early on are prioritized.

My dad came from an era where strength, smarts, determination, independence, and integrity made a man like him believe he was invincible. He lost his own father at age two and had a very strong and independent mother, my grandmother Marie, who raised two very responsible boys. Such honorable characteristics made him an amazing man, husband, and father. Yet he was so independent and a servant to others that he avoided:

- Asking for help
- Recruiting advocates
- Practicing self-care
- Taking action to slow the progression when he became aware of potentially devastating ailments

"We are better together" applies throughout life, and it's especially important as we age to manage the often-overwhelming amount of information and tasks related to maintaining our health.

If you are fortunate to have the support of friends and family, leverage them! You can also request support from a local church or community center. Many nonprofit organizations offer personal services, social activities, and educational programs for people sixty and older. They want you to live longer, feel better, and slow aging.

Have someone who has your back join you at your doctor's appointments. This person can help you ask questions, assess your health status, and make lifestyle modifications that will support your longevity.

Stay Connected in the Community

Staying connected with your community is vital during times of grief. The support, understanding, and shared experiences can provide immense comfort. For me, my community of women in the Heart Link Network offered a safe space to express my feelings, receive encouragement, and find solace in knowing I wasn't alone. Their empathy and strength were incredibly comforting, reminding me that even in the darkest times, there is light in connection.

Thanks to my connection with a community like this, I certainly felt compassion, support, love, and prayers during my grieving process. It also helps to know we're not alone.

I remember when one member shared her story of loss and how the network helped her heal, showing the power of shared experiences and mutual support. I encourage you to share your story with others and lean on those around you. You might find that opening up about your experience not only aids your healing but also strengthens the bonds within your community.

A Note on Self-Compassion

Grief comes in all shapes and sizes, affecting each of us differently. It's a deeply personal journey that requires patience, compassion, and support. Grief is healthy.

Throughout your grieving process, practice self-compassion. Allow yourself to feel whatever comes up without judgment. Be gentle with yourself on the hard days and permit yourself to enjoy the good ones. Remember that grief is not a linear process, and it's okay to have setbacks. Treat yourself with the same kindness and understanding you would offer to a dear friend going through a similar experience.

Practicing self-compassion has meant allowing myself to grieve on my terms. Some days, I cry; some days, I laugh at old memories; and others, I sit in silence, reflecting on the amazing human being I am lucky to call Dad.

In my journey through grief, I've learned to appreciate the small moments, to lean on my faith and community, and to find strength in vulnerability. These lessons continue to guide me as I honor my loved ones and learn to live on with the memories of how they affected my life for the better.

Caprice's story put a smile of encouragement on my face. There is camaraderie in experiencing grief with others who have gone through it.

> "Rejoice with those who rejoice, weep with those who weep." Romans 12:15 ESV

Lessons Learned

For a believer, there are no accidents, no coincidences. We live in a fallen world, but God sifts the circumstances of our lives through His loving fingers so we can bear it. How do we learn and grow if we aren't tested and tried?

> "My brethren, count it all joy when you fall into various trials, knowing that the testing of your faith produces patience." James 1:2-3 NKJV

> "Blessed is the man who remains steadfast under trial, for when he has stood the test, he will receive the crown of life, which God has promised to those who love him." James 1:12 ESV

This is the time when He holds your hand through the "wilderness" and uses the pain and suffering to strengthen you and fortify your faith so you can stand firm through trying times and be used to help others weakened by the harshness of life.

> "But may the God of all grace, who called us to His eternal glory by Christ Jesus, after you have suffered a while, perfect, establish, strengthen, and settle you." I Peter 5:10 NKJV

"See the Forest for the Trees"

There is a tendency to miss the "whole" picture because of the little distractions amplified by grief and diminish the victories you've achieved. I am reminded of the song "Count Your Blessings and Name Them One by One" by Guy Penrod. Behind the veil of grief is God's overflowing and bountiful purpose for your life, waiting to be released.

Return to the journal you started to track how far you've come. Your list of accomplishments is impressive.

- Your faith has been strengthened through prayers, meditating on the Holy Scriptures, and being encouraged by seeing the promises of God in your grief be fulfilled.
- You've created your very own holistic approach to the physical and emotional effects of grief through aromatherapy and face reflexology.
- You've been able to start exercising and eating more nutritionally to support your physical and emotional healing.
- Most of all, you sought out your faith and secular community for support and to support others!

Establishing a Daily Routine for Continued Spiritual and Physical Wellness: Continue to Grow and Progress

Managing grief is "a marathon, not a sprint." It's a state of being you can't escape; it's part of you. But it doesn't have to "drive the bus" and dictate the direction of your future.

Continue to practice a simple daily routine that includes aromatherapy, reflexology, and faith-based practices. Keep in mind the peace and calm it brings you day and night. Relish the emergence or growth of your faith, the things you learned about yourself, and the resilience and strength of character you developed.

Morning Ritual

As you step into the quiet of your morning, before you get out of bed and before the day rushes in, set your intentions in a moment of prayer or meditation on scriptures. This isn't just about asking for strength to get through the day (though that's perfectly fine) but about centering yourself in your faith, reaffirming your trust in God, the One who walks this path with you.

It might overwhelm you at first but keep it simple. Here's a suggestion based on what I try to do every day. Some days, it's not easy, but then I think about the calm and peace I enjoy afterward and how much easier I can deal with the feelings that well up when I'm reminded of the "old days" and the wonderful memories with Doug, Joanne, Ethan, and my mom, people I valued and loved more than anything on earth.

Start with a drop each of wild orange and peppermint on your hands to inhale deeply. This should get your "motor running" as you welcome life's adventures today. If you shower in the morning, do that leisurely as you wash off sleep and refresh your body.

Then, slowly take your face serum of a diluted blend of frankincense and lavender and apply it all over your face and neck, making sure to enjoy every relaxing stroke. Once done, take your knuckles and stimulate your entire face and neck area, activate the blood flow, and wake up your nervous system and organs for proper function, such as hormone balancing. Do this for three to five minutes slowly and firmly.

Throughout the Day

Peppermint is a great energizer. Drop a drop in your water bottle (doTERRA only—I can't vouch for other brands). Keep your custom blend of essential oils close by as the day unfolds. When you feel your grief surge or stress mount, take a moment to inhale the calming benefits of lavender or the energizing peppermint, then stroke the stress-relief points on your forehead. Pair this with a few deep breaths, allowing the aromas to calm your mind and bring your focus back to how well you're thriving following the steps in this book.

Evening Reflection

How did your day go today? Baths with sea salt soaked in essential oils that you already have can help wash away the cares of the day. My favorite thing to do is to fill a half-gallon or a gallon glass jar with Epsom salt or Himalayan sea salt. Then, I put the empty essential oil bottles in the jar upside down so all the leftover oils can drip into the sea salt. This way, I use every last drop!

While in the bath, think about the moments of sadness, maybe even the anger at the unfairness, that you overcame today because you had God's promises in your heart to bring to mind and the tools you prepared and carry with you when you're not home.

With gratitude, reflect on moments throughout the day of victory where you felt peace, saw the beauty of God's creation, or experienced kindness. Let this be a time of letting go, of trusting that you are cared for, even in your deepest grief.

Guided Recipes and Face Reflex Points

The PDF I've included for you to print out and carry in your bag or briefcase includes aromatherapy recipes for grief, health, and beauty, along with a face stimulation points plan, scriptures, prayers, and music.

Continue to integrate these into your daily routine and let them be reminders of your resilience, your capacity for healing, and your deep connection to your faith, your heart, and the healing and hope they bring.

Remember, consistency is effective, and perfection is not the goal. These practices are meant to comfort and nurture you and be part of your day, not another source of stress.

As you conclude this chapter with a heart filled with gratitude and thanksgiving for how far you've come in your journey of restoration, making great use of the tools here and finding yourself trusting God's plan for your life, having been called to be used for His glory and your good, give yourself an A+ for your obedience to allow Him to take charge.

**"For many are called, but few are chosen."
Matthew 22:14 NKJV.**

Visit the Resource page

CHAPTER 11

Embracing A New Normal

Embracing a new normal, a journey not back to who you were but forward to who you have become, remade by the storm of loss, soaked in the downpour of grief, transformed to thrive in grief after the loss.

The clouds have parted, though not all at once, just enough to let slivers of sunlight touch your face. The light reveals the storm's effects and shows the new path forward. You see yourself not as you were but as what you have become, a victor, not a victim.

Redefining Identity After Loss: Identity Shifts

Loss, particularly of someone or something integral to your life, often leads to an identity shift. You might question who you are without this person or thing that was a cornerstone of your existence. It's like looking in the mirror and realizing that the reflection has altered, changed in stark and subtle ways, but still seeing a familiar face. Instead of reclaiming who you were before the loss and navigating this shift, it's about understanding and embracing who you are now in this altered environment.

The church's music ministry sang "You've Already Won," a song by Shane and Shane that struck a chord in me as I thought about the "wilderness" I've traveled and the "giants" I've faced.

The song talks about how we don't know what God is doing in our circumstances, but we can be sure He's already won because it is His battle.

Losing my mother in April 2023 made me furious. I'm not angry that she went home to be with the Lord Jesus. I'm happy for her. But I'm furious at how her flesh and blood treated her for the love of money. She was eighty-seven and widowed twenty-plus years. She was ready to be with the Lord.

> **"For the love of money is a root of all kinds of evil, for which some have strayed from the faith in their greediness and pierced themselves through with many sorrows."**

This information comes from two sources. One is my friend, Dr. Eunice Choi, for whom Becky, my mom's daughter, works. The other is Jen Niere Manaloto, who cared for my mom in the Philippines.

I believe I was told in late 2022 or early 2023 that Becky, my sister, and David, my mom's son, were planning on selling the house in the Philippines, which I bought my mom and stepdad thirty-plus years ago. I heard Becky bragged they could get a million dollars for the home.

I found this humorous since I bought the house from an ex-patriot for about $30K. It's a lovely little house with a good-sized backyard. My dad made it very comfortable and secure, considering the area. It's not in a bad area of Angeles City, Philippines, where the American base used to be, but security is important in a foreign country. Despite the good maintenance of the home, they had never done any significant remodeling.

After I heard Becky was sure they could get a million dollars for it, I looked up properties on Philippine Zillow and saw brand-new homes three times the size, priced at around $650K. Dream on, Becky!

They moved her to a $560 per month one-bedroom apartment on the third floor to get my mom out of the way of getting this imagined million dollars. I was told it was so small that my mother's bed wouldn't fit, so they had her sleeping on an ancient futon that Becky's daughter, Niki, used to sleep on as a child. Niki is forty years old today!

Becky and David were already divvying up the money among themselves. It's pretty amusing to learn that they couldn't sell the home unless they informed and included all the parties, which means me.

Taking her out of the comfort of her home, her garden, the memories of her husband and granddaughter, Joanne, I knew my mom would not be happy. To her, that was punishment.

How much longer would my mom have lived? Her health was poor, and she was fragile. There was no need for them to sell the house now. Except for their greed, they could have waited. Were they so hard up for money to ignore my mom's welfare, happiness, and comfort?

But God. God and His mercy. For this, I'm grateful. Here's why: it wasn't long after they moved her to the one-bedroom apartment on the third floor that the doctors diagnosed her with cancer in all her internal organs. Within two to three months of being cruelly taken from her home and being diagnosed, she went home to be with Jesus. Praise the Lord! He does "make all things work together for good, to those who love Him." You will find the complete verse in Romans 8:28.

I was told by Eunice, according to Becky, that as my mom lay in bed taking her last breath, she had her face and arms toward Heaven as she said, "I am ready. Take me, Lord." That is mercy! I thank God she didn't suffer much. Here's what the Bible said about dying. As we take our last breath on earth, our next breath is in Heaven with Jesus.

> **"For we walk by faith, not by sight. We are confident, yes, well pleased rather to be absent from the body and to be present with the Lord." 2 Corinthians 5:7-8.**

I still get angry and cry when I think about the cruelty perpetrated on my mother by her children. I have to rely on the power of God in the name of Jesus for strength and the ability to forgive them.

When you wrestle with forgiveness, turn to your faith for support. Scriptural meditation and prayer using essential oils like frankincense for spiritual uplifting to help you find peace and forgiveness.

To Recap: Remember these five do-it-yourself steps to restore calm amid the storm, improve sleep and recharge the brain, fortify health, and strengthen your body.

Step 1: Essential Mindset™

Aromatic oils can enhance clarity and cognitive function, helping you reflect and focus during self-exploration. The essential oils I listed in Chapter Five are a good starting point. Incorporating aromatherapy with praying and meditating on the scriptures is an excellent way to support the mindset.

When I pray, I feel cleansed. I cry. I cry tears of joy, tears of sorrow, tears of gratitude and thanksgiving, tears of adoration and praise for God. Crying is release; release is freeing.

Step 2: Essential Beauty™

Let's call out the elephant in the room and admit that we want to heal our minds and bodies and restore our appearance, too, so we can regain our self-confidence.

The internal and emotional destruction caused by grief manifests in our skin, the body's biggest organ. Perhaps it doesn't seem important now, but soon, you will look in the mirror and have to acknowledge and admit that you look twenty years older! I know because it happened to me.

The essential oils in Chapters Five and Six are the best way to start healing from the inside out. Please watch the videos as much as possible. I will then show you how to use the essential oil blends.

Step 3: Essential Stimulation™

Using your knuckles, you can gently press or rub the reflex points on your face that correlate to emotional balance and internal health. Firm pressure awakens the flow of blood and the lymphatic system and stimulates collagen production.

Step 4: Mindful Breathing and Exercise

Take a few minutes to breathe correctly to oxygenate the brain and the cells and tissues, and practice movement, not necessarily strenuous exercise, just movement; maybe dance to the music you like, setting a tone of equilibrium and readiness to face each day,

Step 5: Nutrition and Hydration

Eating nutritious foods and drinking water are great ways to nourish the body, keep a healthy weight, and increase energy. Make sure you take quality vitamins and supplements.

These healing practices do more than soothe; they heal, restore, rejuvenate, and rebuild self-confidence.

Embracing Change

Embracing this new life that you never thought you would ever have to live, a life that you had not planned to have, requires a willingness to see change not as a loss but as a metamorphosis—an evolution into a version of yourself that only exist because of what you've overcome, by the grace of God.

Change after a loss can be daunting. It's like walking on a tightrope, uncertain if you can reach the other side. All you know is that each step forward is a step into wholeness.

With each essential oil that calms your spirit, each reflex point stimulated, grounding your body, each scripture and prayer fortifying your soul and spirit, each cleansing breath, and each restorative practice of health and wellness, you equip yourself to thrive in this new normal.

I embraced change wholeheartedly. Not because I wasn't in grief and no longer cared about the loss of Doug, Joanne, and my mom. I had to decide whether to trust God's will for my and Ethan's life or continue to sulk and be angry about what I no longer have.

> **"Trust in the Lord with all your heart and lean not on your own understanding. In all your ways acknowledge Him, and He will direct your paths." Proverbs 3:5-6 NKJV.**

God's hand is on my life. He put people in my life to get me through the tough times and continues to do so. He has met all my needs and more.

> **"The Lord is my shepherd; I shall not want. He makes me to lie down in green pastures; He leads me beside the still waters. He restores my soul; He leads me in the paths of righteousness For His name's sake." Psalms 23:1-3 NKJV.**

Yes, I miss Doug, Joanne, and my mom every minute of the day. But I have the Blessed Hope that I will see them again. We will reunite and be together for eternity! Do you know how long eternity is? Forever!

> **"... looking for the Blessed Hope and glorious appearing of our great God and Savior Jesus Christ," Titus 2:13 NKJV**

> **"For the Lord Himself will descend from Heaven with a shout, with the voice of an archangel, and with the trumpet of God. And the dead in Christ will rise first. Then we who are alive and remain shall be caught up together**

> with them in the clouds to meet the Lord in the air. And thus we shall always be with the Lord."
> I Thessalonians 4:16-17 NKJV

Embracing the Future

Acknowledge your loss. It has equipped you with resilience and wisdom. These are not just memories but foundational stones for your future. As you reflect on your grief, consider the valuable relationships that have emerged and the accomplishments that brought you joy and fulfillment.

Incorporating Healing Practices into Your Goals for the Future

As you move forward and consider the healing practices you've adopted and want to incorporate into your long-term goals, deepen your knowledge of essential oils and create your healing blends. Part of my work with women is to guide them in using essential oils to care for themselves in greater depth, restoring, rejuvenating, and establishing a graceful aging journey.

Similarly, if reflexology has become a significant part of your healing, consider sharing the practice with others whom these protocols can help. Combine aromatherapy and face reflexology with the grounding power of your faith through prayer and the Holy Scriptures.

Creating a Vision for the Future

I've heard of people writing a letter to their future selves. You can do the same and get confirmation of what you have achieved and how the holistic modalities of aromatherapy, reflexology, and faith have contributed to your restoration. This letter can be a powerful motivational tool.

In setting goals and casting a vision for your future, allow yourself to feel the excitement of possibilities. Embrace the potential for joy, the opportunities for growth, and the continuation of your healing journey.

Maintaining Your Healing Practices Long-Term

The healing practices you've learned are not just for the aftermath of grief—you can sustain them over a lifetime. This commitment supports your immediate healing and fosters ongoing emotional and spiritual wellness.

Sustaining these practices goes beyond the routine application of essential oils or the periodic practice of reflexology. It's about embedding them into daily life.

A morning ritual of diffusing lemon or peppermint oil to invigorate your senses and kick-start your day or an evening routine of massaging your feet with lavender oil to calm your mind before sleep. Over time, these rituals become moments you look forward to, reminding you to pause, reflect, and care for yourself.

Remember, these practices equip you with tools to manage the difficulties of daily life. Viewing your healing as a lifelong journey shifts the focus from a healing destination to a continual growth, learning, and adaptation process.

Celebrating Small Victories on the Path to Recovery

Look forward to completing the tapestry that is you to a time when you feel "healed." The tiny stitches, the minor victories along the way, genuinely enrich the process and deserve celebration. Each step you take in healing, no matter how small, is a meaningful act of courage and strength. Recognizing these moments bolsters your spirit and reaffirms your path toward a fuller, joy-filled life.

Recognizing Progress

Cultivate a habit of recognizing your minor victories by journaling. Each night, dedicate a few minutes to reflect on your day. Write even the most minor win.

Did you get out of bed when you didn't feel like it? Write it down. Did you choose a healthy meal over something less nourishing because you knew it would make you feel better? Celebrate that choice. Over time, this journal will remind you of your progress and be a tool to lift your spirits even on brutal days because you will see how far you've come.

Lori Raupe is a friend who is no stranger to grief and has found journaling and writing down daily experiences, feelings, thoughts, and questions is a healthy and healing way to reminisce all the beautiful memories and release the pain of loss.

Lori's Story: A Journal of Healing

My parents faced significant health challenges as 1998 began. In January, my dad underwent surgery for cancer, and shortly after, my mom had heart surgery and nearly died. By March, I was exhausted from balancing work, family, and caring for my parents in two locations over two hours from home. But it felt different on Monday morning, March 16th—almost like a return to routine. I was so grateful that it seemed the worst was behind us.

The weekend was picture-perfect. We went to my parents' home to check on Dad and visit Mom, who was still recovering away from home. We went shopping and walked through the mall, holding hands and laughing like we always did. We tried on all kinds of crazy outfits before deciding what to get. We spent Saturday night with Dad, making sure he had everything he needed.

One of my sweetest memories is being in bed with Jennifer in my parents' guestroom that night. As we snuggled together, she hugged my neck as she had done so many times, almost a little too tight. She told me how much she loved me and that I was the "best mommy ever." Her words would have to last a lifetime, and twenty-six years later, the memory still brings bittersweet tears of joy to my eyes.

When we visited her that Sunday morning at the rehab center, Mom was getting better. I'll never forget the image of Jenna handing Mom the tulips and seeing their delight. She was dressed in her new sage green outfit we had gotten the day before; it made her green eyes stand out so beautifully. Mom had told her that. Jenna made everything fun; there was never a dull moment when she was around. I loved seeing how Mom and Dad would look at her with a smile of approval. That weekend was a gift from God that we all cherished.

On Monday morning, I peeked into Jennifer's room before leaving for work. She was sleeping peacefully, and I thanked God for her as I prayed for her day. Then, I went to Jami's room. She was already awake, and we had a quick conversation. I asked her to let her sister sleep just a little longer. Life felt almost normal again. I left my home, never knowing how my life was about to change.

Life is fragile and ever-changing. You never expect to get a call that changes your life forever. This one did. The call came with the kind of panic that grips your heart and freezes your breath. Jennifer and her best friend had been in an accident, and one of them was in critical condition. I alternated in thinking which one and prayed that both would be all right as I rushed to the hospital. I prayed harder than I ever had, begging God for a miracle. But when I got there, I saw her again with her eyes closed. Only this time, they would never open. There would never be laughter, the kind that makes your belly hurt, and tears of pure joy run down your face. There would never be the life we had known up until that moment.

Nothing can prepare you for the moment when your child dies. There are no words for the emptiness that swallows you whole. I couldn't escape the pain; my heart didn't just feel broken—it was broken. I was broken. It wasn't long before I turned to journaling, even though it felt almost useless to try and write down emotions that seemed so vast, so impossible to contain on paper.

Those early days felt like being caught in a terrible nightmare. I felt like a Rumba moving through tasks on autopilot, bumping into walls of pain. Picking out a burial place, a casket, and the music for her service—from one decision to the next, bouncing aimlessly—painful ... painful experiences. Everywhere we went, people would say, I'm so sorry for your loss. I hate framing death with the word "loss." Yes, it is a loss, and not that anyone knew how I felt; people don't know what to say. But in no way could loss describe all of the emotions you go through when your child dies.

Jennifer wasn't lost!

Just a day before, she had been so alive. Jenna, as I called her, had eaten her leftover chocolate pie from the day before, said, "Life is short. Ya gotta eat dessert first!" Dad and I laughed and shook our heads in unison. She ran outside to pick the pink tulips for Nana that were growing in their garden. It was like they had been waiting for that moment in time. Now, looking back so many years ago, it was all surreal.

There are many snapshots of memories that I cherish, but there are never enough. Journals are a gift—a way to remember, a space to reconnect with your memories and your precious loved ones. Journaling allowed me to remember her life, not just focus on the day of her death. This was an epiphany for me; I had more joy when I recalled the joyful memories rather than the one painful day that seemed to be in a loop running relentlessly in my mind.

As the fog of early grief started to lift, my journal became a safe place. I wrote about the moments I had forgotten—her sweet, small voice when she was little, how she opened her arms for a hug, and the funny things she'd say to make us laugh. She called her dress-up shoes high heels. I will never forget; I don't want to ever forget.

One day, I found myself writing about the hours she'd spent making fudge for the school bake sale. She ate the first batch before she wrapped the second. We laughed about it forever. It was a simple memory, but I found myself smiling as I wrote.

At that moment, it was like Jennifer was still with me.

Eventually, I started writing letters to Jenna. They weren't always coherent, and the pages were tear-stained. I sometimes asked her,

"Why did you have to leave?" as if it were her choice. I asked God, "Why her?" He answered, "Why not her?" I told him I didn't like his answer! He was okay with that, and I felt His love.

As time passed, I found myself flipping through my old journal entries, surprised at how my grief had shifted. It hadn't gone away, but it had changed. In the early days, my writing was full of raw emotion. But over time, my words started to reflect moments of peace, small signs of healing.

I wrote, "Today was hard, but not as hard as I thought. I laughed for the first time in what feels like forever. I immediately thought of your laughter, Jenna, but it was with joy this time. I miss you, but I think you'd be happy to see me smile again." The page had tear stains.

My journals became filled with love, grief, and the things I wished we had experienced had she lived—scattered sentences mixed with confusion and gratitude—simple gratitude for friends dropping off food and their comforting words. Sometimes, that was all I could write.

Journaling helped me put a name to the storm of emotions—grief, guilt ... disbelief. There was no anger, as some would tell me I would feel, just overwhelming sadness. The act of naming—putting words to the pain—became the first small step toward healing. Writing allows you to see your progress, even when you don't feel like you are moving forward.

Writing eventually helped me let go of some of the pain. I wrote, "In Ecclesiastes, it speaks of a time to mourn, and a time to dance. Is it time to dance?" I knew I had to write to Jennifer's best friend and tell her it was okay for her to start living again, so I did. She has always been so special to us.

It didn't happen all at once and wasn't perfect or linear. I could pour my grief onto the page and leave it there, even if it was only for a moment.

May I encourage you to write, even when it seems pointless and the words don't come easily? Whether you journal about your day, note everything you're grateful for, write a letter to your loved one, or share cherished memories, writing can become your lifeline.

Through a beautiful prayer, healing takes place when you allow the Holy Spirit to help you where you have heart wounds. It has been a beautiful experience in my life and so many others. This experience taught me more questions to write in my journal. You can modify them to be more personal. Here are a few:

- Jesus, how do you feel about being with me right now? (Notice the first thing that comes into your awareness.)
- Jesus, what is something about you that you want me to know today?
- Jesus, can you give me wisdom about how you see grief?
- Jesus, how can my broken heart be healed?
- Jesus, what treasured thoughts or memories would you want me to have today?

Grief is not something you "get over." It's something you carry with you, and writing can help you find a way to carry it but not let it break you. Keep writing, remember, and know that healing is a journey, not a destination. It may lead you to create something good from your pain.

Dad shared his wisdom with me on the day our Jenna died. He said, "Jennifer has been spared all of the heartaches of this life, and for that, we can be grateful." It was a comfort to me that day, but today, some twenty-six years later, I understand more as I have faced more grief in my life. I hope and pray his words bring comfort to you.

> **"The righteous perishes, And no man takes it to heart; Merciful men are taken away, While no one considers That the righteous is taken away from evil." Isaiah 57:1 NKJV**

Visit the Resource page

CHAPTER 12

Real Stories, Real Victories

The stories in this chapter will renew your faith if your loss and grief weakened it. And if you're not a follower of Jesus but still made it through the book—despite all the references to God, Jesus Christ, prayer, scripture, and hymns born from the suffering and triumphs of those who entrusted their lives to Him—you were meant to read this book. Jesus is knocking on the door of your heart; He wants you to trust Him with your present and future.

Each story is a unique journey of pain, discovery, healing, and evolution, shared here to encourage and inspire you and tell you that, like us, God has a plan for your life. He will use your brokenness to heal others through your experience and the Good News (Gospel) of Jesus Christ.

Because of God's grace and mercy, I am here. My opinion about my "love story" with God is that He got the wrong end of the stick—though He called me back from where I was. He is faithful, and I belong to Him! Let me tell you why I know this and why my spiritual foundation is/was strong.

> "Behold, I have engraved you on the palms of My hands; your walls are continually before Me." Isaiah 49:16 ESV

Growing up in a Christian home, you would think I could never become a prodigal. My mom took me to all her women's group activities from a young age.

The women's group often visited the central prison in the Philippines, Muntinlupa, and ministered to prisoners. The prisoners at this main prison filled the cottage industry with products for export. I used to take home purses made from materials native to the Philippines.

They also visited patients in mental institutions. That was sad for me. The place had an unpleasant smell, and the staff didn't provide proper care for the patients. I don't know if it did much for the residents who seemed hopeless and without care from loved ones.

As a family, we were very involved with our church. I sang in the choir, and my dad played the guitar. We attended Bible studies and events, including camping and vacation Bible school during school breaks. We were at church for several days during the week.

At one of these camping trips, I was baptized at age six.

My mom received Christ as her Savior in the church where I grew up. When she first walked into the church, she told me she was pregnant with me. We were so involved that we considered the pastor and his family our extended family.

My spiritual training was derailed and rendered meaningless when, at age nine, my dad took us all to Saigon, Vietnam, where he worked for RMK-BRJ, a construction company.

We lived in Saigon on Cong Ly Street from 1966 to 1970. We went to church on Sundays, but again, we were not significantly involved. As faithful as my mom was to tithe to our old church, there was no Bible reading or praying at home.

In 1970, the country began to fall into the hands of the communists. My parents sent us back to the Philippines when I was thirteen. There was a time between thirteen and fifteen years of age when

I took care of my siblings, six and eight years younger than me by myself without adult supervision.

Shortly after I graduated from high school, at age fifteen, my parents took us to Bangkok, Thailand.

They bought a cocktail lounge called the Executive Room on Patpong 1 Street in Bangkok. Patpong 1 has over 300 competing businesses, including cocktail lounges, go-go bars, and restaurants. Patpong 2, a slightly shorter version, has the same type of businesses, a supermarket, and a couple of high-priced restaurants.

My dad took a job offshore at an oil rig in Singapore, so my mom needed help, and I was it. I tended the bar, waited tables, cleaned before and after we opened, and even sang with the band. Working in a world of adults was intimidating for a fifteen-year-old, but it toughened me. I think I grew up too fast.

Two years later, when I was seventeen, my parents bought the go-go bar called Crystal Palace at the end of the street from us. I managed that, and my mom managed the Executive Room.

There was no church in Thailand at all, no Bible, no praying. My spiritual life was on the decline. My journey began by breaking God's moral laws. Without a second thought, I was living a prodigal life. I broke every commandment and didn't even flinch. I didn't think about God or whether I offended Him. Adultery, fornication, lying, cheating, you name it; I was guilty of all of it. I'll spare you the gory details.

Quite a shocking transformation from a child deeply entrenched in the Christian faith at an early age. Jesus was everything to me. When I got sick, I asked my mom to pray for me instead of taking me to the doctor.

The extent of God's patience came to a screeching halt in 1993, approximately ten years after I met and married Gary, a multi-millionaire who owned a chain of retail gasoline stations in Southern California.

Marrying Gary was the worst decision I've ever made, bar none. But I loved him. I dedicated my efforts to helping him with his company. The decision to help him run his company would ultimately work against me.

Looking back, I realize I wasn't happy in the marriage. I was so busy learning the business that I had no opportunity to know whether the marriage was good. Did it give me what I needed as a wife and a woman? Gary's being Jewish, but not a devout one, offered no influence on my spiritual life.

I was busy running the five trucks the company used to deliver gasoline to the various gas stations. I negotiated fuel prices daily and worked with the ten supervisors, who each managed a group of gas stations. I never really had the luxury of time to examine my marriage and how I felt about it.

I gave my all to the marriage. The big mistake I made was not including Jesus. I didn't even realize how important faith is in sealing my marriage bond with the saving grace and presence of Jesus Christ.

> **"Husbands, love your wives, just as Christ also loved the church and gave Himself for her, So husbands ought to love their own wives as their own bodies; he who loves his wife loves himself."**
> **Ephesians 5:25, 28 NKJV**

Missed opportunities. Gary had three young children with his first wife, lives I could have influenced for the Kingdom. But how could I have encouraged Gary to the Christian faith when I neglected my own relationship with Jesus?

In the eighties through the nineties, the powers-that-be who regulated gasoline storage tanks were hot and heavy on pollution from leaking underground tanks.

There were also many problems with independent operators, many foreigners, concerning gas taxes among the independent gas station owners: pollution, leaking storage tanks, alcohol or ethanol blending, tax evasion, and fraud. The authorities targeted independently owned companies because of their limited ability to fight against a barrage of government lawyers.

Gary had over 150 gas stations in Southern California and had a big target on his back. He was defiant. He didn't believe the government would go beyond fines, penalties, and maybe a civil suit.

So, it was a shock to Gary when they filed a criminal case against him, me, and all of his companies. I'm included as his wife, and I worked in the business with him. It's a negotiating tactic to include the wife to get the husband to fold.

Unfortunately for me, I married a spineless, selfish, self-centered narcissist who didn't have a problem pointing his finger at me. By the way, I didn't make any special deals to testify against Gary, which angered my mom.

When I realized Gary had thrown me under the bus and that I did not have the financial resources to defend myself, Doug, my husband, a friend at that time, took my case, knowing he may never get paid one cent for his legal services.

When the DA's office arrested and picked me up in early 1993, Doug asked the man, "What do I do with her daughter?" Joanne was twelve years old at that time. The man gave Doug two options: "One, you can call child protective services or take her home." Doug has never had children of his own, and this would be an enormous commitment.

But God. This is Doug's life verse.

> **"He has shown you, O mortal, what is good. And what does the Lord require of you? To act justly and to love mercy and to walk humbly with your God." Micah 6:8 NIV**

Doug took Joanne home!

You would think betrayal by a spouse you loved and served for nearly ten years and expected to spend the rest of your life with, and incarceration would be the worst thing to happen to anyone. I won't lie. It was, but it wasn't. When I remember those sad days, I saw God's hand in everything. Unfortunately, even as the Lord redeems us, we won't necessarily escape the consequences of our sins, but He protects and shields us and, most of all, walks us through it.

> **"Surely it was for my benefit that I suffered such anguish. In Your love, You kept me from the pit of destruction; You have put all my sins behind Your back." Isaiah 38:17 NIV**

They took me to jail in Los Angeles when I was first arrested. It's been so long, but I think it was called Sybil Brand. It might have also shut down. It was in such bad shape, dirty and unpleasant. They say the women there try to befriend you to get information to bargain for their case. I agree.

There are no words to express the pain of separation from my then twelve-year-old daughter, Joanne. The anguish was so thick and heavy, and there were days I didn't know if I would be able to hold it together.

But God.

Because the case was also federal, they quickly transferred me to the federal jail, MDC, Metropolitan Detention Center, in the heart of Los Angeles, California. The federal facility was better and cleaner. The supervising officers gave me charge of the kitchen and gave me my room. I felt safe. The cops liked me because I didn't play games and kept the kitchen and the unit clean.

Through the kitchen access via meal deliveries, contraband is passed between male and female inmates who live on different floors. The supervising cops knew I wasn't into that, so they put me in charge. Talk about being hated.

While at MDC, I started reading the Bible, joined Bible studies, and rededicated my life to Jesus. Every day, I listened to the radio to learn what God had to say and how He wanted me to live. My favorites were Chuck Smith, founder and pastor of Calvary Chapel in Costa Mesa, California, and Jack Hayford, pastor of a church in Los Angeles.

Jack Hayford always ends his message with the song "I Will Restore" by Richard Johnson.

I hung on to the words of this song as if God were saying them to me directly. I owned them as a promise from Him.

The state judge sentenced me to four years and three months, and the federal judge made it concurrent with his sentence—praise God! The state wanted consecutive sentences, but God's hand was on the federal judge's heart that day. He told the assistant district attorney who objected to concurrent sentences, "I see she is remorseful. What the state gave her is more than enough."

After the sentencing, they moved me to the Chino Women's Facility (CWF). I was given a great job as a clerk in the office. There, I could attend church and take part in many other activities that strengthened my faith. CWF was laid back, more like a campus than a prison. The Manson girls and Betty Broderick were there.

They later moved women to the new prison in Chowchilla, California. There goes campus life! It wasn't as nice—it was brand new but cold—a concrete jungle. I was placed in a 200-women unit with enormous bathrooms. I emphasize this because I cleaned the filthy bathrooms three times a day. When asked, "Why?" I said, "Because I want to use a clean bathroom." Which is the truth.

My bunkmate was a sweet young Armenian girl who was in there for murder. She escaped. I believe her family paid someone off. That was the rumor among the inmates and guards, anyway.

Not one of the 199 other women who were there for various crimes, some violent, bothered me, or even looked at me the wrong way. I was safe. I focused on the Lord, Bible studies, praying, living the right way, minding my business, and cleaning.

> **"Because you have made the Lord, who is my refuge, Even the Most High, your dwelling place, No evil shall befall you, Nor shall any plague come near your dwelling; For He shall**

give His angels charge over you, To keep you in all your ways." Psalms 91:9-11 NKJV

Doug did his best to bring Joanne once a week. This was difficult, time-consuming—five hours and thirty minutes each way—and costly, but he was faithful to do so. I appreciated and loved this godly man who fearlessly confronted persecution from the district attorney's office. He nearly lost his law practice and license, and losing his home forced him to move in with his parents and Joanne.

In case you're wondering, I had no family member to speak of. My parents went back to the Philippines, and my siblings were upset that I refused to allow my daughter to go to the Philippines with them, so they used that as an excuse not to visit or help me. Doug didn't want her to go, either.

They released me in January 1998. Praise the Lord, I came out stronger in my faith. I established intimacy with God, the Father, Jesus, my Savior and Lord, and the Holy Spirit, my Guide, and my Light.

Stay reading; it gets better.

I, too, had to move into Doug's mom's house. I had nowhere else to go. "How is that better?" you asked. Hang in there; it does get better.

Remember, the song said: "I will restore."

When I got home, Doug told me he had kept a couple of boxes that he needed to throw out, but he wanted to look through them with me first. We found bonds. In the old days, I bought municipal bonds for investment. They were in trust for my daughter's education. I had completely forgotten them.

I called Masako, my friend and then bank manager of Manufacturer's Bank in Los Angeles, California, and told her what we found. She asked us to come to the bank right away. The first "restore": The bonds were worth $60,000. Between that and Doug's savings, he was able to buy the condo so we could move and unburden his parents.

Once we settled into the new home, I considered returning to work to regain a sense of usefulness and help Doug with the financial burden of rebuilding his law practice. "What should I do?" I thought.

While pondering, a conversation with my friend Susan Greenberg came to mind. During one of her visits, as we caught up on family life, she mentioned that her sister-in-law was opening a medical billing company. She didn't go into details, and I didn't ask questions; I just said, "That's great!"

For some reason, my thick skull kept it in my memory banks. It sounded interesting, so I went online to learn what a medical billing company does and how to start one. I had to go to school to learn the basics! Okay, so I went back online to find a school. I found one in Garden Grove. The tuition was $8,000, but I could get in with 10 percent down. I went home and asked Doug for the money.

After I started the classes, I felt hopeful even though I didn't know how I would offer the service and who would be interested in giving a newbie with absolutely no experience in healthcare a chance or the trust to do the job well.

One concern at a time. I still owed the school $7,200! A couple of weeks into it, I went to the owner, Ragu Singh, and asked him if I could work off the balance doing administrative work for the school. Second "restore": He said: "Yes!"

Finally, graduation came. Ragu asked me if I would collaborate with his doctors' offices doing their billing. I declined and told him I wasn't ready. He then asked if I would continue teaching, so I did, teaching the curriculum for several months.

One day, while hanging out with the other teachers, I expressed my sentiment and concern about finding doctors to do billing for. When I started school, I didn't think about how I would market and advertise the service. I didn't have a plan, nor did I have a clue.

Then Jeff (bless his heart!) said, "Grace, Dr. Ha just opened a clinic around the corner on Garden Grove Blvd.!" No sooner had he said that I was out the door. Third "restore": Dr. Ha and his partners have been open for three months, and they have claims that need to be sent out to get payments from the various insurance companies. I was hired. Yay!

That was mid-1998 when God gifted me with Dr. Ha, a believer, a godly, honest, hardworking doctor, who, even during my loss in 2021, continued to support Doug's company with his business. Twenty-six years later, I count Dr. Ha as one of God's fulfillment of His promise.

Why I believe this to be a "restore" for me is Dr. Ha never asked for any references, a resume, billing or coding experience, or even to do a background check, nothing. He hired me on the spot!

Meanwhile, Doug bought the condo for $170,000; four years later, he sold it. Fourth "restore": He sold the house for almost $500,000! He took the profit and bought the house I'm living in today.

Thank You, Lord. Blessed and praise be Your name! You alone deserve honor and adoration.

This house was not the original one Doug bought. The other house in Villa Park was two weeks away from closing escrow. One day, the realtor told us that the house two houses down was being converted into a halfway house for mentally unstable people. We immediately canceled the escrow.

We started looking again and found this house. It was, and still is, a better house—bigger, in a better location, and in better condition. But what mattered most was how God communicated through it.

When we moved in 2004, we needed new air conditioning. You saw my story about Case Bennett in Chapter 3. We contracted with his company to install it. One day, before installation, they needed to look and make sure what tools to bring, so they came to the house with us. Doug, Case, Brian, his employee, and I were standing at the door when Brian, a pagan, piped up and said: "Hey guys, isn't this in your Bible? Your address in your condo is 304, that's seven. Your address here is 412, that's seven! Doesn't that mean something in your Bible?"

Mind you, I'm pretty sure Brian has never cracked open a Bible. Doug and I looked at each other, duh! I didn't recognize that God completed His promise to restore us.

Seven in the Bible is completion! God just told us through a pagan, "I've completed my promise to restore you!" He spoke through a donkey; why not a pagan?

> **"Then the Lord opened the mouth of the donkey, and she said to Balaam, 'What have I**

> done to you, that you have struck me these three times?'" Numbers 22:28 NKJV
>
> "Numbers in Biblical times were often symbolic of a deeper meaning and significance. Seven is especially prominent in the Bible, appearing over 700 times. From the seven days of Creation to the many "sevens" in Revelation, the number seven connotes such concepts as completion and perfection, exoneration and healing, and fulfillment of promises and oaths." -Dolores Smyth, Christianity.com.

Despite myself, my lostness, and depravity, God kept me in the palm of His hand. He dusted me off, cleaned me up, and restored me to Himself by the precious sacrifice of my Savior, Jesus Christ. He also gave me a wonderful husband beyond words.

> "For the eyes of the Lord are on the righteous, And His ears are open to their prayers ..." I Peter 3:12 NKJV.

Thanking God for the Intercessory Work of Jesus on our Behalf

> We thank you that having bore the sin of many, Christ makes intercession for transgressors, Isaiah 53:12 (ESV) and prays, not only for those who were given to him when he was on earth, but also for all those who will believe in him through their word; that they may all be one. John 17:20-21 (ESV)

> That we have an Advocate with the Father, even Jesus Christ the righteous, 1 John 2:1 (ESV) who is therefore able to save to the uttermost all those who draw near to God as a Father, through him as a Mediator, since he always lives to make intercession for his people. Hebrews 7:25 (ESV)

> That we have a High Priest chosen from among men and appointed to act on behalf of men in relation to God, to offer gifts and sacrifice for sin, who can deal gently with the ignorant and wayward; Hebrews 5:1-2 (ESV) and that he has become the source of eternal salvation to all who obey him. Hebrews 5:9 (ESV)

Finding New Purpose After Loss

Remember Ghesi Stojanov, one of my angels in Chapter 3? Well, some years back, she lost her baby boy. She was safe, but the car accident took the life of her little one.

When Ghesi was comforting me, she said she was blessed to have a friend who told her it was a privilege that God had entrusted her with a valuable testimony of resilience and overcoming through her faith. amid the immense grief of burying her baby.

At the end of 2013, while living in Perth, Australia, with her husband, Sasha, doctors diagnosed Ghesi with triple-positive aggressive breast cancer a month after her thirty-third birthday. The findings required her to undergo one year of chemotherapy, six weeks of radiation, and a double mastectomy.

While undergoing treatments, she discovered her voice and the power she had in her life as her advocate through the breast cancer process, which kick-started her career as a Transformational Coach.

This cancer diagnosis gave birth to her non-profit organization, Pinkies Up for Breast Cancer. She recently renamed it Pinkies Up for Wellness to help people with terminal and chronic diseases find alternative, complementary care and tools the organization vetted. Her faith kept her walking according to God's purpose for her life.

And then there's Fanny Crosby, who has been blind since she was six weeks old. Fanny went on to write over 9,000 hymns! "What a pity you can't see," people usually said to her. "The first thing my eyes will ever see will be the face of Jesus in Heaven," she'd reply. And this filled her with joy.

> **"Oh, what a happy soul I am. Although I cannot see, I am resolved that in this world, contented, I shall be. How many blessings do I enjoy that other people don't? To weep and sigh, because I'm blind? I cannot, and I won't." - Fanny Crosby**

You read about Peggy and Gus McAulay in Chapter 3. Doug and I saw how faithful Gus and Peggy were to do God's will, teaching us the Bible and going on as if their lives were perfect, setting examples to all of us about how trustworthy God is. In the meantime, they have kids suffering from health issues that seem impossible to overcome. Peggy remains a shining example to many women experiencing grief in many different ways.

GRACE RICHARDSON

There's Victory in Jesus

The stories of families, women, men, and children who lost loved ones, as I did, at the hands of doctors and hospitals across the country. I am a part of the C-19 Facebook group, and this is its purpose:

"Are you separated from your loved one due to the hospital's negligence? Do you need a place to connect with others going through similar experiences without being silenced? It's time to stop the mistreatment of our loved ones. Hospitals used to be places of healing and compassion.to get better, but now it seems that's not the case. COVID-related only, please."

The group is a place for the bereaved to find each other, comfort, console, encourage, support, and inform one another through faith, prayers, and truth found only in His Holy Word.

The C19 group has members from different states and all walks of life, with different faiths but the same broken hearts. The encouragement we get from each other helps us cope and tells us that we are not alone. The similarities of the circumstances bond us very deeply. We pray for each other, and we encourage each other with scriptures.

The power of community in healing is in sharing grief, the shared practices of our faith, and the accompanying self-care. These community engagements are simple yet of great value, reinforcing a bond and reminding each member that they are not alone in pain. This shared journey does not dilute the personal experiences of grief but enriches them, providing a multi-faceted support system that can adapt to meet each member's changing needs.

My Final "Restore"

As hard as Todd fought me through his lawyer to keep me from my right to see Ethan, they couldn't fight God. Slowly, I saw Ethan more and more. It wasn't easy. I ate a lot of humble pies along the way, but my obedience to the Lord paid off.

I honestly believe Todd would rather have me out of Ethan's life altogether. However, God has a different plan. He is the only one who knows what He has in store for me and Ethan. In the meantime, He's in charge, and I won't go off again using man's way.

But God. Today, my relationship with Todd is better. I am seeing Ethan more. Ethan and I continue to pray for his dad's heart to soften and allow him to spend more time with me. We also pray that my relationship with Todd continues to improve. There's still the issue of control. I am more involved in Ethan's life but am on a "need to know" basis only still. Ethan's prayer is to be able to go to my church and become a "swordsman." There are about 150 plus children of different ages and degrees of memorization, beginning with memorizing verses and chapters.

God Will Not Allow Those Who Love Him Without Help

A Family's Betrayal

The deepest wounds came from the people who should have cared about me the most, who should have been there for me—my own family!

Doug was incredibly generous to my family. When my sister Becky's husband Dave got a job at Delta Airlines, he didn't have a car. He was riding a bicycle. Doug got up at midnight, and drove him to his new job at the L.A. Airport from Orange County. Doug never complained. He just did it.

When Niki (who is Becky's daughter, though Becky continues to pretend to be her sister) was acting out in ninth grade, my mother called me from the Philippines in a panic. "You have to take her," she said. "She's getting off the school bus and doing who knows what. I'm afraid she's going to get pregnant."

Doug didn't hesitate. We took Niki in. For three years Doug drove her to and from school every day. We helped her with homework. Meanwhile, her actual mother, my sister Becky, had nothing to do with her. We raised Niki until she graduated high school.

One day, I walked into my living room and found a strange young Filipino man sitting there. "Who are you?" I asked. "What are you doing here?" "Oh, I met Niki online," he said casually. "I'm here to see her."

That was the straw that broke the camel's back. I immediately called Becky and told her, "You need to take Niki. I don't want to walk into my home again and find a stranger." So, Becky finally took over her care.

Another time, my cousin, Virgie and her husband Corky sold a motorcycle to Becky and Dave. They were supposed to make monthly payments, but suddenly the payments stopped. My mother asked Doug if he could write a legal letter under another attorney's name to scare them into paying. Doug did. They got scared. They paid.

Doug also volunteered to buy Niki a $2,000 car. But Niki's boyfriend decided to paint it with regular house paint. Black house paint. Of course, it ruined the car. Then they complained that the car doesn't run. Now the car was ruined and worthless and can't be returned. Doug was out $2,000.

At the same time, my mother was at our house visiting. Prior to her coming, I was telling Joanne her "ma" is getting older and we need to spend more time with her. So, Joanne took her out one day. While they were out, my mother asked Joanne, "What did your mother pay you to take me out?"

Joanne was hurt, but she didn't say anything to my mother. And then my mother said to Joanne, "I'm so glad Niki is standing up for herself about the car and refusing to pay Doug."

When Joanne got home, she told us. Doug was stunned. He went directly to my mom's room and asked her, "Why would you say that? I'm out $2,000. Why would you support Niki after she and her boyfriend ruined the car?"

My mother made a huge story out of it. She told my brother and sister that Doug yelled at her, that he was cruel to her. Doug doesn't yell. He's an attorney, he uses words. My mom never corrected the story. My siblings took her side or at least used it as an excuse to be upset with us; despite everything Doug had done for them and demanded that Doug and Joanne apologize to my mother.

I said no. "They're not apologizing. They did absolutely nothing wrong." I repeatedly asked my mom to correct what she did but she would not.

And that was the end of our relationship.

When Doug and Joanne went to Heaven, my mom told my siblings, "You need to go see your sister. She's suffered a great loss."

But they didn't come. They sent wilted flowers instead and only because my mother forced them to. No phone call. No visit. No comfort. Nothing.

To this day, they won't speak to me because I won't apologize for something that never happened.

And here's the worst betrayal my brother and sister did. My sister, I'm not surprised, but my brother…. He did a lot of things with my mom. He took her traveling to different countries. In 2023, two years after Doug and Joanne died, my brother and sister decided they want to sell my mom's house in the Philippines. First, it's the house I bought my parents thirty years ago. My mom was 87 years old. She had lived in that house for over thirty years, twenty years as a widow, surrounded by her memories. She had a yard where she could walk and pray every day. I guess they wanted or needed the money. So, they moved her into a tiny apartment on the third floor. They gave her a used futon that had belonged to Niki when she was 12 years old who is now in her 40s. My mother, at 87, frail and weak, was left sleeping on a 28-year-old futon.

This little apartment became her prison. Unable to walk, have the comfort of her memories and deprived of the exercise and prayer time that she normally enjoyed. She was thin and sickly.

Praise God, no more than two or three months later, she was diagnosed with cancer all over her internal organs. In God's faithfulness, He swooped her in His arms and took her home.

To me, that was a huge blessing. I believe God said, "Come on, Aila, I'm going to take you home. You don't need to suffer anymore at the hands of your children."

She went to be with the Lord in April 2023. I got a text from my brother: "Mom went home to be with the Lord." I just thanked him. I have not spoken to him or heard from him since the text and don't think I will at all.

I heard from my friend Eunice Choi that when my mom passed away, she had her arms raised up to the sky, to Heaven, and she said something like, "Jesus, I'm ready, take me home."

I just don't understand how my siblings could do that to their own mother. I guess in the end, nothing else matters, money talks. But I forgive them for what they did. I must. Usually, tragedy, loss, bring family members together, but I guess not this family.

Blood relations doesn't always mean a family. I learned that the hard way. The people who showed up for me—Case and Cindy, Ghesi, Ro, and so many others—they were my true family, God's family. They were the hands and fe**et of Jesus when my own flesh and blood turned their backs.**

> "There is a friend who sticks closer than a brother." Proverbs 18:24 NKJV

> **"Be anxious for nothing, but in everything by prayer and supplication, with thanksgiving, let your requests be made known to God." Philippians 4:6**

Remember when I told you that my daughter, Joanne, was my tech and graphics and how I felt crippled without her? Well, the blessing came in the form of my Virtual Assistant, Dakota Dixon! By God's will, I asked Melissa Esguerra if anyone was helping her with her tech and graphics, and she gave Dakota a ringing endorsement. I consider her a gift from the Lord and an answer to His promise that He will never leave me without help, and I need not be anxious or worried.

> **"Fear not, for I *am* with you; Be not dismayed, for I *am* your God. I will strengthen you, Yes, I will help you, I will uphold you with My righteous right hand." Isaiah 41:10**

God Is in the Story!

The stories here are sad yet inspiring. They are triumphant stories of individuals who, amid their deepest sorrows, disappointments, and defeats, discovered new paths and purposes that reshaped their lives in ways they never expected.

As you consider these stories and reflect on your journey, remember that finding a new purpose isn't about forgetting your loss but integrating it into your life's larger narrative. A few lessons emerge from their journeys that might light your way if you grapple with similar issues. Find what resonates with your needs, whether through the calming scent of essential oils, the therapeutic touch of reflexology, engaging in your faith and secular community, or the grounding act of prayer and scripture reading.

Finally, hold onto hope—the kind of hope forged in the fire of honest confrontation with your deepest pains and doubts. This hope carries the promise to endure and eventually emerge stronger, with faith not unscathed but undoubtedly victorious.

> *"We are* **hard-pressed on every side, yet not crushed;** *we are* **perplexed, but not in despair; persecuted, but not forsaken; struck down, but not destroyed—"** **2 Corinthians 4:8-9 NKJV**

As this book concludes, remember the lessons shared through my story, through Ghesi, Fanny, and the many others who held onto their faith through their pain—and especially through Ethan, whose voice reminds us that even children can find hope in the darkest valleys. Each story is a testament to the resilience of the human spirit and the transformative power of integrating healing practices and faith into the journey of grief.

As you move forward, carry with you the possibility of renewal, the potential for new beginnings, and the promise that from the depths of sorrow can appear new purposes and unbelievable joys.

Look forward to the next chapter of your life. Accept and welcome the continuous odyssey of healing guidance that will enrich your road to recovery.

Embracing the Future

Acknowledge your loss; it has equipped you with resilience and wisdom. These are not just memories but foundational stones for your future. As you reflect on your grief, consider the valuable relationships that have emerged and the accomplishments that brought you joy and fulfillment.

Incorporate Healing Practices into Your Goals for the Future

As you move forward and consider the healing practices you've adopted and want to include in your long-term goals, deepen your knowledge of essential oils and create your own healing blends. Part of what I do to help women is to guide them in using essential oils and face reflexology to care for themselves in greater depth.

Consider sharing aromatherapy and face reflexology with the grounding power of your faith through prayer and the Holy Scriptures with others going through hard emotional challenges.

Creating a Vision for the Future

I've heard of people writing a letter to their future selves. What has been achieved? How have the practices of aromatherapy, reflexology, and faith contributed to restoration? This letter can be a powerful motivational tool.

In setting goals and casting a vision for your future, allow yourself to feel the excitement of possibilities. Embrace the potential for joy, the opportunities for growth, and the continuation of your healing adventure.

Maintain Your Healing Practices Long-Term

The healing practices you've learned are not just for the aftermath of grief—they can be sustained over a lifetime. This commitment supports your immediate healing and fosters ongoing emotional and spiritual wellness.

A morning ritual of diffusing lemon or peppermint oil to invigorate your senses and kick-start your day or an evening routine of massaging your feet with lavender oil to calm your mind before sleep. Over time, these rituals become moments you look forward to, reminding you to pause, reflect, and care for yourself.

Remember, these practices are meant to equip you with tools to manage the ups and downs of daily life. View your healing as a lifelong journey to shift the focus from a destination of being healed to a continual growth, learning, and adaptation process.

Sustain these practices and go beyond the routine application of essential oils, the periodic practice of reflexology, mindful breathing, exercise, or praying and reading the Bible. It's about embedding these practices into your daily life.

Recognize Progress

Cultivate a habit of recognizing your small victories by journaling. Each night, dedicate a few minutes to reflect on your day. Write down even the most minor win. Lori's story in Chapter 11 shows the benefits and the healing power of putting your thoughts, emotions, happy memories, and goals on paper. It motivated Lori to write a book honoring her daughter, Jennifer.

Remember the last trip you took with your beloved? Did you get out of bed when you didn't feel like it because you wanted to celebrate a special occasion with your family? Write it down. Did you choose a healthy meal over something less nourishing because you knew it would make you feel better? Celebrate that choice. Over time, this journal will remind you of your progress and be a tool to lift your spirits even on brutal days because you will see how far you've come.

Celebrate Small Victories on the Path to Recovery

Each step you take in healing, no matter how small, is a meaningful act of courage and strength. Recognize these moments, celebrate them to bolster your spirit and reaffirm your path toward a fuller, joy-filled life.

Testimonies of Triumph

Here are some of my heroes, my prayer partners. Knowing how others are walking their paths through grief can be incredibly motivating.

Consider my friend of eighteen years, Eunice Choi, a chiropractor, who felt like the color had drained from her world after losing her dad, especially in a reckless way. She was consumed with anger that the nursing facility didn't give her father the care he needed and deserved.

Her daily victories of coping amid and beyond her anger come from a praying, faith-filled mom. She uses aromatherapy to calm her nerves and anchor her daily, along with prayers and scripture reading. Now and then, she still gets angry and blames herself, but she realizes that her dad is in Heaven, and they will one day be reunited.

Crystal Velasquez is a photographer friend whose marriage ended in divorce after she uncovered her husband's years of infidelity. He was a despicable person, and her teenage son and young daughter saw his mistreatment and heard his cruel words throughout the process. All while also going through the grief of losing her dad. Despite this, as a woman of faith, Crystal has been sustained by her belief in God and her mother's unchanging support.

I met Chanda, who lost her mom a year ago, at the Smart Method gym. They were very close, and Chanda didn't get out of bed for a year. Her son and husband forced her to get up, wash her face, and join a gym. They knew that exercise would recharge her brain and balance her emotions. She continues to support her body with exercise and proper nutrition.

Lynda Bergh, whom you read about in the earlier chapter, is an excellent example of a true survivor. Her mindset, through her faith and her tenacity, has proven her a worthy opponent of colon cancer. She was in remission, but it has come back. Yet, she pushes through with her care and continues to serve her community through a sex trafficking nonprofit organization while continuing to run her private investigation business. She also wrote a book to help parents and grandparents prevent their kids from being trapped and duped online.

Each story, each small victory shared, adds to the truth that healing is possible and a reality. It's important to remember that these victories are stepping stones of grief to forming the foundation of a new chapter in your life, where joy and pain coexist, giving the other depth.

But there's one more voice you need to hear, the most important one of all.

Throughout this book, I've shared my journey through grief. But I made a mistake in the first edition. I left out the voice of the one who was affected most deeply, my grandson, Ethan.

He was five years old when he lost his mom and his Papa, four days apart. He didn't fully understand what was happening or why they weren't coming back. All he was told was they went to Heaven.

In the next chapter, Ethan speaks for himself, his memories, his letters to his mom and Papa, and his message of hope for other kids walking through the same dark valley.

His voice matters. His story deserves to be told. And I believe it will touch your heart in ways my words cannot.

CHAPTER 13

Ethan's Story

Introduction

My name is Ethan. I'm nine years old. When I was five, my mom and Papa went to Heaven. It was the saddest thing that ever happened to me.

For a long time, nobody asked me how I felt about it. Nobody asked me what I remembered. Nobody asked me how I get through every day since they went to Heaven.

But now my Grandma is writing a new edition of her book, she asked me if I wanted to write my own chapter. She said, "Ethan, there are other kids out there who are going through what you went through or other worse things. Maybe your words will help them."

So, this is my chapter. These are my words. This is my story.

Remembering Mom

My mom was beautiful, kind, loving, and gentle. She was everything that was good in my life.

When my mom was alive, my dad could be mean but my mom was always there to protect me. She kept me safe. She made sure I was okay. Life was good when she was around because I knew she wouldn't let anything bad happen to me.

But then she died. And everything changed.

Without my mom there to protect me, life became so much harder. Some days are more difficult than other days. I hear words now that hurt me—bad words I'm not allowed to say. My dad calls me stupid; he tells me I'm an idiot. He uses the F-word and the S-word when he's angry, at me and at my Grandma. Those words make me feel small and scared, like I'm a bad person.

On the days when I'm not with Grandma—especially nights and weekends—I feel afraid. Sometimes I worry that he might hurt me because he has. I just want to be somewhere safe.

When I'm with Grandma during the week, I remember what it feels like to be safe and loved again. Grandma never calls me names. She never uses bad words. She tells me I'm smart and loved and important. She teaches me the Bible and prays with me every morning, just like my mom used to do. With Grandma, I can breathe. With her, I don't have to be afraid.

But I miss my mom every single day. Every single hour, really. Sometimes every minute.

I miss her beautiful voice. I miss her hugs. I miss her protection. I miss the way she made everything okay. I miss how safe I felt when she was alive. I miss feeling like someone loved me more than anything in the world. I miss her big arms when she hugs me and she hugs me all the time.

Life is so hard without her. Sometimes I get really sad and I cry, and I just want my mom back. I want her to hold me and sing to me and tell me everything will be okay. I want to smell her and feel her arms around me. I want to hear her voice one more time.

I wish she didn't go to Heaven so soon. I needed her to stay longer. I still need her. I'll always need her.

But God PROMISED I will see her again and be with her forever. That's not just a hope—that's a PROMISE. And God doesn't break His promises. The Bible says so, and my mom taught me that we can trust God's Word.

> **"At the right time, I, the Lord, will make it happen." Isaiah 60:22 NLT**

This is my favorite verse. Grandma taught it to me, and I say it to myself on hard days. God has the right time for everything. And at the right time, I'll see my mom again. At the right time, sadness, being afraid, it will be over.

I hold on to that promise on the really hard days—knowing that one day, I'll be with my mom again in Heaven. She'll hold me with her big arms, and I'll be safe forever. No one will say mean things to me. No one will hurt me. I'll just be with my mom, and everything will be okay again. Forever.

> **"And God will wipe away every tear from their eyes; there shall be no more death, nor sorrow, nor crying. There shall be no more pain, for the former things have passed away." Revelation 21:4 NKJV**

Until then, I will try to remember her voice. I will try to remember her hugs. I will hold on to my Grandma, who loves me like my mom did.

Letter to Mom

Dear Mom,

I miss you so much. Every single day. I wish you were still here with me.

I remember when you used to homeschool me. You were so patient with me, even when I didn't understand something. You would explain it in a different way until I got it. You never made me feel dumb. You always made me feel smart.

I remember when you used to read the Bible to me at night. You would tell me stories about Jesus and about how much God loves me. You taught me that Jesus is my Friend and that He's always with me, even when I can't see Him.

I remember when you used to sing to me. Your voice was so beautiful. Sometimes when I'm sad, I try to remember what your voice sounded like. I don't want to forget.

I remember when we used to go places together. You always took me with you. You never left me behind. You always wanted me with you, and that made me feel so special and loved.

I remember your hugs. They were the best hugs in the whole world. When you hugged me, I felt safe. I felt loved. I felt like nothing bad could ever happen to me because you were there.

I remember your smile. You smiled at me all the time. Even when you were tired or stressed, you still smiled at me. Your smile made me feel happy.

Mom, I want you to know that I'm okay. I'm sad a lot, but I'm okay. Grandma takes good care of me. She loves me just like you loved me. She reads the Bible to me and prays with me and teaches me about Jesus, just like you did.

Sometimes I cry because I miss you so much. But Grandma tells me that it's okay to cry. She says that crying doesn't mean I'm not strong. It just means I loved you a lot. And I did. I do. I love you so much, Mom.

I know you're in Heaven with Jesus now. I know you're happy and safe and not hurting anymore. And I know that one day, I'm going to see you again. I'm going to hug you again. I'm going to hear your voice again. And we're going to be together forever.

Until then, I'm going to try to make you proud. I'm going to be kind. I'm going to love Jesus. I'm going to do my best in school. I'm going to help other people. I'm going to be the kind of son you would be proud of.

I love you, Mom. I'll love you forever. Till we meet again.

Your loving son, Ethan

Remembering Papa

Papa was my best friend. He taught me so many things.

He used to take naps with me every day. We had a little corner in the office where we napped together while mom and Grandma worked, where he would tell me stories or watch TV with me. Sometimes we would just be quiet and rest together. I felt so safe with my Papa.

Papa used to take me for walks with Grandma every afternoon. We would walk around the neighborhood, and Papa would show me things. He would point out different plants and tell me their names. He would show me how things work. He was always teaching me something.

My Papa taught me about gardening. He showed me how to plant seeds and how to water them and how to take care of them so they would grow. He taught me the names of all the tools. He taught me how to be patient and wait for things to grow.

Papa also taught me about building things. He showed me how to use tools safely. He taught me to "measure twice, cut once." That means you should check your work before you finish it. I still think about that when I'm building with Legos.

Papa was patient with me. He never got mad at me. He never yelled at me. He was always kind and gentle. He made me feel special and loved.

I miss Papa so much. I miss taking naps with him. I miss going on walks with him. I miss my baths and my Bible story reading with him and Grandma. I miss learning from him. I miss his voice and his laugh and the way he would explain things to me, I even miss his jokes.

Sometimes when I'm building Legos, I feel like Papa is right there with me, teaching me. I can almost hear his voice saying, "Measure twice, cut once." It makes me feel close to him.

My Papa loved me. I know he did. And I loved him too. He wasn't just my grandpa, he was my teacher, my protector.

I'm so glad I got to have Papa in my life, even if it wasn't for very long. He taught me so much. He showed me what it means to be patient and kind and gentle. He showed me what it means to love someone.

Letter to Papa

Dear Papa,

I miss you. I miss you so much it hurts sometimes.

I miss taking naps with you. Do you remember how we used to nap and watch TV together every afternoon? Sometimes you would tell me silly stories that made me laugh so much. Other times we just played, you, mom and Grandma played music and watched me sing and dance. Sometimes we just rested together quietly as we listened to mom and Grandma work. I even miss the times when you cleaned in the back yard and in the house and you would have me help you. I always felt so safe with you.

I miss going on walks with you and Grandma. You always held my hand. You always made sure I was safe. You would show me things and teach me about them. You made everything interesting.

I miss working in the garden with you. You taught me so many things about plants and how they grow. You taught me how to use tools. You taught me to be patient and careful. You taught me that good things take time.

Papa, I want you to know that I still remember everything you taught me. When I build Legos, I think about what you used to say: "Measure twice, cut once." When I'm working on something, I try to be patient and careful, just like you showed me.

Grandma tells me stories about you. She shows me pictures to make sure I remember you. And I do. I remember you every single day.

I wish you were still here. I wish I could take one more nap with you as I listen to your comforting voice. I wish I could go on one more walk with you. I wish I could work in the garden with you one more time.

But I know you're in Heaven with Jesus. I know you're happy there. And I know that one day, I'm going to see you again. We're going to take walks together again. We're going to build things together again. And we're never going to be separated again.

Until then, I'm going to try to make you proud. I'm going to use the things you taught me. I'm going to be patient and kind and gentle, just like you were. I'm going to remember you every single day.

I love you, Papa. Thank you for loving me. Thank you for teaching me. Thank you for being my best friend.

I can't wait to see you again.

Your grandson, Ethan

Life Now

I will never forget my mom and Papa. They taught me so much. What I remember most is after my Papa and Grandma bathed me at night, he would read the Bible stories to me. My mom spent so much time teaching me about school and Jesus and how to be kind to people. I learned so much from both of them, and I will never forget them. I won't let myself forget.

Life is lonely sometimes. Everything changed when they went to Heaven. I used to have such a happy life. Every day, my mom, Papa, and Grandma worked in the office together. I was there with them. Papa and I took naps and watched TV, and then in the afternoon, he and Grandma would go for a walk and take me with them. My mom took me with her when she went to do things with her friends. When my mom and Grandma went to events, they would always take me and Papa with them. I had so much fun, and life was good.

Since my mom and Papa have gone, I sometimes feel alone and afraid, especially on nights and weekends when I'm not with Grandma. I don't always have someone to protect me the way they did. The best time these days is when I am with Grandma. She loves me so much and she does so much for me. I am really happy that my Grandma is still here with me.

I think God left my Grandma here because He knew I needed her. I tell her this when she feels sad too. Sometimes I see her crying, and I just hug her and tell her I love her. I know she misses my mom and Papa too. We miss them together, and that makes it a little easier.

Now that my Grandma takes care of me five days a week, we read the Bible together every morning and we pray together. She teaches me how to pray, how to talk to God like He's my Best Friend, because He is. I love to read the Bible with her because she tells me stories and gives me examples so I can understand it better. I talk to my Grandma about everything. She makes me feel happy. I feel better when my Grandma reminds me about my Papa and mom and the things we used to do together. She also talks about how my mom was when she was a little girl. We look at pictures of mom and Papa when they were little. I love to know about them when they were little like me.

I think my mom and Papa would be really happy to know that I spend so much time with my Grandma these days. We almost got separated, but God made it so that we didn't. God answered my prayers. He kept me and Grandma together.

I want people to know that I was so sad to lose my mom and Papa. I'm still sad. But I also KNOW—not think, not hope, but KNOW, that one day I will see them again because the Bible says so. Jesus promised that if we believe in Him, we'll live forever in Heaven. My mom and Papa believed in Jesus, and so do I. So, I KNOW I'll see them again.

> "Jesus said to her, 'I am the resurrection and the life. He who believes in Me, though he may die, he shall live. And whoever lives and believes in Me shall never die.'" John 11:25-26 NKJV

That promise is what keeps me going on the hard days. It's not just a nice thought, it's TRUE. God promised it, and God doesn't lie.

My mom and Papa are in Heaven right now, waiting for me. They're not gone forever, they're just there first. And one day, I'll get to be with them again, and we'll never be apart ever again.

My Talents - What I Love to Create

One of the things that helps me when I'm sad is creating things. When I draw or build or paint, I don't think about the sad stuff as much. I just think about what I'm making, and that makes me feel better.

Drawing with Pencil

My favorite thing to do is draw with pencil. I'm really good at it. I draw cartoon characters, and I can make them look exactly how I want them to look.

People say that drawing with pencil is harder than painting, but I think it's easier. With a pencil, you have so much control. You can make the lines exactly right. You can shade things to make them look real. You can erase and fix things until they're perfect.

I draw all the time. I draw cartoon characters all the time. I can spend hours just drawing and creating new adventures for them.

My Grandma would watch me and say, "That's really good, Ethan! You're so talented!" I love hearing her say that. It makes me remember my mom's voice when she says those words to me.

My Comic Books

I created a cat hero. He's a character I made up, kind of like the Dog Man, which is one of my favorite book series by Dav Pilkey.

I also created other characters like The Bark Knight. I made up my own stories about them, and I draw their adventures. It's really fun because I get to decide what happens. I can make them do anything I want. They can fight bad guys, save the day, or just have funny adventures.

My Grandma helped me turn my drawings into real comic books. I made two comic books.

The first one is called "The Cat Kid" (Book One). It's about The Cat Kid and his adventures in Cat City. He meets characters like Flip-O-Rama, Petey's Dad, and The Bark Knight. There's a villain named LD (Lobster Dog) who causes trouble. It's a funny story with lots of action.

The second one is called "Cat Kid and the Bark Knight Rises" (Book Two). This one continues the story. The Cat Kid and The Bark Knight team up to fight crime in their neighborhood. There's an "End Song" where all the Super Buddies come together. It's about friendship and working together to stop the bad guys.

Both of my comic books were being prepared to be published together as one book by a publisher named Lori Raupe. The book is called "Cat Kid - Book One," and it's supposed to come out in January 2026. I couldn't believe my comic books are going to be real books that other kids can read! When Grandma told me, I was so excited. I kept asking, "Really? Really? For real?"

We recently learned that Amazon will not allow my comics to be sold as it violates some kind of a law? I'm not sure what it's called "fringemen something?". Anyway, I have to go back and create new characters that don't look like someone else's character. I can't copy my favorite comic book writer's comic books. So, I now have new characters that I have started to work on. Stay tuned!

My comic books aren't about being sad or about my mom and Papa going to Heaven. They're just fun adventure stories. But Grandma says that other kids who are going through hard things might see my comic books and think, "Wow, Ethan lost his mom and Papa, but he can still make cool stuff. Maybe I can too."

I hope that's true. I hope other kids see my comic books and know that even when really bad things happen, you can still create things and have fun and do what you love.

Painting

I also paint sometimes. I use watercolors and acrylic paints. I paint pictures of things I see, like trees or the sky, or pictures from my imagination, like dragons or superheroes.

Painting is fun because you can mix colors and make new colors. I like mixing blue and yellow to make green, or red and white to make pink.

But I'm better at drawing with pencil. Drawing with pencil is harder than painting, but that's why I like it more. It's a challenge, and I'm good at it.

Grandma puts some of my paintings on the fridge. Some of them she frames and hangs on the wall. That makes me feel really good.

Building with Legos

I LOVE building with Legos. I can build really fast. Grandma says I can finish a big Lego set in less than an hour, which is way faster than most kids. I have a whole collection of Minecraft scenes.

I love following the instructions and seeing the picture on the box turn into a real thing. I've built cars, spaceships, castles, and all kinds of buildings. My favorite sets are the ones with lots of pieces because they're more challenging.

Sometimes I don't follow the instructions. I just build whatever I want. I make my own creations, like a spaceship that can turn into a robot, or a house with secret rooms.

Building reminds me of Papa. He used to help me with projects. He taught me how to use tools and how to build things. When I'm building Legos, I remember him showing me how to be careful and patient and how to follow steps.

I think about what I learned from Papa when I'm building. I check to make sure all the pieces fit before I move to the next step.

Building makes me feel close to Papa. It's like he's still teaching me things.

How Creating Helps Me

When I'm drawing or painting or building, I don't think about the sad stuff as much. I don't think about my mom being gone or Papa not being here, or the hard things I go through when I am away from my grandma.

My talents are gifts from God. Grandma always tells me that. She says God gave me the ability to create things so I can bring joy to other people and to myself.

I think that's true. When I make something, I feel happy. And when other people see what I made, they smile. That makes me happy too.

I am still looking forward to my comic books being published, and that will be the coolest thing ever. But even if they weren't, I would still draw and create because it makes me feel good. It helps me be less sad. It helps me remember my mom and Papa in happy ways.

If you're going through something hard, I think you should try creating something. It doesn't have to be drawing or painting or building. It could be anything—writing, singing, dancing, making up stories, building with blocks, or anything else you love.

When you create something, you're making something new that didn't exist before. And that's really special. It reminds you that even when bad things happen, you can still do good things.

God gave us talents so we can use them. So don't be afraid to try. Even if you don't think you're good at it, just try. You might surprise yourself.

And who knows? Maybe one day your creations will help other people too—just like I hope my comic books will help other kids who are sad or going through hard things.

> **"For we are God's handiwork, created in Christ Jesus to do good works, which God prepared in advance for us to do." Ephesians 2:10 NIV**

My Message to Other Kids

If you're reading this and you lost someone you love or maybe going through something hard, I want you to know you're not alone.

I know how you feel. I know what it's like to miss someone so much it hurts. I know what it's like to cry yourself to sleep at night.

I know what it's like to be afraid how someone will treat you from one day to the next, I know what it's like to wish things could go back to the way they were.

But I also want you to know something else: it's going to be okay. Maybe not today. Maybe not tomorrow. But one day, it's going to be okay.

Here are some things that help me:

Talk About Your Feelings

Don't keep your sadness inside. Talk to someone you can trust, maybe your grandparent or your teacher? Tell them how you feel. Tell them what you're thinking about. Tell them what you're scared of. When I talk to my Grandma about my mom and Papa, it makes me feel better. She doesn't tell me to stop being sad. She doesn't tell me to get over it. She just listens. And sometimes, that's all you need, someone who will just listen.

It's Okay to Cry

Crying doesn't mean you're weak. It doesn't mean you're a baby. It just means you loved someone a lot, and you miss them.

I cry sometimes. I cry when I think about my mom. I cry when I remember Papa. And that's okay. Grandma tells me that Jesus cried too when His friend, Lazarus, died. If Jesus cried, it's okay for us to cry too.

Remember the Good Times

When you think about the person you lost, try to remember the happy times. Remember the fun things you did together. Remember the way they made you laugh. Remember the way they made you feel loved.

I think about the times my mom reads to me and how tight she used to hug me. I think about the times my Papa and I planted strawberries together and built things. I think about the walks we took and the funny things we talked about. My Papa can be funny and silly, too, like me. Those memories make me smile, even though they also make me sad.

Do Things That Make You Happy

It's okay to have fun, even when you're sad. It's okay to laugh, even when you miss someone. The person you lost would want you to be happy. They wouldn't want you to be sad all the time.

I draw. I build. I play. I do things that make me happy. And when I'm doing those things, I don't feel as sad.

Believe in Heaven

This is the most important thing: if you believe in Jesus, you're going to see the person you lost again. That's not just a nice story, it's TRUE. It's a promise from God, and God always keeps His promises.

My mom and Papa are in Heaven right now. They're happy. They're safe. They're not hurting anymore. And one day, I'm going to be with them again. Forever.

That promise is what gets me through the hard days. When I'm really sad, I remind myself: "I'm going to see them again. This isn't goodbye forever. It's just goodbye for now." My Grandma and I talk about this and it makes us joyful.

> **"Jesus said to her, 'I am the resurrection and the life. He who believes in Me, though he may die, he shall live. And whoever lives and believes in Me shall never die. Do you believe this?'" John 11:25-26 NKJV**

Do you believe it? I do. And if you believe in it too, then you have hope. Real hope. The kind of hope that helps you get up in the morning. The kind of hope that helps you smile again. The kind of hope that helps you live your life, even when you miss someone so much.

You're Stronger Than You Think

I want you to know something else: you're stronger than you think you are.

I didn't think I could survive losing my mom and Papa. I didn't think I could keep going. But I did. And you can too. Don't forget there are other people who love you and they want to help you.

You're going to have bad days. You're going to have days when you don't want to get out of bed. You're going to have days when you cry and cry and cry.

But you're also going to have good days. You're going to have days when you laugh. You're going to have days when you feel happy. You're going to have days when you remember that life is still beautiful, even though someone you love is gone.

And little by little, the good days will start to outnumber the bad days. Little by little, the pain will get easier to carry. Little by little, you'll learn how to live with the sadness instead of being crushed by it.

Hold On to That Promise

If I could tell you one thing, the most important thing, it's this: hold on to the promise of Heaven. Hold on to the promise that you're going to see the person you lost again.

That promise is what keeps me going. That promise is what helps me get out of bed in the morning. That promise is what gives me hope when I feel sad. That promise is like the arms of Jesus hugging me and keeping me safe.

And that promise is for you too.

So, hold on to it. Don't let go of it. On the bad days, when you feel like you can't go on, remember the promise. Remember that this isn't the end. Remember that one day, you're going to be reunited with the person you love, and you're never going to be separated again.

"At the right time, I, the Lord, will make it happen." Isaiah 60:22 NLT

My Grandma always tells me: "Ethan, God has a plan. God has a purpose. God knows what He's doing, even when we don't understand."

So, hold on. Keep going. Keep believing. Keep hoping.

It's going to be okay. I promise.

> **"The Lord is my shepherd; I shall not want. He makes me lie down in green pastures; He leads me beside the still wa**ters. He restores my soul."
> Psalm 23:1-3 NKJV

Ethan and His Faith Amazes Me!

Ethan said something to me recently that pierces my heart every time I think about it. He said, "Grandma, when I see my mom in Heaven, I'm going to ask her why she married my dad."

No child should have to ask that question. It's not an emotion that a child should have towards a parent.

As I listen to Ethan talk about his pain as he struggles with the verbal abuse, the profanity, the fear and the daily meanness he faces when he's not with me, I carry a burden of guilt. I was a prodigal for so many years. I didn't recognize the stewardship God entrusted to me of my daughter Joanne. She didn't grow up in church. She didn't get the Word of God. She didn't get the Biblical guidance every daughter deserves from her mom.

So, when it came time for her to choose a husband, she didn't have a godly foundation and example to guide her. I don't know why she chose Todd. I don't know what she saw in him. But I know I failed to equip her with the godly wisdom to recognize a God-honoring man.

And yet—God is so good. So faithful. So redemptive.

Because out of that union came Ethan. A good and godly boy. A child who loves Jesus with his whole heart. A boy destined to become a man after God's heart who will use his pain today to bring hope to other hurting children.

And when Joanne, Todd, and Ethan moved in with us after Ethan was born, something miraculous happened. Joanne gave her life to Christ. She was saved. She was baptized. She became a woman of God who raised her son to know and love Jesus. Doug and I prayed and we saw the answer. What a faithful God we serve.

So even though I was not a good person in those early years, even though I was a horrible mother during Joanne's formative years, God still brought the fruit of a saved child out of it. He redeemed my failures. He restored what the locusts had eaten.

> **"I will restore to you the years that the swarming locust has eaten." Joel 2:25 NKJV**

I just thank God. I thank God for His faithfulness as Husband to this widow, according to His promise. I couldn't ask for anyone better. He has spoiled me to no end. He is also Father to Ethan, as His Word declares.

> **"A Father to the fatherless, a Defender of widows, is God in his holy dwelling." Psalm 68:5 NIV**

God doesn't waste our pain. He doesn't abandon us in our failures. He redeems. He restores. He brings beauty from ashes.

That's the God we serve. And that's the hope I cling to for Ethan's future.

CONCLUSION

As we draw to a close, I want to take a moment to reflect on the path we've traveled together through the pages of this book. We've sailed the turbulent waters of grief, exploring how the intertwined practices of faith in God, aromatherapy, face reflexology, mindful breathing, exercise, nutrition, and proper hydration can offer you restoration and a strong foundation for healing. It's been a journey about coping with loss, understanding, and embracing the deep emotional transformations it can manifest.

We've covered a lot of ground together. From the basics of aromatherapy and the targeted techniques of face reflexology to the soul-soothing power of scripture meditation and the support of your church and your local community, each element is a step toward holistic healing. While distinct, these practices share a common thread—each offers a way to touch the heart, soothe the mind, and nurture the body in distress.

The beauty of this holistic approach lies in its capacity to help you navigate grief and foster personal growth and the blooming or deepening of your faith. As you've learned to blend essential oils, apply pressure to reflex points, draw strength from your faith, breathe properly, and nourish your body, you've been crafting a new, resilient version of yourself—one refined by the fires of loss but emerging stronger, more compassionate, and more aware of those around you.

The road to recovery is neither straight nor predictable, and healing is not a destination but a continuous adventure. I encourage you to keep these practices close to your heart and adopt them into your daily routines. Remember, each day is a new opportunity to apply what you've learned and honor your progress and setbacks as essential parts of your healing process.

Now, I call on you to commit to this journey of recovery and self-discovery. Be patient and gentle with yourself, recognize that healing takes time, and each small step is a victory. I also encourage you to connect with others who are walking this path. Share your stories, your struggles, and your successes.

Your faith, your newfound holistic means of supporting your body and brain, and your personal sojourn to victory could light the way for someone else in their darkest hour. As Ethan wrote in his message to other kids: "Hold on to that promise. It will get you through." If a child who lost his mom and Papa at age five can hold onto hope, so can you. Their stories might inspire you to continue and channel your grief into fulfilling God's plan for your life, which will be used for your good and His glory!

I sincerely thank you for allowing me to join you in your healing expedition. Sharing such a deeply personal part of your life has been a privilege. Please remember that you are never alone.

Finally, let me leave you with a message of hope. While grief is a part of life, it also brings the seeds of significant personal growth and a deeper connection with your Creator. Each day you practice faith, aromatherapy, face reflexology, healing breath, exercise, and nourishment, you embrace a renewed sense of purpose and joy. There is light ahead, and it shines from the strength within you, reflecting your courage and your heart's capacity to heal.

I pray that God, the One who knew you before He formed you in your mother's womb, the One who loves you through Christ Jesus will reveal Himself to you as He continues to hold your hand and walk you through the "wilderness."

May you walk forward in peace and strength, carrying with you the lessons of love and loss and knowing where your help comes from. May you know joy unspeakable. May God bless you and prosper all you do in this journey to a renewed life filled with hope and trust for new beginnings, in Jesus' name. Amen!

> **"Fear not, for I *am* with you; Be not dismayed, for I *am* your God. I will strengthen you; yes, I will help you; I will uphold you with My righteous right hand." Isaiah 41:10 NKJV**

Visit the Resource page

EPILOGUE

THRIVING IN GRIEF

Is this the beginning or the end? That depends on how you see your own experience and its effects on the rest of your life.

To me and Ethan, it's the beginning, the open door that we chose to step into. However, there are two doors. One leads to ongoing incredible pain and suffering of loss, festering anger towards the horrible destructive cards we were dealt, ignoring the fact that God numbers our days and the Father wanted Doug and Joanne home. It is, after all, what every believer strives for—to be in the presence of the Almighty God and our Lord and Savior Jesus Christ.

The other door is the path that God has directed us to.

Remember what His word says?

> **"Trust in the Lord with all your heart, And lean not on your own understanding; In all your ways acknowledge Him, And He shall direct your paths." Proverbs 3:5-6 NKJV**

To be used for His glory, to have the gift of dwelling with Him forever is more than just hope. The icing on the cake? We get to spend eternity with those who've gone before us too!

Doug used to say, "If God never gave us anything more than salvation, He has already given us too much." The one who follows Jesus Christ will understand what that means.

Gratitude is a huge part of thriving. The Bible says:

> "Rejoice always, pray without ceasing, in everything give thanks; for this is the will of God in Christ Jesus for you." 1 Thessalonians 5:16-18 NKJV

The Blessing in Disguise

When Corrie ten Boom and her sister Betsy arrived at Ravensbrück concentration camp, they were assigned to a barracks so overcrowded and infested with fleas that Corrie was miserable. The fleas were everywhere—biting, crawling, making life even more unbearable than it already was.

But Betsy remembered the Scripture they had just read: **"Give thanks in all circumstances" (1 Thessalonians 5:18).** She insisted they thank God for everything—even the fleas. Corrie thought her sister had lost her mind. Thank God for fleas? How could anything good come from these horrible pests?

Yet something remarkable happened. In their flea-infested barracks, Betsy and Corrie were able to hold open Bible studies. Women gathered around them, hungry for hope and comfort. They prayed together, worshipped together, and found strength in God's Word. And strangely, the guards never interfered. They never came in to stop them or punish them, even though such gatherings were strictly forbidden and could mean death.

Corrie couldn't understand why they had this unusual freedom—until much later, when another prisoner explained: the guards refused to enter their barracks because of the fleas.

The very thing Corrie had despised, the thing she couldn't imagine being grateful for, was the protection that allowed them to minister to hundreds of desperate women. The fleas were a blessing in disguise.

Seeing the Fleas in Ethan's Story

When I think about Ethan's story, I see the fleas.

I see the unimaginable losses—his mom, his Papa, both gone within four days. I see the years with a father who couldn't love him the way he needed. I see the confusion, the pain, the stolen childhood.

For years, I asked God: Why? Why did this precious boy have to suffer so much? Why couldn't You protect him from this pain?

I couldn't see any blessing. I could only see the fleas.

But now, looking back, I'm beginning to see what I couldn't see before.

Because of everything Ethan endured, he has a depth of compassion that most nine-year-olds don't possess. He understands loss. He understands what it means to need comfort, to need someone to show up, to need grace.

Because of his suffering, he's learning resilience. He's learning that even when life breaks your heart, you can still get up in the morning. You can still laugh. You can still create and dream and hope. He's channeling his story into comic books that will help other grieving children—turning his pain into purpose.

He has a Grandma who will fight for him with everything she has. He has safety. He has stability. He has someone who sees him, hears him, and loves him fiercely.

And because he walked through the valley of the shadow of death at such a young age, Ethan will grow up knowing—truly knowing—that God is with us even in the darkest places. That faith isn't just for the easy days. That Jesus holds us together when everything falls apart.

The fleas haven't disappeared. The pain of losing his mom and Papa will always be part of Ethan's story. But I'm learning to trust that God can use even the worst things—especially the worst things—to bring about something beautiful.

I don't know yet what all of that beauty will look like. Ethan is only nine. His story is still being written, but we know the Author.

I do know this: the boy who lost so much is learning to thrive anyway. He's creating comics. He's asking deep questions. He's loving and being loved.

And that, dear reader, is the blessing hidden in the fleas.

Ethan is going to be okay. More than okay.

Life Today - God's Restoration Continues

Today, as I write these final words, I'm overwhelmed by God's faithfulness. When I lost Doug and Joanne in September 2021, I couldn't see past the crushing pain. I couldn't imagine a future. I couldn't fathom how Ethan and I would survive, let alone thrive.

But God had a plan far greater than I could have imagined.

Ethan's Creative Healing

Ethan has channeled his grief into something beautiful and redemptive. He creates comic books designed to help other children laugh even as they navigate their own grief journey. These aren't just drawings from a child processing pain—they're tools of healing, crafted by someone who understands loss in a way most nine-year-olds never will.

When I watch Ethan draw and write, pouring his heart onto the pages, I see God's hand at work. I see a boy who could have been destroyed by trauma instead using his story to bring hope to other hurting children.

> **"Let no one despise your youth, but be an example to the believers in word, in conduct, in love, in spirit, in faith, in purity." 1 Timothy 4:12 NKJV**

Ethan is turning his pain into purpose. Just like his Grandma Grace.

The Book's Impact - God's Global Reach

Thrive in Grief has received recognition I never expected and certainly don't deserve—but God does. This book, born from the darkest season of my life, has been honored with:

- Gold Medal from Global Book Awards
- Trophy and public recognition on stage from International Impact Book Awards (winner in two categories)
- Book of the Year 2025 from ChristLit

- 2025 Awardee American Book Honor Recognition from Litfest America

I also reached #2 on the Amazon Bestseller list. These are milestones that still leave me in awe.

But the awards aren't what matter most. What matters is that God is using my pain to reach women around the world who are drowning in their own grief. Women who thought they'd never smile again. Women who couldn't get out of bed. Women who felt abandoned by God.

The reviews and testimonies I've received tell the real story. Women write to me saying, "I finally feel understood." "You gave me hope when I had none." "Your story saved my life." "I thought I was the only one who felt this way."

These aren't my victories—they're God's. He took my shattered heart and turned it into a vessel of hope for hundreds of women globally. Women from different countries, different backgrounds, different losses—all finding comfort in knowing they're not alone.

This is what **Romans 8:28 looks like in action: "And we know that in all things God works for the good of those who love him, who have been called according to his purpose."**

These awards and the lives being touched by this book are God's goodness being revealed and His purposes fulfilled.

My Continued Education - Equipped to Heal

After Doug and Joanne went to Heaven, I could have given up. I could have let grief consume me. Instead, I chose to equip myself to help others heal.

My journey to help others didn't end with my own healing. I knew that if I was going to serve women globally through virtual coaching, courses, books, and podcasting, I needed to offer more than my personal story. I pursued four doctoral degrees—in functional, natural, holistic, and nutritional medicine—and combined them with my certifications in clinical aromatherapy and face reflexology. These weren't just credentials to hang on a wall; they were tools to build something greater: a whole, integrative, evidence-based methodology that honors both science and Scripture.

My 27 years working with medical doctors taught me the importance of treating the whole person, and now I was weaving that clinical expertise with the face reflexology and essential oils that had been so healing in my own grief journey. The result became my proprietary AromaReflex Healing™ approach—a five-pillar framework that addresses the physical, emotional, and spiritual ravages of loss.

I wanted women everywhere to have access to healing that was both clinically sound and deeply Biblical, whether through podcasting, teaching, or one-on-one coaching.

I also earned my LEHP (Licensed Ecclesiastical Holistic Practitioner) certification—another tool in my arsenal to serve women with excellence and integrity.

I know Doug and Joanne would be so proud. They're watching from Heaven, cheering me on, celebrating every woman I help, every life transformed, every heart healed.

My Mission Today

Today, I help women ages 45-70 who are struggling with grief, loss, and life transitions. I show them that there is a Calm Within the Storm ™. I tell them they shouldn't have to live in pain and desperation. They shouldn't have to suffer alone. With this book and the resources I offer they won't have to.

I can serve women globally through virtual connections from the comfort of their own homes, they can access the tools and support they need to not just survive their grief, but thrive in it.

I've helped hundreds of women worldwide discover that grief doesn't have to be the end of their story. It can be the beginning of a deeper faith, a renewed purpose, a more authentic life, and a new chapter.

Graceful Wellness Co continues to grow. The book continues to land in the hands of women who want to heal and be supported. In the meantime, I homeschool Ethan five days a week, teaching him not just academics but character, faith, and resilience. We do devotions together every morning, just as his mom did with him. We focus on our relationship with Jesus most of all.

What Restoration Looks Like

This is what restoration looks like. This is what thriving in grief means.

God took a prodigal daughter who spent years lost in darkness and brought her back to Himself.

God took a woman who was incarcerated and gave her a second chance—and then a third, and a fourth, and more chances than I can count.

God took a widow and a grieving mother and gave her a platform to help others heal.

God took a grandmother fighting for her grandson and brought them back together—not just surviving, but thriving.

God took the worst season of my life—losing Doug and Joanne four days apart—and turned it into the greatest testimony of His faithfulness.

My life, Ethan's life today truly represents God's goodness revealed and purposes fulfilled.

I have my grandson Ethan with me five days a week. He's safe. He's loved. He's creating beautiful art that will help other children. He's building an intimate relationship with Jesus. He's thriving.

I have a thriving business helping women around the world heal from grief using natural medicine and Bible-based practices.

I have an award-winning book that's reaching people I'll never meet, in places I'll never go, bringing hope to hearts I'll never see—but God sees them all.

I have four doctoral degrees and professional certifications that equip me to serve with excellence and compassion.

I have a story of redemption that can only be explained by God's grace.

The Journey Continues - Living with Hope

I wish I could tell you that after all the blessings God poured into our lives, everything became easy. I wish I could say that Ethan and I are living happily ever after with no more struggles, no more tears, no more hard days.

But that wouldn't be true.

The truth is this: Ethan and I are still dealing with challenges. We're still navigating the ongoing difficulties with his father. We still face days that are harder than others. We still cry. We still miss Doug and Joanne with an ache that never fully goes away.

But here's what's different now: we face these challenges with hope instead of despair. We walk through the hard days with faith instead of fear. We know that God is with us, and we trust that He will continue to carry us through.

Still in the Battle

Ethan and I are still dealing with his father. That hasn't changed. The verbal abuse, the profanity, the meanness—it's all still there when Ethan is with him on nights and weekends.

There are days when Ethan comes to me looking defeated and small. There are days when I hold him while he cries because of something his father said to him. There are moments when I want to rage against the injustice of it all—Why does this little boy have to suffer so much? Why can't his father just love him the way he deserves to be loved?

But then I remember: God is fighting this battle for us. Not me. Not Ethan. God.

> "The Lord will fight for you; you need only to be still." Exodus 14:14 NIV

Every morning before Ethan starts on his schoolwork, we read the Word of God together, and then we pray together. And one of the things we pray for—every single day—is Ethan's father. We pray that God will change his heart. We pray that God will soften him. We pray that one day, Ethan's father will see the precious gift God gave him in his son.

We don't pray for revenge. We don't pray for him to be punished. We pray for redemption.

Because that's what Jesus taught us to do. Jesus said, **"Love your enemies and pray for those who persecute you." (Matthew 5:44 NIV)**

So that's what we do. We pray. We trust. We wait for God to move.

And some days, that's really hard. Some days, I want to take matters into my own hands. Some days, I want to fight fire with fire.

But God keeps reminding me: **"Vengeance is mine, I will repay, says the Lord." (Romans 12:19 NKJV)**

So I let go. I release my anger. I trust God to do what I cannot.

And Ethan is learning this too. He's learning that even when people hurt us, we can still pray for them. We can still hope for them. We can still trust that God can change even the hardest hearts.

Because of Ethan's anger that he says he has, in our morning prayers, I make him say what the fruit of the Holy Spirit are found in **Galatians 5:23-23 "But the fruit of the Spirit is love, joy, peace, patience, kindness, goodness, faithfulness, gentleness, self-**

control; against such things there is no law." Then I ask him to say the verse of how God expects us to live each day: Micah 6:8 "To do justice, to love mercy and walk humbly with our God." Then I tell him to recite the verse in **1 Thessalonians 5:16-18 "Rejoice always, pray without ceasing, give thanks in all circumstances; for this is the will of God in Christ Jesus for you.**

I do this at the end of our prayer every day. Why? Because the word of God does not return void. I want every word to be engraved in his heart, mind and spirit. I have been called to participate in stewarding this boy and I will not fail him.

The Power of Community in the Long Haul

One of the most important lessons I've learned through all of this is that community isn't just for the crisis—it's for the long haul.

When Doug and Joanne first died, people showed up. They brought food. They prayed. They helped with the house. They sat with me while I cried.

But as the months turned into years, some people drifted away. And that's okay—that's normal. Life moves on.

But there are a few people who stayed. People like Ghesi, Cindy, Yvette, Case, Lynda, and so many others. They didn't just show up for the funeral. They showed up for the long, hard years that followed.

They're still showing up now.

When I'm overwhelmed they pray for me. When Ethan has a hard day, they check in on him. When I need encouragement, they send me a text or call me on the phone.

This is what the body of Christ looks like. This is what community is supposed to be.

If you're in the thick of grief right now, don't isolate yourself. I know it's tempting. I know it feels easier to just shut the world out and deal with your pain alone.

But you need people. You need community. You need the body of Christ to hold you up when you can't stand on your own.

And if you're reading this and you're on the other side—if you're the friend, the family member, the church member—please don't disappear after the funeral. Please keep showing up. Keep praying. Keep checking in.

The first few weeks are hard, but the first few years are harder. Grief doesn't end when the casseroles stop coming. Grief goes on and on, and we need you to go on with us.

Using Our Pain to Help Others

One of the most profound truths I've learned through this journey is that God wastes nothing.

Not our pain. Not our tears. Not our suffering.

He uses it all.

When I write on social media or meet with women one-on-one, I share my story. I share the pain of losing Doug and Joanne. I share the struggle of fighting for Ethan. I share the ongoing challenges we still face.

And do you know what happens? Women come up to me with tears in their eyes and say, "Thank you. I thought I was the only one."

That's the power of testimony. That's the power of sharing your story.

Your pain can become someone else's hope. Your struggle can become someone else's encouragement. Your victory can become someone else's inspiration.

> **"Praise be to the God and Father of our Lord Jesus Christ, the Father of compassion and the God of all comfort, who comforts us in all our troubles, so that we can comfort those in any trouble with the comfort we ourselves receive from God." 2 Corinthians 1:3-4 NIV**

This is why I wrote this book. This is why I shared my story. Not because I've arrived. Not because I have it all figured out. But because I know what it's like to be in the pit, and I know that God can pull you out.

I know what it's like to lose everything, and I know that God can restore what was lost.

I know what it's like to feel like you'll never smile again, and I know that God can bring joy back into your life.

If my pain can help even one person keep going, then it was worth it.

The Purpose of Ongoing Suffering

You might be wondering: If God is so good, why does He allow the suffering to continue? Why hasn't He fixed everything yet?

I've wrestled with that question many times.

And here's what I believe: God doesn't waste our suffering. He uses it to refine us, to shape us, to make us more like Jesus.

> **"Consider it pure joy, my brothers and sisters, whenever you face trials of many kinds, because you know that the testing of your faith produces perseverance. Let perseverance finish its work so that you may be mature and complete, not lacking anything." James 1:2-4 NIV**

I am not the same person I was four years ago. Grief has changed me. Suffering has shaped me. The ongoing battle has refined me.

I'm stronger now. I'm more compassionate now. I'm more dependent on God now.

And I wouldn't trade that for anything.

Yes, I would give anything to have Doug and Joanne back. Yes, I would love for Ethan's father to treat him with kindness and respect and value him. Yes, I would prefer an easier life.

But I also know that this hard, painful, ongoing journey has brought me closer to God than I ever was before. It has forced me to my knees. It has taught me to trust Him completely.

And that is a gift.

Thriving While Still Struggling

Here's the paradox: You can thrive and still struggle at the same time.

Thriving doesn't mean everything is perfect. Thriving doesn't mean you never cry. Thriving doesn't mean you've moved on and forgotten.

Thriving means you're still here. You're still fighting. You're still believing. You're still trusting God even when you can't see the way forward.

Ethan and I are thriving. Our lives are full of joy, purpose, and hope. We laugh. We create. We dream. We serve. We love.

But we're also still struggling. We still face hard days. We still deal with challenges. We still walk through valleys.

And that's okay.

Because God is with us in the valleys. He's with us in the struggles. He's with us in the ongoing battles.

> **"Even though I walk through the darkest valley, I will fear no evil, for you are with me; your rod and your staff, they comfort me." Psalm 23:4 NIV**

This is the message I want you to take away from this book: You don't have to wait until everything is perfect to thrive. You can thrive right now, right where you are, even in the middle of the mess.

You can grieve and hope at the same time. You can cry and still smile. You can struggle and still trust God.

That's what thriving in grief looks like.

A Final Word

To the grandparents fighting for your grandchildren: Keep standing. Keep trusting. Keep fighting. Keep praying, your prayers are not wasted.

To the children walking through grief: You're not alone. Jesus is right there with you. The flames won't destroy you.

To those who feel betrayed and forgotten: The pit is not the end of your story—it's preparation for your purpose.

To everyone who's been praying and waiting: God sees every tear. He hears every prayer. Keep trusting.

To anyone facing impossible giants: The battle belongs to the Lord. You don't have to be big enough—God is fighting for you.

And if God can bring beauty from Ethan's story—and from mine—He can bring beauty from yours too—no matter how many fleas you're facing right now.

To You, Dear Reader

If you're reading this and you're still in the pit of grief, I want you to know: God has a plan for you. You may not see it yet. You may not believe it's possible. But I'm living proof that God can take the most devastating losses and create something beautiful.

Ethan and I are living proof that you can lose everything and still find joy.

We are living proof that thriving in grief isn't just possible—it's promised to those who trust God in the powerful name of Christ Jesus.

This is where thriving begins.

This is where purpose is found.

This is where God's goodness is revealed.

Our lives today—Ethan's and mine—represent the faithfulness of a God who never abandons His children, even in the darkest valleys.

And He won't abandon you either.

> **"For I know the plans I have for you, declares the Lord, plans to prosper you and not to harm you, plans to give you hope and a future."**
> **Jeremiah 29:11 NIV**

May you find that hope. May you discover that future. May you learn to thrive in your grief, just as we have.

And may the God of all comfort hold you close every step of the way.

With love and hope,

Grace Richardson, DNM, DNHM, DFM, PhD
Award-Winning Author of *Thrive in Grief*
Founder of Graceful Wellness Co.
Creator of AromaReflex Healing™ and Calm the Storm Within™

RESOURCE PAGE

Introduction

YouTube Playlist: https://tinyurl.com/introduction-videos
Google Photos Folder: https://tinyurl.com/introduction-pictures

"Blessed be the God and Father of our Lord Jesus Christ, the Father of mercies and God of all comfort, who comforts us in all our tribulation, that we may be able to comfort those who are in any trouble, with the comfort with which we ourselves are comforted by God."

Intro video
Grace Richardson and Ethan Martinez

Chapter 1

YouTube Playlist: https://tinyurl.com/chapter1-videos
Google Photos Folder: https://tinyurl.com/chapter1-pictures

1) God Is In the Story
https://youtu.be/ryD3D9X2myk?si=GL-JRSWtHX02AIPy

2) Trust In God
https://youtu.be/sTcQGzpN3PA?si=coZCmZS27JyWl-Ku

3) Legal papers

4) Woman escapes C-19 hospital Treatment
https://www.theepochtimes.com/article/hospital-holocaust-woman-escapes-covid-19-hospital-treatment-protocols-says-

others-not-so-lucky-4728030?est=AAAAAAAAAAAAAAAZv
Auch8J28zJ4pMJs2RQB%2Fp5xE5B9sbvskXuc0ZKXjXNU7A5

5) Greg Eyerly article
https://www.theepochtimes.com/its-truly-unreal-stories-of-negligence-at-the-hand-of-covid-19-hospital-treatment-protocols-continue-to-surface_4694066.html

6) Ethan videos

Chapter 2

YouTube Playlist: https://tinyurl.com/chapter2-videos
Google Photos Folder: https://tinyurl.com/chapter2-pictures

1) "What A Friend We Have In Jesus"
Https://youtu.be/g5uisBMZ3Tc?si=SW1r473ALZTNVCaI

2) Together
https://youtu.be/lOtMqixroVw?si=GDM5DCeKLYbTQX88

Chapter 3

YouTube Playlist: https://tinyurl.com/chapter3-videos
Google Photos Folder: https://tinyurl.com/chapter3-pictures

Photos Personal and community
Videos Personal and community

Chapter 4

YouTube Playlist: https://tinyurl.com/chapter4-videos
Google Photos Folder: https://tinyurl.com/chapter4-pictures

Grief and learning how to support your body videos

Chapter 5

YouTube Playlist: https://tinyurl.com/chapter5-videos
Google Photos Folder: https://tinyurl.com/chapter5-pictures

Elizabeth Oliver video
Lynda Bergh Herring video

Emotional support recipes
Essential oil blending videos

1)"Come, Jesus, Come"
https://youtu.be/UViC6DllCeA?si=4dxHxqzEbw0Zhx30

Chapter 6

YouTube Playlist: https://tinyurl.com/chapter6-videos
Google Photos Folder: https://tinyurl.com/chapter6-pictures

Skin serum recipes
Blending videos

Chapter 7

YouTube Playlist: https://tinyurl.com/chapter7-videos
Google Photos Folder: https://tinyurl.com/chapter7-pictures

Ethan's videos
Face reflexology videos

Chapter 8

YouTube Playlist: https://tinyurl.com/chapter8-videos
Google Photos Folder: https://tinyurl.com/chapter8-pictures

Ethan's videos
Breathing videos
Exercise videos
Simone LeCompte Smartfit Method Yorba Linda and Costa Mesa, California

Chapter 9

YouTube Playlist: https://tinyurl.com/chapter9-videos
Google Photos Folder: https://tinyurl.com/chapter9-pictures

Various information and videos

Chapter 10

YouTube Playlist: https://tinyurl.com/chapter10-videos
Google Photos Folder: https://tinyurl.com/chapter10-pictures

1)"Scars In Heaven"
https://youtu.be/btcCKQii-oU?si=LvMRLEvwJOEhlyO5

Chapter 11

YouTube Playlist: https://tinyurl.com/chapter11-videos
Google Photos Folder: https://tinyurl.com/chapter11-pictures

1)Caprice Crebar and Lori Raupe video

2)"Knowing What I Know About Heaven"
https://youtu.be/ga_RB4I88So?si=ll3fonqcpWPb8RR4

Chapter 12

YouTube Playlist: https://tinyurl.com/chapter12-videos
Google Photos Folder: https://tinyurl.com/chapter12-pictures

1)"In the Garden
https://youtu.be/w572Nk__-34?si=-cfxolxc__FIUgpO

2) "Softly and Tenderly"
https://youtu.be/3_dMzucjEaw?si=lIzo0phlZ79QqNjr

2)"Why Me, Lord?" - Kris Kristofferson
https://youtu.be/g2u_rEcWW8M?si=xOdq8e5iF2xH13Ia

2) "The Goodness of God" - CeCe Winans
https://youtu.be/9sE5kEnitqE?si=jOiBISWvavTZW8Oh

3) Ghesi Stojanov and Elizabeth Oliver video

4) Ghesi Stojanov video

ACKNOWLEDGEMENTS

It took a village!

I thank the LORD of heaven's armies (Sabaoth) for all the protection and for fighting my battles for me, my LORD of provisions(Jireh) for sustaining me with overflowing abundance, my LORD Who sees me(El Roi), my LORD Who heals me and Ethan (Rapha), my LORD Who keeps His covenants with me(El-Berith), my LORD and source of strength(Eyaluth),my LORD and shield that protects me (Magen), my LORD the Redeemer (Gaol), my LORD my Deliverer (Palet), my LORD of Peace (Yahweh-Shalom), my LORD who sanctified me (Yahweh-M'Kaddesh). Thank You, I give You all the glory!

A heartfelt "thank you" and much love and appreciation to Case and Cindy Bennett, Joseph and Allison Newsome, Glen Pallas, Robert T Ha MD, Eunice Choi,DC, LAc and her mom, Eunice and Heath Hamaguchi, Ro and Greg Lerman, George Gutierrez, Raul Mendez, Heather Bailey, Glenda Godinez, Ghesi and Sasha Stojanov, John and Yvette Kronick, Seth Kronick, Jenny Tsai, Robin Hu, Caprice Crebar, Misty Loreto, Lynda Bergh-Herring, Diana Sabatino, Luz Sellers, James and Anastasia Lander, Genevieve, Richard and Maggie Dobiesz, Joe, Rachel and April Rodriguez, Elizabeth Oliver, Dakota Dixon, Crystal Velasquez, Anthony Macias, Rigo Jacobo, Mitch Haynam, Mary Barnett, Renee Ascencio, Shannon Eggleston, Jacqueline Cortes Sammons, MD, Pastor Jack Hibbs, Evan and Melissa Esguerra, Jim and Julie Boswell, Glenn and Kathy Linde, Peter and Lisa Mouzakis, Dan and Jaclyn Canzone, Peggy McAulay, Mitch and Wendy Pedersen, Andrea Ortiz, Dawn Carpenter, Glenda Godinez, Ketan G. Bhakta, MD, Harry and Eva Lowenstein, Rosie and John Trani

ABCS OF SALVATION

If after reading this book, you were drawn to Jesus Christ, Lord and Savior, please use the following as a guide to know how to receive Him into your life and make Him your personal Savior. Feel free to contact me at www.thriveingrief@gmial.com for help or guidance to how to find a doctrinally sound church that will help you grow in your faith. You can also go to: https://rockharborchurch.net/grow-connect/church-locator/

If you don't know how to secure your salvation, this simple and easy to follow "ABCs of Salvation" will guide you on how to accept Jesus Christ as your Lord and Savior. He is the only Way to Heaven!

You might be wealthy, but it cannot be exchanged for your soul. Whatever you have here on earth, they are nothing and there is no forever on Earth.
The Kingdom of Heaven is more valuable than anything else.
It is appointed that we will die physically, and we will be judged (Hebrews 9:27).
You only have two destinations: Heaven or Hell.
Hell has no exit and Heaven has only one door – Jesus

So how can you receive Jesus and be saved?

A – ADMIT that you are a Sinner

We all have sinned.

17 For if by one man's offence death reigned by one; much more they which receive abundance of grace and of the gift of righteousness shall reign in life by one, Jesus Christ.)

18 Therefore as by the offence of one judgment came upon all men to condemnation; even so by the righteousness of one the free gift came upon all men unto justification of life.

19 For as by one man's disobedience many were made sinners, so by the obedience of one shall many be made righteous.

20 Moreover the law entered, that the offence might abound. But where sin abounded, grace did much more abound:

21That as sin hath reigned unto death, even so might grace reign through righteousness unto eternal life by Jesus Christ our Lord.
Romans 5:17-21 KJV

And no matter how you try to be good, you will still fail.

For all have sinned, and come short of the glory of God;
Romans 3:23 KJV

We are unclean.

But we are all as an unclean thing, and all our righteousnesses are as filthy rags; and we all do fade as a leaf; and our iniquities, like the wind, have taken us away.
Isaiah 64:6 KJV

B - BELIEVE on the Lord Jesus Christ

God gave His only begotten Son Jesus Christ to save us. And through His blood, our sins are washed away.

For God so loved the world, that He gave His only begotten Son, that whosoever believeth in Him should not perish, but have everlasting life.
John 3:16 KJV

Only by His grace and not by works.

8 For by grace are ye saved through faith; and that not of yourselves: it is the gift of God:

9 Not of works, lest any man should boast.

10 For we are his workmanship, created in Christ Jesus unto good works, which God hath before ordained that we should walk in them.
Ephesians 2:8-10 KJV

There is no other way but only through Jesus Christ alone.

Jesus saith unto him, I am the way, the truth, and the life: no man cometh unto the Father, but by me.
John 14:6 KJV

God commended His love toward us.

But God commendeth His love toward us, in that, while we were yet sinners, Christ died for us.
Romans 5:8 KJV

If we have Jesus Christ living in us, we will live eternally.

He that hath the Son hath life; and he that hath not the Son of God hath not life.
1 John 5:12 KJV

In the power of our Lord Jesus Christ.

For I verily, as absent in body, but present in spirit, have judged already, as though I were present, concerning him that hath so done this deed, In the name of our Lord Jesus Christ, when ye are gathered together, and my spirit, with the power of our Lord Jesus Christ, To deliver such an one unto Satan for the destruction of the flesh, that the spirit may be saved in the day of the Lord Jesus.
1 Corinthians 5:3-5 KJV

By the blood of our Savior Jesus Christ

Not by works of righteousness which we have done, but according to his mercy he saved us, by the washing of regeneration, and renewing of the Holy Ghost; Which he shed on us abundantly through Jesus Christ our Saviour; That being justified by his grace, we should be made heirs according to the hope of eternal life.
Titus 3:5-7 KJV

C – CONFESS with your mouth

Now that you accepted that you are a sinner and believe in the Lord Jesus Christ, confess with your mouth your sins and that you believe in Him. Let Him come to you and accept Him as your Lord and Savior.

If we confess our sins, He is faithful and just to forgive us our sins, and to cleanse us from all unrighteousness.
1 John 1:9 KJV

9 That if thou shalt confess with thy mouth the Lord Jesus, and shalt believe in thine heart that God hath raised Him from the dead, thou shalt be saved.

10 For with the heart man believeth unto righteousness; and with the mouth confession is made unto salvation.

11 For the scripture saith, Whosoever believeth on Him shall not be ashamed.
Romans 10:9-11 KJV

Now do the Sinner's Prayer:

Holy, and gracious, Father, I recognize and acknowledge I am a miscreant not deserving of Your grace and I ask forgiveness of my sins. I know Your Son is the Truth, the Light, and the Way, I give myself freely to His control and welcome Him into my heart. I ask You to walk with me and guide me, teach me Your way and your truth. Thank You for the gift of Your Son's sacrifice on the cross that I may live. Thank You for Your forgiveness and for accepting me as Your child. Amen.

Now that you are saved and you have Jesus Christ living in you, you should not stop there. What is next? Follow Him, His words, submit yourself, and don't forget to

D - DEPART from evil

This is not part of the step to secure salvation, but it is a way of proving yourself that you are now truly of Christ. Forget your past and follow Him.

Depart from evil, and do good; seek peace, and pursue it.
Psalms 34:14 KJV

Therefore, if any man be in Christ, he is a new creature: old things are passed away; behold, all things are become new
2 Corinthians 5:17 KJV

GRACE RICHARDSON

(For he saith, I have heard thee in a time accepted, and in the day of salvation have I succoured thee: behold, now is the accepted time; behold, now is the day of salvation.)
2 Corinthians 6:2 KJV

Your Story Can Light Someone's Path

Dear Reader,

You've journeyed through these pages, discovering how to transform grief into growth through the Essential Steps™ system. Now, you have an opportunity to help others find their way to healing.

By sharing your experience with this book on Amazon, you'll guide fellow travelers through their darkest valleys. Whether you found hope in the aromatherapy protocols, renewal through face stimulation techniques, or comfort in spiritual wisdom, your review could be the lighthouse another grieving soul needs.

A few minutes of your time could change someone's life.

Share your story at [Amazon Review Link]

Click this link to opt in for the BONUS workbook (PDF):

https://thriveingrief.com/workbook

REFERENCES

"8 Ways to Use Essential Oils in Your Skincare Routine." 2022. Clean Rebellion. June 16, 2022. https://cleanrebellion.com/8-ways-to-use-essential-oils-in-your-skincare-routine/.

"19 Bible Verses to Bring Comfort in a Time of Loss." 2023. September 26, 2023. https://get.tithe.ly/blog/19-bible-verses-to-bring-comfort-in-a-time-of-loss.

"44 Bible Verses about Trusting God In Difficult Times." n.d. https://bible.knowing-jesus.com/topics/Trusting+God+In+Difficult+Times.

"50+ Bible Verses for Healing - Powerful Scripture Quotes." n.d. Bible Study Tools. https://www.biblestudytools.com/topical-verses/healing-bible-verses/.

Apoussidis, Esther. 2023. "Reflexology: A Soothing Path to Relieve Burnout and Overwhelm." *MindBody Oasis* (blog). September 17, 2023. https://mindbodyoasis.co.uk/2023/09/17/reflexology-a-soothing-path-to-relieve-burnout-and-overwhelm/.

Atsumi, Toshiko, and Keiichi Tonosaki. 2007. "Smelling Lavender and Rosemary Increases Free Radical Scavenging Activity and Decreases Cortisol Level in Saliva." *Psychiatry Research* 150 (1): 89–96. https://doi.org/10.1016/j.psychres.2005.12.012.

Brandenberger, Holly. 2024. "Aromatherapy for Grief and Loss." Science of Essentials. August 29, 2024. https://www.scienceofessentials.com/blog/aromatherapy-for-grief-and-loss.

Cacciatore, Joanne, Kara Thieleman, Ruth Fretts, and Lori Barnes Jackson. 2021. "What Is Good Grief Support? Exploring the Actors and Actions in Social Support after Traumatic Grief." Edited by Manuel Fernández-Alcántara. *PLOS ONE* 16 (5): e0252324. https://doi.org/10.1371/journal.pone.0252324.

"CeCe Winans - Believe For It (Deluxe Edition)." n.d. https://fts.lnk.to/BFIDeluxe.

Chapman, Morris. n.d. "I Will Restore." YouTube. https://www.youtube.com/watch?si=Okk7Ma2vXUNQP8wi&v=W2D_btjTao4&feature=youtu.be.

"Collagen: What It Is, Types, Function & Benefits." n.d. Cleveland Clinic. https://my.clevelandclinic.org/health/articles/23089-collagen.

"Complicated Grief: Finding Hope and Healing Through Faith." 2019. Tacoma Christian Counseling. December 12, 2019. https://tacomachristiancounseling.com/articles/complicated-grief-finding-hope-and-healing-through-faith.

Embong, Nurul Haswani, Yee Chang Soh, Long Chiau Ming, and Tin Wui Wong. 2015. "Revisiting Reflexology: Concept, Evidence, Current Practice, and Practitioner Training." *Journal of Traditional and Complementary Medicine* 5 (4): 197–206. https://doi.org/10.1016/j.jtcme.2015.08.008.

"Ethical and Sustainable Aromatherapy Guide." n.d. Aromatics International. https://www.aromatics.com/blogs/learning-guide-ethical-and-sustainable-aromatherapy.

"Explore the Riches of Church's 'Top Seven' Methods of Prayer." 2023. Crux. June 18, 2023.

https://cruxnow.com/commentary/2023/06/explore-the-riches-of-churchs-top-seven-methods-of-prayer/.

"Faith Based Retreats for Bereaved Parents." n.d. While We're Waiting. https://whilewerewaiting.org/.

"Fanny Crosby: The Girl Who Couldn't See But Helped The World To Sing." n.d. Goodreads. https://www.goodreads.com/book/show/59345880-fanny-crosby.

Flarey, Dominick. 2024. "Christian Counseling and Grief." *AIHCP* (blog). February 9, 2024. https://aihcp.net/2024/02/09/christian-counseling-and-grief/.

"From Traumatic Beginnings to Hopeful Endings - Mary's Story of Loss, Grief, and Faith in God That Kept Her Moving Forward." 2020. Jen Roland. December 3, 2020. https://jenroland.com/2020/12/03/from-traumatic-beginnings-to-hopeful-endings/.

Fung, Timothy K. H., Benson W. M. Lau, Shirley P. C. Ngai, and Hector W. H. Tsang. 2021. "Therapeutic Effect and Mechanisms of Essential Oils in Mood Disorders: Interaction between the Nervous and Respiratory Systems." *International Journal of Molecular Sciences* 22 (9): 4844. https://doi.org/10.3390/ijms22094844.

"God Is In This Story - Katy Nichole and Big Daddy Weave." n.d. YouTube. https://www.youtube.com/watch?si=iX1mHPNHmpVANq1Z&v=R_zI1Iy5_EQ&feature=youtu.be.

"Grief Support: Give Yourself a Break." 2023. *ShareLife* (blog). May 31, 2023. https://sharelife.com/grief-support-give-yourself-a-break/.

"How the Immune System & Digestive System Work Together." 2021. Solgar. October 12, 2021. https://www.solgar.com/blog/lifestyle/immune-system-digestive-system-work-togther/.

"How You Can Be (Literally) Sick With Grief." 2023. Cleveland Clinic. January 26, 2023. https://health.clevelandclinic.org/can-grief-make-you-sick.

Khot, Mish. 2022. "Facial Reflexology: How It Helps Your Whole Body." *Avaana Answers* (blog). October 25, 2022. https://avaana.com.au/blog/benefits-of-facial-reflexology/.

Kuriyama, Hiroko, Satoko Watanabe, Takaaki Nakaya, Ichiro Shigemori, Masakazu Kita, Noriko Yoshida, Daiki Masaki, et al. 2005. "Immunological and Psychological Benefits of Aromatherapy Massage." *Evidence-Based Complementary and Alternative Medicine* 2 (2): 179–84. https://doi.org/10.1093/ecam/neh087.

Mabilog, Patrick. 2016. "Forgiveness: Why Holding onto That Grudge Will Only Hurt You." March 31, 2016. https://www.christiantoday.com/article/forgiveness-why-holding-onto-that-grudge-will-only-hurt-you/83008.htm.

Marciniak, Traci. 2016. "5 Steps to Create Your Own Healing Space." Miller-Dwan Foundation. December 13, 2016. https://mdfoundation.org/5-steps-to-create-your-own-healing-space/.

Matera, Riccardo, Elena Lucchi, and Luca Valgimigli. 2023. "Plant Essential Oils as Healthy Functional Ingredients of Nutraceuticals and Diet Supplements: A Review." *Molecules* 28 (2): 901. https://doi.org/10.3390/molecules28020901.

"Matthew Henry's Method for Prayer | Learn to Pray the Bible." n.d. Matthew Henry. https://www.matthewhenry.org/.

Michel, Ann, and Heidi A. Campbell. 2023. "6 Traits People Value in Online Faith Communities - Lewis Center for Church Leadership." March 21, 2023. https://www.churchleadership.com/leading-ideas/6-traits-people-value-in-online-faith-communities/, https://www.churchleadership.com/leading-ideas/6-traits-people-value-in-online-faith-communities/.

"Mindfulness for Grief and Loss." 2024. Mindful. March 18, 2024. https://www.mindful.org/mindfulness-for-grief-and-loss/.

Norman, Laura. 2015. "DIY Foot Reflexology For Your Best Sleep Ever." Mindbodygreen. August 5, 2015. https://www.mindbodygreen.com/articles/diy-foot-reflexology.

Pagán, Camille Noe. 2024. "Aromatherapy & Essential Oils for Stress Relief." WebMD. April 6, 2024. https://www.webmd.com/balance/stress-management/aromatherapy-overview.

Query, Amy. 2022. "9 Powerful Stories of Emotional Strength in the Bible." Deep Spirituality. January 11, 2022. https://deepspirituality.com/emotional-strength-stories/.

Rádis-Baptista, Gandhi. 2023. "Do Synthetic Fragrances in Personal Care and Household Products Impact Indoor Air Quality and Pose Health Risks?" *Journal of Xenobiotics* 13 (1): 121–31. https://doi.org/10.3390/jox13010010.

Rari, Don. 2023. "Benefits of Essential Oils." Doni Rari: Rare Gifts. March 11, 2023. https://donirari.com/blog/benefits-of-essential-oils/.

"Rediscovering Faith After Personal Loss." 2024. Spiritual Care Support Ministries. January 25, 2024. https://www.scsm.tv/rediscovering-faith-after-personal-loss/.

Richmond, Christine. 2023. "6 Ways Exercise Can Help When You're Grieving." SilverSneakers. November 3, 2023. https://www.silversneakers.com/blog/ways-exercise-can-help-when-grieving/.

Safai, Yalda. 2022. "Grief and the Body: Symptoms, Coping Strategies, and Outlook." Healthline. July 25, 2022. https://www.healthline.com/health/grief-physical-symptoms.

Scrimgeor, Alex. 2023. *Facial Reflexology for Emotional Well-Being.* https://www.simonandschuster.com/books/Facial-Reflexology-for-Emotional-Well-Being/Alex-Scrimgeour/9781644115862.

Shirley, Madison. 2022. "The Benefits of Goal Setting During Grief." *Ericshouse* (blog). January 2, 2022. https://www.ericshouse.org/the-benefits-of-goal-setting-during-grief-by-madison-shirley/.

"Spafford – The Story Behind the Hymn 'It Is Well with My Soul.'" 2021. *Christian Discipleship Lessons* (blog). June 28, 2021. https://www.cocdiscipleship.org/middle-ages/horatio-gates-spafford-the-story-behind-the-hymn-it-is-well-with-my-soul/.

Sutton, Jeremy. 2023. "Integrative Therapy: Definition, Techniques, & Examples." PositivePsychology.Com. May 25, 2023. https://positivepsychology.com/holistic-therapy/.

Symth, Dolores. 2024. "What Does the Number 7 Mean in the Bible and Why Is It Important?" Christianity.Com. November 19, 2024. https://www.christianity.com/wiki/bible/what-is-the-biblical-significance-of-the-number-7.html.

Taylor Chavoustie, Cynthia. 2018. "What Is Aromatherapy and How Does It Help Me?" Healthline. May 15, 2018. https://www.healthline.com/health/what-is-aromatherapy.

Taylor, Justin. 2015. "22 Benefits of Meditating on Scripture." The Gospel Coalition. March 13, 2015. https://www.thegospelcoalition.org/blogs/justin-taylor/22-benefits-of-meditating-on-scripture/.

"The Role of Faith in Grief." 2024. Butterflies + Halos. January 11, 2024. https://butterfliesandhalos.com/blogs/news/the-role-of-faith-in-grief#:~:text=Embracing%20the%20role%20of%20faith%2C%20healing%2C%20and%renewed%20purpose.

https://www.azquotes.com author/15737-Marianne_Williamson/tag/forgiveness

"Therapeutic Massage, Esthetics, and Yoga." n.d. Precision Wellness. https://ptmassagespringfieldmo.com/.

"Top 20+ Comforting Bible Verses about Grief and Loss." n.d. Bible Study Tools. Accessed December 9, 2024. https://www.biblestudytools.com/topical-verses/bible-verses-for-overcoming-grief/.

"Unleashing the Power of Sweet Slumber: Mastering the Art of Better Sle." 2023. The Sleep Spot. May 18, 2023. https://thesleepspot.co.nz/blogs/sleep-science-1/unleashing-the-power-of-sweet-slumber-mastering-the-art-of-better-sleep.

Veda, Ayushi. 2023. "Energize and Elevate Mood with a Rainbow Diet: 9 Colorful Foods." Scoop360.In. August 10, 2023. https://scoop360.in/energize-and-elevate-mood-with-a-rainbow-diet-9-colorful-foods/.

Wane, Ousmane, Luis F. Zarzalejo, Francisco Ferrera-Cobos, Ana A. Navarro, Alberto Rodríguez-López, and Rita X. Valenzuela. 2023. "Generation of Typical Meteorological Sequences to

Simulate Growth and Production of Biological Systems." *Applied Sciences* 13 (8): 4826. https://doi.org/10.3390/app13084826.

"What Is Stress?" n.d. Cleveland Clinic. https://my.clevelandclinic.org/health/diseases/11874-stress.

Williams, Jane, Gillian W. Shorter, Neil Howlett, Julia Zakrzewski-Fruer, and Angel M. Chater. 2021. "Can Physical Activity Support Grief Outcomes in Individuals Who Have Been Bereaved? A Systematic Review." *Sports Medicine - Open* 7 (April):26. https://doi.org/10.1186/s40798-021-00311-z.

Williams, Lista. n.d. "Grief and Faith: The Relationship Between Grief and Belief." What's Your Grief? https://whatsyourgrief.com/grief-and-faith-grief-belief/.

Wilson, Debra Rose. 2017. "20 Anti-Aging Oils to Add to Your Routine." Healthline. November 21, 2017. https://www.healthline.com/health/beauty-skin-care/essential-oils-for-wrinkles.

———. 2019. "Pressure Points On and For the Face." Healthline. August 30, 2019. https://www.healthline.com/health/pressure-points-for-face.

"Your Guide to Choosing High Quality Essential Oils to Make Pure, Organic and Therapeutic Blends." n.d. Isabella's Clearly. https://www.isabellasclearly.com/blog/the-ultimate-guide-to-choosing-high-quality-essential-oils.

Zampitella, Christina. n.d. "Incorporating Religion & Spirituality into Grief Counseling." PESI. https://www.pesi.com/blog/details/2123/incorporating-religion-spirituality-into-grief-counseling.